# Rose Murray's
## New Casseroles and Other One-Dish Meals

Macmillan Canada

Toronto

**Canadian Cataloguing in Publication Data**

Murray, Rose, 1941-
  Rose Murray's new casseroles and other one-dish meals

Includes index.
ISBN 07715-7392-8

1. Casserole cookery. I. Title. II. Title: New casseroles and other one-dish meals.

TX693.M87   1996                  641.8'21                  C96-930956-2

Macmillan Canada wishes to thank the Canada Council, the Ontario Arts Council and the Ontario Ministry of Culture and Communications for supporting its publishing program.

Cover photograph:  Doug Bradshaw
Food styling:  Olga Truchan
Cover and inside design:  Gord Robertson
Page composition:  Michael Kelley

Pictured on the cover:  Herbed Chicken Breasts in a Loaf of Bread (p.92), Tomato and Cheese Tart (p.207), Spicy Shepherd's Pie with Feta-Potato Topping (p.119), Mussel Stew with Roasted Garlic Mayonnaise (p.31), and Old-Fashioned Turkey Pot Pie (p.97).

Macmillan Canada
A Division of Canada Publishing Corporation
Toronto, Canada

1 2 3 4 5     00 99 98 97 96

Printed in Canada

# Contents

## Recipes

To the memory of my father, George Varty, and for Muriel, Allen and John who all knew my mother's good cooking.

# Introduction

A STEW quietly sits burbling away on the back of the stove while it fills the house with irresistible aromas. A casserole is tucked away in the refrigerator ready to be popped into the oven to come out crusty golden on top. A few simple ingredients join together in a wok or skillet to form a colorful shiny whole of interesting shapes. These are the immediate sensual appeals of one-dish meals. There are, however, many more far-reaching attributes.

For centuries, one-pot meals have been so important that they have become the classic dishes that come to mind when you conjure up the food of many countries—Paella, Hungarian Goulash, Britain's pies, Pot-au-Feu, Pad Thai, Jambalaya, Moussaka, even Lasagna.

In many cases, these meals were peasant dishes and, consequently, were economical, using only what was at hand. They were hearty to fill up men who worked in the fields. They were easy and quick to put together by the women who toiled alongside. The meals were easy to serve because, like Paella, they were often cooked and eaten on the spot with the family gathering around the cook pot. Or the dishes were often portable—made ahead in the house to be carried out to a vineyard or forest.

Most of the attributes of one-dish cooking—ease, convenience, economy, portability, advance preparation—are just as important to our modern lifestyle as they were in days gone by. Because most of us no longer do heavy physical labor, I've lightened up the heartier dishes by using less fat and more vegetables. I've also added new tastes and flavor combinations. We can take advantage of our modern equipment: electric stoves, microwave ovens (however, in this book, I don't refer to it much since a casserole doesn't stay hot if reheated in a microwave oven, and a soup or a stew needs more attention in a microwave than it does on the stove-top or in a conventional oven), wonderful pots and pans, refrigerators and especially our freezers. Most of these one-dish meals can be made ahead and refrigerated or frozen, ready for a day when time is at a premium or for casual entertaining after a long day at work.

We may no longer toil alongside our husbands in fields and vineyards, but most women work outside the home. More and more couples are cooking together, especially on weekends when they prepare a nice array of weekday meals. These one-dish recipes are just right for this kind of big-batch cooking. Sometimes at-home mothers cook together and carry home a supply of one-pot suppers so that they can have more variety and more economical meals.

We may no longer carry midday meals to the fields but we have new places to take them—the chalet in ski season, the cottage, potluck suppers and family reunions. One-dish meals are definitely easier to transport and serve and, despite our modern conveniences, I would hope we still feel it's important to enjoy the company of friends and family around a dish such as Paella or Pot-au-Feu with crusty bread and wine, much like people did years ago.

Here is a variety of make-ahead, self-contained meals: big casseroles to delight a number of friends tomorrow or to freeze in small amounts for future family meals; long-simmering soups and stews to warm you on cold, windy days, or on any day you need comforting. There are small, quick skillet dinners and stir-fries, easy enough for novice cooks, and lovely elegant dishes for all your entertaining. I hope through my recipes you will come to discover all the wonderful attributes of one-dish cooking.

# Casseroles

Back in the 1950s, during the height of the can-opener era, the casserole was in its prime. You might remember unkindly the ubiquitous tuna-noodle-mushroom soup-potato-chip concoction when you hear the word. For anyone under 40, casseroles might have a negative connotation because they fell into disfavor as being too homely during the so-called "gourmet" period of the 1970s and were considered too soggy for the crispness of *nouvelle cuisine,* which we thankfully have got out of our systems.

I'm sorry if casseroles have had a bad rap because I think these one-dish meals are fantastic for many reasons. They're friendly, soothing, convenient to make and serve. They make wonderful baby or new-neighbor presents. They go to potluck dinners in style and make easy juggle-on-your-lap buffet dishes because they can usually be eaten with only a fork. They're perfect for working mothers and entertaining alike since the meals can be made ahead. They're great for families on the go because many of the following casseroles can be frozen in single servings, ready to accommodate each member's schedule.

Although casseroles may take a little longer to make and dirty more dishes since the ingredients often have to be separately precooked, these dishes do allow for pots and pans to be washed well ahead of serving time.

## Great Hints for Make-Ahead Casserole Suppers

- When cooking pasta for a casserole that is not going to be baked right away, cook until barely *al dente,* then add 2 cups (500 mL) cold water to boiling pasta before draining.
- Remember that pasta or rice tends to absorb moisture as it sits in a casserole; be sure there is enough liquid in the casserole.
- Refrigerate cooked dishes to cool before wrapping. If freezing a casserole, be sure it is wrapped well in foil and a freezer bag to prevent freezer burn.
- Frozen dishes can fool you when it comes to their heating time, especially

hearty casseroles like lasagna. Thaw in the refrigerator overnight and allow plenty of heating time, double-checking the centre before serving. The deeper the dish, the longer it will take. You can reheat frozen cooked entrées: keep them well covered and always use a moderate oven (about 350°F/180°C). In general, a medium-deep casserole will take about 1½ hours. Dishes that have lots of liquid, such as soups and stews, can be warmed up over direct heat in a saucepan, but be sure to stir often.

- If you know you're going to freeze a casserole and don't want to lose the baking dish to the freezer for weeks, line the dish with foil before adding the food. Cover and freeze until solid, remove from dish, overwrap well and return to freezer. (To use, place frozen food, still in its liner, back in the dish.)
- Label food with not only the name of dish but also the reheating instructions to save time later.
- Do not overcook foods that are made ahead because they will cook a little more when reheated.
- Most casseroles, stews and main-dish soups will keep up to 2 days in the refrigerator and are best frozen no longer than 3 months. Thaw in the refrigerator or microwave oven; room temperature thawing encourages the growth of bacteria.
- Check the temperature of your freezer; it should register 0°F (–18°F) on a freezer thermometer.
- Use less garlic, pepper and cloves than usual if freezing a dish because freezing intensifies these seasonings.
- Use more onion, salt and herbs if freezing a dish because these tend to lose flavor during freezing.
- Omit bread crumb toppings if freezing a dish because these become soggy.
- It is better to add potatoes when reheating a dish since they change texture when frozen.
- Use only regular or parboiled rice if freezing a dish since quick-cooking rice becomes very mushy.
- Bath towels are great for transporting casseroles to potluck suppers because they not only insulate but also brace the dishes and keep them from slipping. Towels can also catch any drips that do get away.

# Casserole Dishes and Pans

CASSEROLE DISHES and Dutch Ovens: I like to oven-bake most one-pot meals because they need little or no stirring. While skillet suppers are essentially fuss-free, you do need to peek under the lid occasionally to see that nothing is sticking or scorching, especially if the sauce is somewhat sweet or contains pasta. Also, I prefer the oven because the pot is fully surrounded by heat, which means more even cooking.

For oven-baking, it's convenient to have a Dutch oven or flameproof casserole that can go both onto the stove top and into the oven.

I also have a number of shallow oval gratin dishes that look prettier on the table than the regular rectangular or square ones. If I call for a shallow 8-cup (2 L) baking dish, use an 11- x 7-inch (2 L) baking dish if you don't have a gratin dish. A 13- x 9-inch (3 L) glass baking dish is equivalent to a 12-cup (3 L) gratin dish. Actually, casseroles are more forgiving than cakes and the like if you don't have just the right dish.

Cast-Iron Skillets: A well-seasoned cast-iron skillet is perfectly nonstick. Since nonstick skillets rarely have ovenproof handles, I prefer a cast-iron one because it can make that trip to the oven after browning ingredients on top of the stove. (I try to use as few pans as possible.) Besides, they're usually cheaper and last forever. I have four of different sizes, including one of my mother's. It must be at least seventy-five years old.

To place nonstick skillets in the oven, wrap the handle in several thicknesses of foil for protection against temperatures up to 400°F (200°C).

The secret to a well-seasoned cast-iron skillet is to first clean a new skillet very well with a soap-scouring pad. Then dry it well, coat the inside with oil and place in a 200°F (100°C) oven for about 3 hours. (Make melba toast while your oven is on.) Then never use detergent on it again. Each time you use it, swish with very hot water, using a brush or nylon scouring pad to remove stubborn bits, soaking if necessary. Rinse well, wipe dry completely and let air-dry before storing.

# Stews and Chili

Ragoût, navarin, daube, cioppino, hot pot, fricassée, jambalaya, blanquette—whatever the name, they all mean stew. Probably invented along with the first clay pots, stew is among the world's oldest dishes. It's that comforting one-dish meal whose rich flavor and inviting aroma still warm anyone's heart on a cold day.

Set down a plate of steaming dark broth, colorful winter vegetables, tender pieces of meat or fish with a sprinkling of fresh parsley on top and you'll find that the most sophisticated gourmand not only eats with relish but reaches for lots of crusty bread to capture every bit of sauce. Add a green salad and perhaps beer or wine, and there need be nothing else for the perfect winter meal.

Stews are flexible and not at all demanding. Easy enough for even the least experienced cook, these slowly braised dishes have the additional appeal of being good make-ahead meals, gaining even more flavor if made one day and reheated another. In addition, stews are economical. Best made with the least expensive meat and vegetables, a stew takes only a couple of pounds of meat to satisfy at least eight hungry people. Compare that to cooking steaks or a roast for the same number.

Early cooks discovered this economy in chili, a southwestern kind of stew. Although nobody knows its exact origin, chili probably evolved from the rigors of Texan frontier life and the love of Mexican food. In any event, it was quickly discovered that small amounts of meat (when chopped and braised with lots of fresh chilies) could easily feed a family.

Since those days, however, chili has been made from a great variety of ingredients—beef, chicken, seafood, vegetables, sausage. Regardless of its main component, chili still remains an economical dish that's easy to make. Like all stews, chili is terrific made one day and warmed up another, making it perfect portable fare for the chalet or cottage.

# Stew- and Chili-Making Hints:

- If you like a thicker sauce (sauce thickens on cooling if made ahead), dissolve some cornstarch or flour in cold water and stir into the bubbling liquid.
- Long-cooking stews done in the oven require less attention, but they all can cook on top of the stove. Stir more often and give them less time, but be sure they're kept at a very low simmer because high heat will toughen the meat.
- All stews and chilis freeze well, but you might like to omit any potatoes; cook them and add to the stew just before serving because potatoes generally become mealy upon freezing.
- Remember that water expands as it freezes. When storing stews, chilis or soups, leave at least 1 inch (2.5 cm) of room at the container top.
- Quite often, buying an inexpensive roast on sale is less costly than buying stewing meat. Remember to buy one big enough to yield the amount of boneless meat called for in the recipe after trimming away fat and sinew.
- Serve chili in a bowl with garnishes of shredded cheese, chopped tomato, olives and sour cream, and if you like, accompany it with crusty rolls or cornbread. Or, spoon chili into taco shells, or roll it up in flour tortillas and sprinkle liberally with cheese before heating through.
- For fun, serve stews or chili in interesting ways as in Chive Popovers (see page 113) or Loaf of Bread (see page 92) or in a pumpkin as in Argentinian Autumn Stew (see page 111). You might use squash, peppers or cabbage as holders. Or, for chili, make tortilla "bowls" by brushing both sides of tortillas with melted butter. Place each in ovenproof bowl, making pleats as needed to fit. Bake in 400°F (200°C) oven for 10 to 15 minutes or until crisp and golden brown. Cool in bowls.
- Try various toppings on stews and chilis to make them company or potluck fare, such as Sage Dumplings (see page 72), Cheddar-Bacon Crust (see page 153), Cornmeal Topping (see page 108) and pastry (see page 142); or make your favorite biscuit recipe and put on hot stew to bake.

Go Withs: Sometimes you'll want to cook rice, noodles or potatoes to go with stews or chili, but crusty bread is usually all you need. A crisp green salad will satisfy the need for a contrasting texture to the usual soft, albeit comforting, stew.

# Main-Course Soups

O F SOUP AND LOVE," a Spanish proverb says, "the first is best." Soup has survived through the ages as a source of warmth and comfort. With the discovery of fire and a heat-resistant cooking vessel to hang over that fire, soup was probably the original one-pot supper.

The name, it is believed, came from the feudal castles of very early medieval times, when crowds of enthusiastic diners enjoying wild boar or venison came up with the idea of dipping great pieces of bread into the meat broth. This they called "sop." In the 12th century, someone tried the meat broth as a separate part of the meal, and the name changed from "sop" to "soupe." In 17th-century France, "soupes" meant chunks of meat or fish boiled with vegetables and one "sopped" the resulting broth. "To sup" meant to eat the evening meal at which soup was traditionally served, and the meal itself became "supper."

Soup soon became a basic daily food that brought the family together around the hearth where it was made. Today, fast-paced lives mean that families don't always eat together, but soup is still perceived as a soothing, cheering food. It's real food with an aroma and flavor that can draw even the busiest family around the supper table. A bowl of hearty homemade soup, a chunk of bread for sopping up every drop, and maybe a bit of cheese and fruit make a perfect supper to help dispel winter chills.

Soup is not only welcome and nourishing to eat, but it's also easy to make and it freezes well.

Inexpensive homemade broths (broths and stocks are made the same way, but a stock is more apt to be a sauce base; however, they are often used interchangeably) are extremely easy to create and make an afternoon home with a simmering pot pay off. However, don't let the lack of homemade broth deter you from making interesting soups, because you can substitute canned broth. And don't let a long list of ingredients put you off either; most soups are not complicated to make.

Enjoy and, as Molière said, "I live on good soup, not on fine words."

# Whole-Meal Soups

# Easy Basic Meat Broth

A good broth or stock makes a good soup. If the broth is too salty or weak, the soup will quickly reflect these flaws. Obviously, a good homemade broth is the best, and it's not difficult to make. However, if time or mood doesn't allow you to prepare your own, the next best bet is canned broth. To make homemade broth, you can use all beef or all chicken. If using all chicken, dispense with the browning.

| | | |
|---|---|---|
| 2¼ lb | meaty beef soup bones | 1 kg |
| ¾ lb | meaty chicken bones (necks, wings, backs) | 375 g |
| 1 | onion (unpeeled), cut in chunks | 1 |
| 1 | carrot (unpeeled), cut in chunks | 1 |
| 1 tbsp | vegetable oil | 15 mL |
| 2 | stalks celery, cut in chunks | 2 |
| 1 | large tomato, coarsely chopped (or 2 canned tomatoes, chopped) | 1 |
| 4 | sprigs parsley | 4 |
| 1 | bay leaf | 1 |
| 1½ tsp | salt (preferably coarse pickling) | 7 mL |
| Pinch | dried thyme | Pinch |

Place bones, onion and carrot in shallow pan and drizzle with oil. Roast in 450°F (230°C) oven for 45 minutes, stirring occasionally.

Transfer contents to large kettle; add celery, tomato, parsley, bay leaf, salt and thyme. Pour in 14 cups (3.5 L) cold water; slowly bring to boil, skimming any scum from surface.

Meanwhile, add 2 cups (500 mL) water to browning pan; bring to boil, scraping up any brown bits from bottom of pan. Add to kettle; reduce heat and simmer gently, uncovered, for 5 to 6 hours or until rich broth develops.

Strain through fine sieve into large bowl, pushing hard on solids. Discard solids and let broth cool. Refrigerate, covered, for up to 2 days or freeze for up to 6 months. Remove fat from top before you use or freeze broth. Makes about 11 cups (2.75 L).

# Hearty Bean Soup with Garlic Toasts

This hearty soup needs little else for a warming winter meal. If you prefer, pass the toasts in a basket rather than pouring the soup over them. If making the soup ahead, undercook the vegetables slightly.

| | | |
|---|---|---|
| 4 | slices side bacon, diced | 4 |
| 1¼ lb | lean pork, cut in ¼-inch (5 mm) wide strips | 625 g |
| 1 | onion, chopped | 1 |
| 2 | EACH carrots and stalks celery, coarsely chopped | 2 |
| 3 | cloves garlic, chopped | 3 |
| 7 cups | chicken broth or water | 1.75 L |
| 1 | bouquet garni* | 1 |
| Half | head cabbage, shredded | Half |
| 4 | potatoes, peeled and cubed | 4 |
| 1 | can (19 oz/540 mL) white pea (navy) beans, drained and rinsed | 1 |
| 6 | thick slices French bread, toasted | 6 |
| 1 | clove garlic, peeled and halved | 1 |

In large saucepan, cook bacon over medium-high heat until crisp. Remove with slotted spoon and set aside.

Brown pork in bacon drippings; remove with slotted spoon and set aside. Add onion, carrots, celery and garlic; cook over medium heat for about 10 minutes or until softened, stirring often.

Add broth and bring to boil. Return pork and juices and bacon to pan; add bouquet garni. Simmer, covered, over low heat for 1½ hours.

Add cabbage, potatoes and beans; cook for 30 minutes or until potatoes are tender. (Soup can be cooled, covered and refrigerated for up to 1 day. Bring to room temperature; reheat over low heat.) Taste and adjust seasoning.

Rub hot toast with cut side of garlic and place in heated bowls; pour soup over top. Makes 6 servings.

---

*To make a bouquet garni, place 2 celery stalks around 3 sprigs parsley, 1 bay leaf, 1 tsp (5 mL) dried thyme and 5 peppercorns in a cheesecloth bag.

# Autumn Soup with Sausage and Lentils

Chock-full of harvest vegetables, this easy supper soup is delicious any time of the year. Serve with crusty bread and coleslaw. A fruit crisp would make a perfect ending.

| | | |
|---|---|---|
| 1 lb | mild Italian sausages | 500 g |
| 2 tbsp | vegetable oil | 25 mL |
| 2 | potatoes, peeled and diced | 2 |
| 2 | carrots, diced | 2 |
| 2 | stalks celery, diced | 2 |
| 1 | small rutabaga, peeled and diced | 1 |
| 1 | onion, chopped | 1 |
| Half | sweet green pepper, diced | Half |
| 5 cups | beef broth | 1.25 L |
| ½ cup | dried red lentils, rinsed | 125 mL |
| 1 tbsp | tomato paste | 15 mL |
| | Salt and pepper | |
| 2 tbsp | chopped fresh parsley | 25 mL |

Cut sausage into 1-inch (2.5 cm) pieces. In large saucepan, heat half of the oil over medium heat; cook sausages for 3 minutes. Add potatoes; cook for about 2 minutes or until browned. Transfer to paper towel-lined dish; set aside.

Add remaining oil, carrots, celery, rutabaga, onion and green pepper to saucepan; cook for 3 to 5 minutes or just until softened.

Stir in broth, lentils, tomato paste, and salt and pepper to taste; bring to boil. Reduce heat, cover and simmer for 20 minutes.

Add reserved sausage and potatoes; cover and simmer for 25 minutes or until vegetables are tender. (Soup can be cooled, covered and refrigerated for up to 2 days; gently reheat.) Taste and adjust seasoning if necessary. Serve sprinkled with parsley. Makes 6 to 8 generous servings.

# Hearty Chili Soup

For little more than the price of a can of chunky soup, you can make this easy vegetarian soup for eight and cut down on sodium, too.

| | | |
|---|---|---|
| 4 tsp | vegetable oil | 20 mL |
| 4 | cloves garlic, minced | 4 |
| 2 | onions, chopped | 2 |
| 1 | can (28 oz/796 mL) tomatoes | 1 |
| 2 | stalks celery, diced | 2 |
| 2 | carrots, diced | 2 |
| 1 | sweet green pepper, diced | 1 |
| 2 tbsp | chili powder, or to taste | 25 mL |
| 1 tsp | EACH dried oregano and basil | 5 mL |
| Pinch | hot pepper flakes, or to taste | Pinch |
| ¼ tsp | EACH salt and pepper | 1 mL |
| 2 | cans (each 19 oz/540 mL) kidney beans or chick-peas (undrained) Shredded Cheddar cheese | 2 |

In large saucepan, heat oil over medium heat; cook garlic and onions for 3 minutes. Add tomatoes, mashing with fork. Stir in 1 tomato can of water, celery, carrots, green pepper, chili powder, oregano, basil, hot pepper flakes, salt and pepper.

Stir in beans and 1 bean can of water; bring to boil. Reduce heat, cover and simmer for 30 minutes for flavors to blend. (Soup can be cooled, covered and refrigerated for up to 5 days or frozen for up to 2 months.) Serve sprinkled with cheese. Makes 8 servings.

# Bacon and Egg Chowder

Hearty enough for supper and quick to whip up for lunch, this chowder has the advantage of being made with ingredients you probably have on hand. Serve with toasted whole wheat rolls and carrot sticks.

| | | |
|---|---|---|
| 5 | slices side bacon | 5 |
| 2 | stalks celery (with leaves), chopped | 2 |
| 2 | EACH potatoes and carrots, peeled and diced | 2 |
| 1 | onion, chopped | 1 |
| 1 tsp | dry mustard | 5 mL |
| 1 tsp | Worcestershire sauce | 5 mL |
| ¾ tsp | dried marjoram | 4 mL |
| ¼ tsp | salt | 1 mL |
| Pinch | pepper | Pinch |
| 2 tbsp | all-purpose flour | 25 mL |
| 3 cups | milk | 750 mL |
| 1 cup | chicken stock | 250 mL |
| 4 | hard-cooked eggs | 4 |

In large saucepan, cook bacon over medium-high heat until crisp; crumble and set aside.

Pour off all but 2 tbsp (25 mL) fat from pan; reduce heat to medium. Add celery, potatoes, carrots, onion, mustard, Worcestershire sauce, marjoram, salt and pepper; cook for 5 minutes. Stir in flour; cook for 1 minute. Add milk and stock; bring to boil. Reduce heat, cover and simmer for 10 to 15 minutes or until vegetables are tender.

Remove whites from yolks and coarsely chop; add to soup and gently heat through.

Finely chop yolks. Serve soup sprinkled with yolks and reserved bacon. Makes 4 to 6 servings.

# Hearty Beef Vegetable Soup

Chopped vegetables and beef simmer in an old-fashioned, stick-to-your-ribs soup which takes only 15 minutes of preparation. A perfect chalet supper for several good friends who will certainly linger if they smell it cooking, this hearty soup also freezes well for future meals. If you wish to dress up the soup a bit for company, garnish each serving with a small dollop of Chive Cream (recipe follows).

| | | |
|---|---|---|
| 2 lb | boneless blade or cross-rib roast | 1 kg |
| 2 lb | soup bones | 1 kg |
| 2 | large onions, chopped | 2 |
| 3 | large carrots, coarsely chopped | 3 |
| 2 | stalks celery, sliced | 2 |
| 2 | leeks (white parts only), sliced | 2 |
| ¾ lb | parsley root,* sliced | 375 g |
| 16 cups | water | 4 L |
| 1 | can (28 oz/796 mL) tomatoes | 1 |
| ½ cup | rice | 125 mL |
| 1 tbsp | EACH packed brown sugar and salt | 15 mL |
| 1 tsp | EACH dried savory and dry mustard | 5 mL |
| ½ tsp | EACH dried marjoram and thyme | 2 mL |
| ¼ tsp | EACH pepper and dried dillweed | 1 mL |

In large kettle, combine beef, soup bones, onions, carrots, celery, leeks, parsley root, water, tomatoes, rice, sugar, salt, savory, mustard, marjoram, thyme, pepper and dillweed; bring to boil. Skim off froth.

Reduce heat to low; simmer, partially covered and stirring occasionally, for 4 hours. Skim fat from surface. Discard soup bones. Remove beef; cut into cubes and return to soup. Makes about 12 servings.

---

**\*Parsley root is available at most supermarkets. If unavailable, substitute 1 large peeled celeriac or 2 parsnips and 2 more carrots.**

# Chive Cream

| ½ cup | light sour cream | 125 mL |
| ½ cup | snipped chives or green onions | 125 mL |
| 2 tsp | white wine vinegar | 10 mL |
| ¼ tsp | EACH salt and pepper | 1 mL |

In small bowl, whisk together sour cream, chives, vinegar, salt and pepper. (Cream can be covered and refrigerated for up to 1 day.) Makes ⅔ cup (150 mL).

# Baked Tuscan Vegetable and Bread Soup

Rather like a stew, this really thick vegetable soup is usually made a day or two ahead in Italy's Tuscany region where its name, Ribollita, means "recooked" or "reboiled." It starts with a rich chicken and vegetable minestrone that's layered in a casserole with crusty bread. When it sits, the flavor develops; then it's baked until steaming and tender inside, crusty and golden on top.

| | | |
|---|---|---|
| 5 cups | chicken broth | 1.25 L |
| 1 lb | chicken breasts, skinned | 500 g |
| 2 | bay leaves | 2 |
| 3 tbsp | olive oil | 45 mL |
| 1 | onion, chopped | 1 |
| 2 | cloves garlic, minced | 2 |
| 2 | EACH carrots and stalks celery, diced | 2 |
| 1 | sweet green pepper, diced | 1 |
| 2 cups | chopped cabbage | 500 mL |
| 1 tsp | EACH dried thyme and rosemary | 5 mL |
| 1 | can (19 oz/540 mL) tomatoes, coarsely chopped | 1 |
| ¼ tsp | pepper | 1 mL |
| 1 | pkg (10 oz/284 g) fresh spinach, chopped | 1 |
| ½ cup | chopped fresh parsley | 125 mL |
| 1 | small zucchini, thinly sliced | 1 |
| 1 | can (19 oz/540 mL) white kidney beans, drained and rinsed | 1 |
| 8 | thick slices stale Italian or French bread | 8 |
| 1 cup | freshly grated Parmesan cheese Olive oil Freshly grated Parmesan cheese | 250 mL |

In large kettle, bring broth, chicken and bay leaves to boil; reduce heat and simmer, covered, for 20 minutes or until chicken is no longer pink inside. Remove and dice chicken, discarding bones; set meat aside. Discard bay leaves. Keep broth warm.

Meanwhile, in large skillet, heat 2 tbsp (25 mL) of the oil over medium heat; cook onion, garlic, carrots and celery for 10 minutes, stirring occasionally. Add remaining oil, green pepper, cabbage, thyme and rosemary; cook over low heat, stirring occasionally, for 10 minutes.

Add vegetable mixture to warm broth. Add tomatoes and pepper; bring to boil. Reduce heat and simmer, covered, for 30 minutes. Add spinach, parsley, zucchini, beans and chicken; cook for 5 minutes. Remove 1 cup (250 mL) of the soup and set aside.

Ladle half of the remaining soup into a 24-cup (6 L) casserole or Dutch oven; cover with 4 slices of the bread and ½ cup (125 mL) cheese. Cover with remaining soup (except reserved); layer with remaining bread. Drizzle reserved soup over top; sprinkle with remaining cheese. (Can be cooled, covered and refrigerated overnight.)

Bake, covered, in 350°F (180°C) oven for 20 minutes (45 minutes if refrigerated); uncover and bake for 20 minutes (45 minutes if refrigerated) or until hot.

Ladle into large warm soup bowls and garnish each with drizzle of olive oil and sprinkle of Parmesan cheese. Makes 6 servings.

# Chunky Chicken Soup with Winter Vegetables

A traditional family Sunday meal in France, chicken in the pot (*poule au pot*) is served in two courses—first the broth, perhaps with noodles or French bread, then the chicken and vegetables. I like to tear the poached chicken into large pieces and return to the broth so that the whole dish is like a chunky soup.

| | | |
|---|---|---|
| 3 lb | fryer or roasting chicken | 1.5 kg |
| | Salt and pepper | |
| 2 | onions, halved | 2 |
| 6 | cloves garlic | 6 |
| 2 | bay leaves | 2 |
| 8 cups | chicken broth | 2 L |
| 1 tsp | dried thyme | 5 mL |
| ½ tsp | dried sage | 2 mL |
| 2 | leeks | 2 |
| 2 | parsnips | 2 |
| Half | rutabaga | Half |
| 4 | carrots | 4 |
| 4 | stalks celery (with leaves) | 4 |
| 2 tbsp | chopped fresh parsley | 25 mL |

Remove fat from chicken. Place chicken in large saucepan: sprinkle chicken inside and out with salt and pepper. Add onions, garlic and bay leaves. Pour in broth; bring to boil, skimming off foam. Add thyme and sage; cover and cook over low heat for 30 minutes.

   Meanwhile, quarter leeks lengthwise; cut into 1-inch (2.5 cm) pieces. Peel parsnips and rutabaga. Cut parsnips, rutabaga, carrots and celery into bite-size chunks. Add vegetables to saucepan; simmer, covered, for 30 to 45 minutes or until vegetables are tender and chicken is falling off bones. Discard bay leaves. Skim off fat. Remove chicken and let cool enough to handle; tear meat into large pieces and return to soup, discarding skin and bones. (Soup can be cooled, covered and refrigerated for up to 2 days. Remove any remaining fat from broth. Heat over low heat.) Serve sprinkled with parsley. Makes 4 servings.

# Mexican Chicken and Corn Soup

As soothing and comforting as the proverbial chicken soup, this colorful main course is made especially interesting with the addition of zesty Mexican flavors. Serve with wedges of warm corn tortillas.

| | | |
|---|---|---|
| 1 tbsp | vegetable oil | 15 mL |
| 1 | onion, thinly sliced | 1 |
| 2 | jalapeño peppers, seeded and diced | 2 |
| 2 tsp | ground cumin | 10 mL |
| ½ tsp | dried oregano | 2 mL |
| 1 | clove garlic, minced | 1 |
| 3 lb | fryer chicken, cut up | 1.5 kg |
| 8 cups | chicken broth | 2 L |
| 2 | carrots, sliced | 2 |
| ⅓ cup | long-grain rice | 75 mL |
| 1 | small zucchini, cubed | 1 |
| 1½ cups | frozen corn | 375 mL |
| | Salt and pepper | |
| 1 | tomato | 1 |
| | Fresh coriander sprigs | |
| | Lime wedges | |

In large kettle, heat oil over medium heat; cook onion, jalapeños, cumin, oregano and garlic, stirring often, for about 5 minutes or until onion is softened.

Add all of the chicken except breasts. Stir in broth; bring to boil over high heat. Reduce heat, cover and simmer for 20 minutes.

Add carrots, rice and chicken breasts; cover and cook for about 15 minutes or until chicken breasts are no longer pink. Skim off fat. Remove chicken and let cool enough to handle. Tear meat into bite-size pieces and return to soup, discarding skin and bones. (Soup can be prepared to this point, cooled, covered and refrigerated for up to 1 day. Remove any remaining fat from top of broth.)

Heat soup, covered, over medium heat until simmering. Add zucchini and corn; simmer, uncovered, for about 5 minutes or until zucchini is tender-crisp. Season with salt and pepper to taste.

Seed unpeeled tomato and cut into large cubes; stir into soup. Serve immediately garnished with coriander. Pass lime wedges to squeeze into hot soup. Makes 6 servings.

# Caldo Gallego
## (Portuguese Potato and Kale Soup)

Kale in Portugal is mild and tender. At country markets, you see women stacking the leaves, rolling them into fat "cigars" and shaving them into tiny shreds on hand-cranked shredding wheels. If you can't find kale, substitute collards, cabbage, spinach, turnip or mustard greens. The sausage is actually chourico in Portugal and is similar to the more widely available Spanish chorizo which may be substituted for it in recipes. For an even heartier soup, substitute chicken stock for the water. Serve with Portuguese corn bread, known as broa.

| | | |
|---|---|---|
| 1 tbsp | olive oil | 15 mL |
| 2 | chicken breasts (about ¾ lb/375 g) | 2 |
| 1 | onion, chopped | 1 |
| 1 | clove garlic, minced | 1 |
| 2 | potatoes, peeled and cut in ½-inch (1 cm) cubes | 2 |
| 8 cups | water | 2 L |
| ½ tsp | salt | 2 mL |
| ¼ tsp | pepper | 1 mL |
| ½ lb | chorizo, pepperoni or other spicy sausage, thinly sliced | 250 g |
| 1 | can (19 oz/540 mL) red kidney beans, drained and rinsed | 1 |
| 3 cups | shredded kale (coarse stems removed) | 750 mL |

In large kettle, heat oil over medium heat; add chicken and brown all over. Remove and set aside.

Add onion and garlic to pan; cook, stirring, for 3 minutes without browning. Add potatoes; cook, stirring, for 2 to 3 minutes or until beginning to color. Stir in water, salt and pepper; bring to boil, stirring to scrape up any brown bits from bottom of pan.

Return chicken to pan; reduce heat and cook, covered, for 20 to 25 minutes or until chicken is no longer pink inside. Remove chicken and let cool enough to handle. Tear meat into bite-size pieces, discarding skin and bones. Set meat aside.

Meanwhile, in skillet, fry sausage over low heat for 10 minutes or until browned; drain well and add to soup. Add beans; cook, covered, for 5 minutes. Add kale and chicken; cook, uncovered, for about 5 minutes or until kale is tender. Taste and adjust seasoning. Makes 4 to 6 servings.

# Beef Borscht

The addition of beans to this hearty Ukrainian soup makes it a main-course hit. My friend and assistant, Sharon Boyd, who is of Ukrainian background, might use green beans when they're in season instead of white. We both agree that this is a good time to try the julienne blade on your food processor. Before serving, taste for salt, pepper, sugar and vinegar, adding more if desired; there should be a hint of vinegar.

| | | |
|---|---|---|
| 1 tbsp | vegetable oil | 15 mL |
| 1 lb | lean beef, diced | 500 g |
| 8 cups | water or beef broth | 2 L |
| 1 tsp | salt | 5 mL |
| 2 tbsp | butter | 25 mL |
| 4 | beets, peeled and julienned | 4 |
| 1 | EACH carrot and parsnip, julienned | 1 |
| 1 | onion, chopped | 1 |
| 2 | large cloves garlic, minced | 2 |
| 2 tbsp | EACH tomato paste and red wine vinegar | 25 mL |
| 1 tsp | granulated sugar | 5 mL |
| 2 | bay leaves | 2 |
| 4 cups | shredded cabbage | 1 L |
| 1 | can (19 oz/540 mL) white pea (navy) beans, drained and rinsed<br>Pepper | 1 |
| 1 tbsp | snipped fresh dill (approx) (or 1 tsp/5 mL dried dillweed)<br>Sour cream | 15 mL |

In large heavy saucepan, heat oil over medium-high heat; add beef and brown. Stir in water and salt; bring to boil. Reduce heat, cover and simmer for about 1¼ hours or until meat is tender.

Meanwhile, in another large saucepan, melt butter over medium heat; cook beets, carrot, parsnip, onion and garlic, stirring, for 5 minutes. Stir in tomato paste, vinegar, sugar and bay leaves; bring to boil. Reduce heat, cover and simmer for 10 minutes.

Add cabbage and beans; simmer for 10 more minutes. Stir into meat mixture. Season with pepper to taste. Simmer for 5 to 10 minutes for flavors to blend. Discard bay leaves. (Soup can be cooled, covered and refrigerated for up to 2 days or frozen for up to 4 months.) Stir in dill. Serve garnished with dollop of sour cream. Sprinkle with more fresh dill if desired. Makes 6 to 8 servings.

# Quick Mushroom, Beef and Barley Soup

This thick, nourishing soup is reminiscent of grandmother's long-simmering version, except that you can make this one in minutes.

| | | |
|---|---|---|
| 2 tbsp | butter | 25 mL |
| ½ lb | mushrooms, sliced | 250 g |
| 1 | clove garlic, minced | 1 |
| 1 tsp | dried marjoram | 5 mL |
| 5 cups | beef broth | 1.25 L |
| 1 | can (14 oz/398 mL) tomato sauce | 1 |
| 2 cups | water | 500 mL |
| 1 | bay leaf | 1 |
| 1 lb | lean ground beef | 500 g |
| 4 | potatoes, cut in ¾-inch (2 cm) cubes | 4 |
| ¾ cup | pot or pearl barley | 175 mL |
| | Salt and pepper | |
| Half | pkg (10 oz/284 g) fresh spinach, chopped | Half |

In large kettle, melt butter; cook mushrooms and garlic over medium-high heat for 5 minutes, stirring often. Sprinkle with marjoram. Stir in broth, tomato sauce, water and bay leaf.

Meanwhile, in skillet, cook beef, breaking up with wooden spoon, until no longer pink. Drain well and add to kettle.

Add potatoes and barley; bring to boil. Reduce heat, cover and simmer for 25 to 30 minutes or until potatoes and barley are tender. Season with salt and pepper to taste. Discard bay leaf.

Stir in spinach; cover and cook for about 4 minutes or just until wilted but still bright green. Makes 6 to 8 servings.

# Lentil and Lemon Soup with Bacon

If you like the fresh taste of lemon, you'll love this simple vegetable soup scented with cumin. Serve with grain bread.

| | | |
|---|---|---|
| 1½ cups | dried green lentils | 375 mL |
| 6 | slices side bacon | 6 |
| 3 | carrots, sliced | 3 |
| 2 | stalks celery, sliced | 2 |
| 1 | onion, chopped | 1 |
| 1 | clove garlic, minced | 1 |
| 5 cups | chicken broth | 1.25 L |
| 1 tsp | grated lemon rind | 5 mL |
| 1 | bay leaf | 1 |
| ½ tsp | salt | 2 mL |
| ½ cup | chopped fresh parsley | 125 mL |
| ¼ cup | fresh lemon juice | 50 mL |
| 1 tsp | ground cumin | 5 mL |

Sort and rinse lentils; set aside. In large saucepan, fry bacon until crisp. Drain on paper towels; cool and crumble.

Discard all but 2 tbsp (25 mL) drippings from pan. Add carrots, celery, onion and garlic; cook over medium heat, stirring, for 5 minutes or until onion is softened. Add lentils. Stir in broth, lemon rind, bay leaf and salt; bring to boil. Reduce heat, cover and simmer for about 45 minutes or until lentils are tender. Discard bay leaf.

Stir in parsley, crumbled bacon, lemon juice and cumin. Taste and adjust seasoning. Makes 6 servings.

# Poached Lamb Shoulder with Root Vegetables

Full-flavored lamb makes a happy companion for storage root vegetables. If you wish, use the same weight of shanks instead of shoulder.

| | | |
|---|---|---|
| 1 | boneless lamb shoulder (about 1¾ lb/875 g) | 1 |
| 1 tbsp | vegetable oil | 15 mL |
| 1 | onion, sliced | 1 |
| | Salt and pepper | |
| 2 | cloves garlic, minced | 2 |
| 1 tsp | dried marjoram | 5 mL |
| ¼ tsp | dried thyme | 1 mL |
| 1 | bay leaf | 1 |
| 12 cups | water | 3 L |
| 1 tbsp | tomato paste | 15 mL |
| Half | rutabaga | Half |
| 2 | EACH potatoes, turnips, carrots and parsnips | 2 |
| ½ cup | chopped fresh parsley | 125 mL |

Trim any fat from lamb but leave meat in one piece. In large saucepan, heat oil over medium heat; add lamb and onion and brown lamb all over, sprinkling with salt and pepper to taste and stirring onion occasionally. Stir in garlic, marjoram, ½ tsp (2 mL) salt, thyme and bay leaf.

Pour in 12 cups (3 L) water and tomato paste; bring to a boil. Reduce heat to low, partially cover and simmer for about 1 hour and 15 minutes or until lamb is tender. Discard bay leaf.

Remove lamb to plate and let cool enough to handle; cut into bite-size cubes.

Meanwhile, remove any fat from top of liquid and simmer broth for 15 minutes, uncovered.

Meanwhile, peel and cut rutabaga, potatoes, turnips, carrots and parsnips into ½-inch (1 cm) cubes. Add to broth; cover and simmer for 15 minutes. Return meat cubes to pan and heat through for about 5 minutes. Taste and adjust seasoning. Stir in half of the parsley. Serve garnished with remaining parsley. Makes about 8 servings.

# Herbed Shrimp and Cod Chowder

This easy chowder makes a quick midweek supper with brown bread and a green salad. Vary the fish according to what's available and good in the market. Salt pork is worth seeking out for its flavor, but if it's unavailable use bacon.

| | | |
|---|---|---|
| ¼ lb | salt pork | 125 g |
| 1 | onion, thinly sliced | 1 |
| ½ tsp | dried thyme | 2 mL |
| ¼ tsp | dried marjoram | 1 mL |
| 1 | bay leaf | 1 |
| 4 | potatoes, peeled and thinly sliced | 4 |
| ⅓ cup | dry white wine | 75 mL |
| 2 cups | milk | 500 mL |
| 1 | bottle (237 mL) clam juice | 1 |
| 1 cup | light cream | 250 mL |
| ⅔ lb | cod, cut in 1-inch (2.5 cm) cubes | 350 g |
| ½ lb | shrimp, shelled and deveined | 250 g |
| ¼ tsp | Tabasco sauce | 1 mL |
| | Salt and pepper | |
| 2 tbsp | chopped fresh parsley | 25 mL |

Rinse salt pork under cold water; dry well and finely dice. In large saucepan, sauté salt pork over medium-high heat until crisp, 5 to 8 minutes. With slotted spoon, transfer to paper towels to drain; set aside.

Pour off all but 2 tbsp (25 mL) drippings from pan. Add onion, thyme, marjoram and bay leaf; cook for about 2 minutes or until onion is softened. Add potatoes; cook over high heat, stirring, for about 5 minutes or until beginning to soften. Add wine; reduce heat and simmer, uncovered, for 3 minutes. Stir in milk, clam juice and cream; simmer, uncovered, for 15 minutes or until potatoes are tender. (Do not let boil.)

Stir in cod and shrimp; simmer, uncovered, for 5 minutes or until fish flakes when tested with a fork and shrimp are pink. Discard bay leaf. Stir in Tabasco sauce. Season with salt and pepper to taste. Serve garnished with reserved salt pork bits and parsley. Makes 4 servings.

---

The word "chowder" is a corruption of the French word *chaudière*, a large heavy pot used by fishermen and farmers to cook soups.

# Mussel Stew with Roasted Garlic Mayonnaise

With the delicious flavor of mussels as its focus, this quick-to-make stew is a great comforter on a cold Friday night. Or, enjoy it for lunch with weekend guests with a loaf of grain bread, a green salad and fresh fruit.

| | | |
|---|---|---|
| 2 lb | mussels | 1 kg |
| ¾ cup | dry white wine | 175 mL |
| 3 | shallots, minced | 3 |
| 3 tbsp | chopped fresh parsley | 45 mL |
| 2 tbsp | butter | 25 mL |
| 2 | leeks, sliced | 2 |
| 1 | fennel bulb, chopped | 1 |
| 2 | cloves garlic, minced | 2 |
| 1 | bay leaf | 1 |
| 1 tsp | dried thyme | 5 mL |
| 3 | potatoes, peeled and diced | 3 |
| 1 | can (28 oz/796 mL) tomatoes, diced | 1 |
| 2 cups | fish stock* | 500 mL |
| 1 lb | fresh fish (cod or haddock), cubed | 500 g |
| | Roasted Garlic Mayonnaise (recipe follows) | |

Scrub and debeard mussels; discard any that do not close when tapped. Place in large saucepan with wine, shallots and parsley. Cover and bring to boil over medium-high heat; cook, shaking pan occasionally, until mussels open, 4 to 5 minutes. Discard any that do not open.

Place strainer over bowl; pour in mussels, reserving liquid in bowl. Remove mussels from shells and discard shells. Set mussels aside.

In same saucepan, melt butter over medium heat; cook leeks, fennel, garlic, bay leaf and thyme for 5 minutes. Add potatoes; cook for 2 minutes, stirring. Stir in tomatoes, mussel liquid and fish stock; bring to boil. Reduce heat, cover and cook for 20 minutes or until vegetables are tender. Discard bay leaf. (Stew can be prepared to this point, cooled, covered and refrigerated overnight; bring to simmer before proceeding. Cover and refrigerate mussels separately.)

Add fish; cook for 5 minutes. Return mussels to pan; cook for 2 minutes. Serve garnished with Roasted Garlic Mayonnaise. Makes 6 servings.

# Roasted Garlic Mayonnaise

| 10 | large cloves garlic (unpeeled) | 10 |
| ½ cup | mayonnaise | 125 mL |

Pierce each garlic clove. Enclose in foil and roast in 375°F (190°C) oven for about 30 minutes or until softened. Let cool; press out garlic and mash. Blend into mayonnaise. (Mayonnaise can be covered and refrigerated for up to 3 days.) Makes ½ cup (125 mL).

---

*Fish stock is simple to make if you have raw fish scraps such as heads and bones. Just simmer, uncovered, in cold water with diced celery, chopped leeks or onions and seasonings for about 30 minutes; then strain through cheesecloth. I often use bottled or canned clam juice instead of fish stock.

# Hearty Meatball Soup

Enjoy this fast main-course soup with crusty bread and a green salad.

| | | |
|---|---|---|
| 1 tbsp | vegetable or olive oil (approx) | 15 mL |
| 4 cups | coarsely shredded cabbage | 1 L |
| 2 | stalks celery (with leaves), sliced | 2 |
| 1 | onion, sliced | 1 |
| 6 cups | beef broth | 1.5 L |
| 1 | can (14 oz/398 mL) tomatoes, chopped | 1 |
| 1 | can (19 oz/540 mL) kidney beans (undrained) | 1 |
| 1 tbsp | chili powder | 15 mL |
| 36 | frozen Basic Meatballs (recipe, page 124) | 36 |
| ½ cup | macaroni | 125 mL |
| | Celery leaves (optional) | |

In large kettle, heat oil over medium-low heat; cook cabbage, celery and onion for 5 minutes, stirring often and adding a bit more oil if necessary.

Stir in broth, tomatoes, kidney beans and chili powder; bring to boil. Stir in frozen Basic Meatballs and macaroni; simmer, covered, for 15 minutes or until vegetables are tender and meatballs are heated through. Serve garnished with celery leaves if desired. Makes 6 servings.

# White Bean and Pepper Soup with Spiced Yogurt

You could, of course, serve this hearty soup without the yogurt garnish, but it does add a nice spark of flavor. Smoked pork hocks, available in delis, farmers' markets and most supermarkets, lend a lovely smokiness.

| | | |
|---|---|---|
| 1 lb | dried white pea (navy) beans (2 cups/500 mL) | 500 g |
| 1 | small smoked pork hock or meaty ham bone | 1 |
| 2 tbsp | olive oil | 25 mL |
| 4 | leeks, sliced | 4 |
| 6 | cloves garlic | 6 |
| ½ tsp | salt | 2 mL |
| 5 | large carrots, thinly sliced | 5 |
| 1 | EACH sweet green and red pepper, cut in short strips | 1 |
| 1 tsp | EACH ground cumin, dried thyme and dried marjoram | 5 mL |
| 1 tbsp | packed brown sugar | 15 mL |
| ¼ tsp | EACH cayenne and black pepper | 1 mL |
| 2½ cups | beef broth | 625 mL |
| ¼ cup | chopped fresh parsley | 50 mL |
| | Spiced Yogurt (recipe follows) | |

Sort and rinse beans. In large saucepan, cover beans with 8 cups (2 L) cold water and let soak overnight in refrigerator. (Or, cover with water and bring to boil; boil for 2 minutes. Remove from heat; cover and let stand for 1 hour.)

Drain beans; cover again with 8 cups (2 L) fresh cold water. Add pork hock; bring to boil. Reduce heat, cover and simmer for about 45 minutes or until beans are tender.

Meanwhile, in large skillet, heat oil over medium heat; cook leeks for 5 minutes. Meanwhile, mince and mash garlic with salt. Add to pan along with carrots; cook for 3 minutes over medium-low heat. Stir in peppers, cumin, thyme, marjoram, brown sugar, cayenne and black pepper. Stir in broth and bring to boil, stirring to scrape up any brown bits from bottom of pan.

Remove hock from beans; cut off and dice any meat, discarding skin and bone. Return meat to pot along with carrot mixture; bring to boil. Reduce heat, cover and simmer for 30 minutes. Taste and adjust seasoning. Stir in parsley. Serve garnished with dollop of Spiced Yogurt. Makes 8 to 10 servings.

# Spiced Yogurt

| | | |
|---|---|---|
| ½ cup | plain yogurt | 125 mL |
| ½ tsp | EACH paprika and ground cumin | 2 mL |
| ¼ tsp | turmeric | 1 mL |
| Pinch | cayenne pepper | Pinch |

In small bowl, whisk together yogurt, paprika, cumin, turmeric and cayenne. Makes ½ cup (125 mL).

# Black Forest–Style Split Pea Soup

Split peas in a hearty soup have been part of our Canadian heritage ever since the voyageurs combined them with salt pork and water. Here, I'm leaving home to give them a bit of German flavor. Accompany with light rye bread and a red and green cabbage slaw dressed with sour cream.

| | | |
|---|---|---|
| 2 tbsp | vegetable oil | 25 mL |
| 2 | EACH onions, carrots and potatoes, chopped | 2 |
| 1 | EACH stalk celery and clove garlic, chopped | 1 |
| 1 | bottle (341 mL) beer | 1 |
| 1 | large smoked pork hock or meaty ham bone | 1 |
| 1 lb | dried green split peas, rinsed and drained (2 cups/500 mL) | 500 g |
| 8 cups | water | 2 L |
| 2 tsp | mustard seeds, crushed | 10 mL |
| 1 tsp | EACH dried thyme and marjoram | 5 mL |
| Pinch | EACH ground cloves and pepper | Pinch |
| ½ lb | European-style weiners or bratwurst, sliced | 250 g |
| 2 tbsp | cider vinegar (optional) | 25 mL |
| | Salt | |
| ¼ cup | chopped fresh parsley | 50 mL |
| | Parsley Croutons (optional), (recipe follows) | |

In large saucepan, heat oil over medium heat; cook onions, carrots, potatoes, celery and garlic for 5 minutes, stirring often. Stir in beer and bring to boil, scraping up any brown bits from bottom of pan.

Add pork hock, peas, water, mustard seeds, thyme, marjoram, cloves and pepper; bring to boil. Reduce heat, cover and simmer for 2 hours, stirring occasionally.

Remove hock; cut off and dice any meat, discarding skin and bone. Return meat to pot along with weiners, vinegar (if using), and salt to taste; heat for 2 to 3 minutes. Stir in parsley. Serve sprinkled with Parsley Croutons, if desired. Makes 8 to 10 servings.

# Parsley Croutons

You can, of course, use other herbs or skip them altogether.

| | | |
|---|---|---|
| 4 | slices Italian or French bread | 4 |
| ½ cup | unsalted butter | 125 mL |
| 2 tbsp | chopped fresh parsley | 25 mL |

Cut bread into ½-inch (1 cm) cubes. In large skillet, melt butter over medium heat; stir in parsley. Add bread cubes; toss until golden brown and crisp, about 5 minutes. Drain on paper towels. Makes 3 cups (750 mL).

---

**To crush mustard seeds, use a mortar and pestle. Or, place in sturdy little plastic bag and crush with rolling pin or bottom of heavy skillet.**

# Smoked Fish and Corn Chowder

A touch of heat and smoked rather than fresh fish lend a new twist to an old favorite. It's delicious with dense corn bread.

| | | |
|---|---|---|
| 2 tbsp | butter | 25 mL |
| 2 | leeks, thinly sliced | 2 |
| 3 cups | diced peeled potatoes | 750 mL |
| Half | sweet red pepper, finely diced | Half |
| 1 | jalapeño pepper, seeded and diced | 1 |
| 2 tbsp | all-purpose flour | 25 mL |
| 2½ cups | chicken broth | 625 mL |
| 1½ cups | milk | 375 mL |
| 2 cups | canned or frozen corn kernels, drained | 500 mL |
| | Salt and pepper | |
| ¼ lb | smoked salmon, trout or mackerel | 125 g |
| | Chopped fresh parsley or chervil | |

In large saucepan, melt butter over medium-low heat; cook leeks, potatoes, red pepper and jalapeño, stirring often, until wilted, about 10 minutes. Sprinkle with flour; cook for 2 minutes, stirring.

Add chicken broth and bring to boil, stirring constantly; cook for 5 minutes, stirring often. Stir in milk; simmer for 3 to 4 minutes. Add corn, and salt and pepper to taste; return to simmer. Turn off heat.

Cut fish into pea-size pieces; carefully add to chowder and heat for 2 minutes without stirring. Serve garnished with parsley. Makes 4 servings.

---

**To prepare leeks, trim off dark green tops and roots. Split lengthwise, spread leaves and hold under cold running water to wash away any sand. Finely slice crosswise.**

# Monda Rosenberg's Oriental Chicken Noodle Soup

This quick and easy recipe is courtesy of my good friend Monda Rosenberg, Food Editor of *Chatelaine* magazine. If you have a few Oriental staples on hand, you can make it whenever you feel like a comforting hot bowl of soup that has lots of flavor. Monda suggests stirring in thick slices of bok choy if you wish, or shrimp and snow peas for a fancier version.

| | | |
|---|---|---|
| 1 cup | dried Oriental mushrooms (about ½ oz/14 g) | 250 mL |
| 6 cups | chicken broth | 1.5 L |
| 2 cups | water | 500 mL |
| 2 tbsp | dry sherry | 25 mL |
| 1 tbsp | soy sauce | 15 mL |
| 1 tsp | sesame oil (preferably dark) | 5 mL |
| ½ to 1 tsp | hot pepper flakes | 2 to 5 mL |
| 2 | cloves garlic, crushed | 2 |
| 1 | piece (1-inch/2.5 cm) unpeeled fresh ginger, thinly sliced | 1 |
| 1 lb | skinless boneless chicken breasts | 500 g |
| 4 | green onions | 4 |
| Half | pkg (450 g) rice noodles (about ¼-inch/5 mm wide), broken up | Half |

Rinse mushrooms in sieve under warm water. Place in bowl and cover with about 1 cup (250 mL) hot water. Let stand to soften while preparing soup. Meanwhile, in large saucepan, combine chicken broth, water, sherry, soy sauce, sesame oil, hot pepper flakes, garlic and ginger; bring to boil. Slice chicken into bite-size strips; stir into rapidly boiling soup. Reduce heat to low so soup is just simmering. Simmer, covered, until chicken is no longer pink, 6 to 8 minutes.

Saving soaking liquid, drain mushrooms. Remove and discard any stems; thinly slice mushrooms if not already sliced. Add mushrooms and liquid to soup. (Soup can be prepared to this point, cooled, covered and refrigerated for up to 2 days; reheat gently.)

Meanwhile, diagonally slice onions into 1-inch (2.5 cm) pieces. Place dry noodles in sieve; rinse with warm water. Stir onions and noodles into soup. Heat until hot and serve immediately. (By the time soup is heated through, noodles will be cooked.) Makes 4 servings.

# Mulligatawny Soup

There are many variations of this interesting Indian soup which derives its name from *mullaga* (pepper) and *tanni* (water or broth). This simplified version is absolutely delicious. Warm some poppadums (thin, crisp bread available in East Indian shops) to go alongside.

| | | |
|---|---|---|
| ¼ cup | all-purpose flour | 50 mL |
| 3 | chicken breast halves | 3 |
| | (about 1½ lb/625 g total) | |
| 2 tbsp | vegetable oil | 25 mL |
| 4 | carrots, cut in ½-inch | 4 |
| | (1 cm) diagonal slices | |
| 4 | parsnips, diced | 4 |
| 2 | onions, chopped | 2 |
| 2 | stalks celery, cut in ¼-inch | 2 |
| | (5 mm) slices | |
| 2 | apples, peeled and diced | 2 |
| 2 tbsp | curry powder | 25 mL |
| ¼ tsp | mace | 1 mL |
| Pinch | cayenne pepper | Pinch |
| 6 cups | chicken broth | 1.5 L |
| 1 cup | light cream | 250 mL |
| | Salt and pepper | |
| 1 cup | hot cooked rice | 250 mL |
| ¼ cup | chopped fresh coriander or parsley | 50 mL |

Place flour in plastic bag; add chicken and shake to coat well, reserving remaining flour.

In large saucepan or kettle, heat oil over medium heat; brown chicken evenly on all sides. Remove chicken and set aside.

Remove any dark brown bits from pan with paper towel. To fat remaining in pan, add carrots, parsnips, onions, celery, apples, curry powder, mace and cayenne; cook, stirring, over medium-high heat until coated with fat. Reduce heat to low; cover and cook, stirring often, for 10 minutes. Sprinkle in reserved flour; cook, stirring, for 2 minutes. Gradually stir in broth.

Return chicken to pot and bring to boil; reduce heat, cover and simmer for 1 hour, stirring occasionally. Remove chicken; cut meat into bite-size pieces, discarding skin and bones. Return to soup. (Soup can be prepared to this point, covered and refrigerated overnight.)

Stir in cream. Season with salt and pepper to taste; heat gently over low heat but do not boil. Place large spoonful of rice and some of the coriander in each soup bowl; ladle soup over top. Makes 8 servings.

# Quick Ham and Bean Soup with Macaroni

Using some of the leftover ham from Sunday dinner, this fresh-tasting soup takes only minutes to put together with ingredients you probably have on hand.

| | | |
|---|---|---|
| 2 tbsp | olive oil | 25 mL |
| 1 | onion, chopped | 1 |
| 1 | sweet green pepper, diced | 1 |
| 2 | cloves garlic, minced | 2 |
| 1½ cups | diced cooked ham | 375 mL |
| 3 cups | water | 750 mL |
| 1 | can (28 oz/796 mL) tomatoes | 1 |
| ½ tsp | dried marjoram | 2 mL |
| ¼ tsp | dried thyme | 1 mL |
| | Salt and pepper | |
| ½ cup | small macaroni | 125 mL |
| 1 | can (19 oz/540 mL) Romano beans, drained and rinsed | 1 |

In large saucepan, heat oil over medium heat; cook onion, half of the green pepper, the garlic and ham for 5 minutes.

Stir in water, tomatoes, marjoram, thyme, and salt and pepper to taste; bring to boil. Add macaroni; cook over medium heat for 5 minutes.

Stir in beans and remaining green pepper; cook for 3 minutes or until macaroni is tender. Makes about 4 servings.

# Pasta

# Two-Cheese Baked Penne with Roasted Vegetables

This is the type of make-ahead casserole I love serving to company. Your family will love it too, and you can easily make it in two 9-inch (2.5 L) square baking dishes to freeze one and enjoy the other now. A crisp green salad goes well with the smooth texture of the two deliciously melted cheeses.

| | | |
|---|---|---|
| 2 | sweet red or yellow peppers, sliced | 2 |
| ½ lb | mushrooms, quartered | 250 g |
| 2 | small zucchini, sliced | 2 |
| 2 | small red onions, cubed | 2 |
| 4 | cloves garlic, minced | 4 |
| ¼ cup | olive oil | 50 mL |
| | Salt and pepper | |
| ½ cup | chopped fresh parsley | 125 mL |
| 2 tbsp | chopped fresh basil | 25 mL |
| | (or 2 tsp/10 mL dried) | |
| ½ tsp | dried rosemary | 2 mL |
| 5 cups | penne pasta with ridges (1 lb/500 g) | 1.25 L |
| 1 | can (28 oz/796 mL) meatless spaghetti sauce | 1 |
| 1 lb | provolone cheese, shredded | 500 g |
| 1 cup | freshly grated Asiago or Parmesan cheese | 250 mL |

In large shallow pan, toss peppers, mushrooms, zucchini, onions and garlic with oil; spread out and roast in 450°F (230°C) oven for about 25 minutes or until softened, stirring once or twice. Season with salt and pepper to taste. Stir in ⅓ cup (75 mL) of the parsley, basil and rosemary.

Meanwhile, in large pot of boiling salted water, cook pasta just until al dente, about 8 minutes. Pour in 2 cups (500 mL) cold water; drain well and cool. Gently combine with spaghetti sauce, vegetables, provolone and half of the Asiago cheese. Transfer to greased shallow 12-cup (3 L) baking dish. Sprinkle with remaining Asiago and parsley. (Pasta can be prepared to this point, covered and refrigerated for up to 1 day, or frozen for up to 2 months. Thaw in refrigerator. Bring to room temperature before heating.)

Bake, covered, in 375°F (190°C) oven for 30 minutes. Uncover and bake for 10 to 15 minutes longer or until bubbly. Makes 8 servings.

# Pasta E Fagioli Casserole

I love the comforting pasta and bean soup that inspired me to develop this recipe. The casserole is the type of thing I might make to serve half tonight to my family and freeze the remainder for another time. It's great with a crisp green salad and fresh fruit.

| | | |
|---|---|---|
| 1 lb | Italian sausage (mild or hot) | 500 g |
| 1 | EACH onion, carrot and stalk celery, chopped | 1 |
| 4 | cloves garlic, minced | 4 |
| 1 tsp | dried oregano | 5 mL |
| ½ tsp | dried basil | 2 mL |
| ¼ tsp | hot pepper flakes | 1 mL |
| 1 | can (28 oz/796 mL) tomatoes, coarsely chopped | 1 |
| 2 tbsp | tomato paste | 25 mL |
| 1 | can (19 oz/540 mL) Romano or kidney beans, drained and rinsed | 1 |
| | Salt and pepper | |
| 5 cups | penne pasta (1 lb/500 g) | 1.25 L |
| ½ cup | EACH freshly grated Parmesan cheese and chopped fresh parsley | 125 mL |
| ½ lb | Fontina or provolone cheese, shredded | 250 g |

Remove casings from sausage. In large skillet over medium-high heat, cook sausage, crumbling with fork, onion, carrot, celery, garlic, oregano, basil and hot pepper flakes until sausage is browned.

Add tomatoes and tomato paste; simmer, uncovered, for 10 minutes, stirring occasionally. Stir in beans, and salt and pepper to taste; cook for 5 minutes.

Meanwhile, in large pot of boiling salted water, cook pasta just until al dente, about 8 minutes. Drain and combine with tomato mixture, half of the Parmesan cheese and half of the parsley. Transfer to greased 13- x 9-inch (3 L) glass baking dish. (If making ahead, cool slightly.)

Sprinkle with Fontina cheese and remaining Parmesan and parsley. (Pasta can be prepared to this point, covered and refrigerated for up to 1 day, or frozen for up to 2 months. Thaw in refrigerator. Bring to room temperature before heating.)

Bake, covered, in 400°F (200°C) oven for 20 minutes; uncover and bake for 10 to 15 minutes or until bubbly. Makes 8 servings.

# Baked Tortellini with Three Cheeses

Packaged tortellini and frozen peas team up with lots of creamy cheese to make this super easy supper.

| | | |
|---|---|---|
| 1 | pkg (350 g) meat- or cheese-filled tortellini | 1 |
| 3 tbsp | butter | 45 mL |
| 1 cup | fresh bread crumbs | 250 mL |
| 2 | cloves garlic, minced | 2 |
| 1 | small onion, chopped | 1 |
| 4 tsp | all-purpose flour | 20 mL |
| 1 cup | milk | 250 mL |
| 1 tsp | dried basil | 5 mL |
| | Salt and pepper | |
| 1 cup | shredded low-fat mozzarella cheese | 250 mL |
| 1 cup | low-fat cottage cheese | 250 mL |
| ½ cup | freshly grated Parmesan cheese | 125 mL |
| 1½ cups | frozen peas | 375 mL |

In large pot of boiling salted water, cook tortellini according to package directions. Drain well and transfer to well-greased 8-cup (2 L) shallow casserole.

Meanwhile, in large skillet, melt butter. Transfer 1 tbsp (15 mL) to small bowl; stir in bread crumbs and set aside.

Add garlic and onion to skillet; cook over medium heat, stirring often, for 4 minutes or until onion is softened. Sprinkle with flour; cook, stirring, for 1 minute.

Gradually stir in milk. Sprinkle with three-quarters of the basil, and salt and pepper to taste. Cook, stirring, for 2 to 3 minutes or until thickened and bubbly. Remove from heat. Stir in mozzarella, cottage cheese and Parmesan until smooth. Pour over tortellini in casserole. Rinse peas under hot water; gently stir into casserole.

Stir remaining basil into bread crumb mixture; sprinkle over casserole. (Pasta can be prepared to this point, covered and refrigerated for up to 6 hours. Remove from refrigerator 30 minutes before proceeding.) Bake, uncovered, in 375°F (190°C) oven for 20 to 30 minutes or until bubbly. Makes 4 servings.

# Macaroni Tomato Pie

This colorful variation on macaroni and cheese makes a quick and easy family supper with a green salad.

| | | |
|---|---|---|
| 1¼ cups | macaroni | 300 mL |
| 1 | egg, beaten | 1 |
| 1½ cups | shredded Cheddar cheese | 375 mL |
| 1 | can (19 oz/540 mL) stewed tomatoes | 1 |
| ¼ tsp | EACH salt, pepper, dried oregano and basil | 1 mL |
| 1 cup | fresh bread crumbs | 250 mL |
| 1 tbsp | butter, melted | 15 mL |

In large pot of boiling salted water, cook macaroni until al dente, about 8 minutes; drain well. Stir in egg and 1 cup (250 mL) of the Cheddar. Spread over bottom and side of greased 9-inch (23 cm) pie plate.

Stir together tomatoes, salt, pepper, oregano and basil; pour into macaroni shell. Sprinkle with remaining Cheddar.

Toss bread crumbs with butter; sprinkle over top, covering edge of macaroni shell. Bake in 350°F (180°C) oven for 25 to 30 minutes or until golden. Makes 4 servings.

# Tex-Mex
# Macaroni and Cheese

Everyone loves macaroni and cheese, and this one has an interesting south-of-the-border twist.

| | | |
|---|---|---|
| 2 cups | macaroni (8 oz/250 g) | 500 mL |
| 2 tbsp | butter | 25 mL |
| 3 tbsp | all-purpose flour | 45 mL |
| 1 tsp | dry mustard | 5 mL |
| ½ tsp | salt | 2 mL |
| ¼ tsp | pepper | 1 mL |
| 2 cups | milk | 500 mL |
| 2 cups | shredded mild Cheddar cheese (½ lb/250 g) | 500 mL |
| ¼ cup | chopped, rinsed, canned or bottled jalapeño peppers (114 mL can) | 50 mL |
| 1 tsp | Worcestershire sauce | 5 mL |
| 1 tbsp | vegetable oil | 15 mL |
| ¼ cup | chopped green onions (about 3) | 50 mL |
| 1 tsp | EACH chili powder and dried oregano | 5 mL |
| 1 | can (7½ oz/213 mL) tomato sauce Chopped green onion tops | 1 |

In large pot of boiling salted water, cook macaroni until al dente, about 8 minutes. Drain and return to pot.

Meanwhile, in medium saucepan, melt butter; whisk in flour, mustard, salt and pepper. Whisking constantly, gradually add milk, whisking until blended. Cook over medium heat, stirring constantly, for 2 to 3 minutes or until thickened. Reduce heat to low; simmer for 1 minute. Remove from heat. Stir in 1½ cups (375 mL) of the cheese, jalapeño peppers and Worcestershire sauce until cheese is completely melted, 1 to 2 minutes.

Stir sauce into drained macaroni. Transfer to greased 8-cup (2 L) deep casserole. Bake, uncovered, in 375°F (190°C) oven for 25 to 30 minutes or until sauce is bubbly.

Meanwhile, in small saucepan, heat oil over medium heat; cook green onions, chili powder and oregano for 1 minute. Stir in tomato sauce and bring to boil. Reduce heat to low; simmer, partially covered, for 10 minutes.

Remove baked macaroni from oven. Spoon tomato sauce over top. Sprinkle with remaining cheese. Serve sprinkled with green onion tops. Makes 4 to 6 servings.

# Tomato Macaroni and Cheese

This is still one of our very favorite pasta dishes—no fancy new ingredients, just old-fashioned flavor and ease.

| | | |
|---|---|---|
| 2 cups | macaroni (8 oz/250 g) | 500 mL |
| ½ lb | Cheddar cheese, preferably old | 250 g |
| 1 | can (19 oz/540 mL) tomatoes, chopped | 1 |
| 1 tsp | EACH granulated sugar, Worcestershire sauce and dry mustard | 5 mL |
| ½ tsp | EACH salt and dried thyme | 2 mL |
| ¼ tsp | pepper | 1 mL |
| ½ cup | dry bread crumbs | 125 mL |
| 2 tbsp | butter, melted | 25 mL |

In large pot of boiling salted water, cook macaroni until al dente, about 8 minutes. Drain well and transfer half to well-greased deep 12-cup (3 L) casserole.

Meanwhile, shred half of the cheese and dice remainder. Sprinkle half of each over macaroni in casserole. Top with remaining macaroni, then remaining cheese.

Stir together tomatoes, sugar, Worcestershire sauce, mustard, salt, thyme and pepper; pour over macaroni. Toss bread crumbs with butter; sprinkle evenly on top. (Casserole can be prepared to this point, covered and refrigerated for up to 1 day. Bring to room temperature.)

Bake, uncovered, in 350°F (180°C) oven for 40 to 50 minutes or until top is golden brown. Makes 4 servings.

# Instant Mac and Cheese

Everyone knows of a university student who practically lived on those boxed macaroni-and-cheese suppers. Well, this one takes only seconds longer to prepare—and tastes much, much better. Round it out with a green salad and whole wheat rolls.

| | | |
|---|---|---|
| 1½ cups | macaroni | 375 mL |
| 1 cup | shredded Cheddar cheese | 250 mL |
| ¼ cup | plain yogurt | 50 mL |
| 1 tbsp | EACH butter and Dijon mustard | 15 mL |
| ¼ tsp | EACH salt and pepper | 1 mL |
| Pinch | hot pepper flakes | Pinch |

In large pot of boiling salted water, cook macaroni until al dente, about 8 minutes; drain well in colander.

Meanwhile, stir together Cheddar and yogurt; set aside.

In same pot, melt butter over low heat; stir in mustard, salt, pepper and hot pepper flakes. Add macaroni and toss to coat. Remove from heat; add cheese mixture and toss. Makes 2 servings.

# Quick Mushroom-Beef Lasagna

This quick and classic lasagna is a family favorite and very easy to put together with oven-ready noodles. Serve with a crisp green salad and whole wheat rolls. If the package of noodles suggests, add 1 cup (250 mL) water to the sauce.

| | | |
|---|---|---|
| 2 tbsp | olive oil | 25 mL |
| 1 lb | mushrooms, sliced (6 cups/1.5 L) | 500 g |
| 1 lb | lean ground beef | 500 g |
| 3 | cloves garlic, minced | 3 |
| 1½ tsp | EACH dried oregano and basil | 7 mL |
| Pinch | EACH granulated sugar and hot pepper flakes | Pinch |
| 1 | can (28 oz/796 mL) crushed tomatoes | 1 |
| 1 | can (14 oz/398 mL) tomato sauce | 1 |
| 1 lb | ricotta cheese, drained if necessary | 500 g |
| 2 | eggs | 2 |
| Pinch | EACH nutmeg and pepper | Pinch |
| 12 to 15 | oven-ready lasagna noodles | 12 to 15 |
| ½ lb | mozzarella cheese, shredded | 250 g |
| ½ cup | freshly grated Parmesan cheese | 125 mL |

In large saucepan, heat oil over medium-high heat; cook mushrooms for 3 minutes. Remove with slotted spoon and set aside. Add beef; cook for about 5 minutes or until no longer pink, breaking up with spoon. Drain off any fat.

Stir in garlic, oregano, basil, sugar and hot pepper flakes. Return mushrooms to pan. Stir in tomatoes and tomato sauce; bring to boil. Reduce heat and cook, stirring often, for 20 to 25 minutes or until thickened.

If not using smooth tub ricotta, whirl with eggs, nutmeg and pepper in food processor or blender until fairly smooth. If already smooth, just beat eggs, nutmeg and pepper together in bowl; stir in ricotta.

To assemble, spread thin base of meat sauce in greased 13- x 9-inch (3 L) baking dish. Cover with layer of noodles, then half of the ricotta mixture, one-third of the remaining meat sauce and one-third of the mozzarella. Repeat layers once. Cover with remaining noodles, meat sauce and mozzarella, being sure noodles are completely covered. Sprinkle with Parmesan. Cover with foil. (Lasagna can be prepared to this point and refrigerated for up to 1 day, or frozen for up to 2 months. Thaw in refrigerator. Remove from refrigerator 30 minutes before heating.)

Bake, loosely covered with foil, in 375°F (190°C) oven for 20 minutes. Uncover and bake for 20 to 25 minutes longer or until bubbly and heated through. Let stand for 10 minutes before serving. Makes 8 servings.

# Easy Layered Lasagna Casserole

This dish has the same wonderful flavor as lasagna but takes less time to make. If you like, you can substitute one can (28 oz/796 mL) meatless spaghetti sauce for the homemade sauce.

| | | |
|---|---|---|
| 1 lb | lean ground beef | 500 g |
| 1 | EACH onion and | 1 |
| | sweet green pepper, chopped | |
| 1 | clove garlic, minced | 1 |
| 3 cups | All-Purpose Cooked Tomato Sauce | 750 mL |
| | (recipe follows) | |
| 4 cups | rigatoni (¾ lb/375 g) | 1 L |
| 1 cup | freshly grated Parmesan cheese | 250 mL |
| 1 cup | shredded Fontina or | 250 mL |
| | mozzarella cheese | |

In large saucepan, cook beef, breaking up with back of spoon, onion, green pepper and garlic over medium heat for 10 minutes or until meat is no longer pink. Drain off any fat. Stir in All-Purpose Cooked Tomato Sauce; bring to boil. Reduce heat, cover and simmer for 15 minutes.

Meanwhile, in large pot of boiling salted water, cook rigatoni until al dente, about 12 minutes. Drain well.

Spread thin base of meat sauce in greased shallow 12-cup (3 L) casserole. Cover with one-third of the pasta, one-third of the remaining meat sauce, and one-third of the Parmesan cheese. Repeat layers twice. Top with Fontina cheese. (Casserole can be prepared to this point, covered and refrigerated for up to 1 day. Remove from refrigerator 30 minutes before heating.)

Bake, covered, in 350°F (180°C) oven for 15 minutes. Uncover and bake for 10 to 15 minutes longer or until bubbly. Makes 6 to 8 servings.

# All-Purpose Cooked Tomato Sauce

This easy all-purpose sauce will keep for several days in the refrigerator or for up to 2 months in the freezer.

| | | |
|---|---|---|
| 1 tbsp | vegetable or olive oil | 15 mL |
| 2 | cans (each 28 oz/796 mL) tomatoes, chopped | 2 |
| 1 | can (5½ oz/156 mL) tomato paste | 1 |
| 4 | cloves garlic, minced | 4 |
| 1 tbsp | granulated sugar | 15 mL |
| 2 tsp | dried basil | 10 mL |
| 1 tsp | dried oregano | 5 mL |
| ½ tsp | EACH salt and pepper | 2 mL |
| ¼ tsp | hot pepper flakes | 1 mL |

In large saucepan, heat oil over medium heat; stir in tomatoes, mashing with potato masher if possible. Stir in tomato paste plus one tomato paste can of water.

Add garlic, sugar, basil, oregano, salt, pepper and hot pepper flakes; bring to boil. Reduce heat to very low and simmer, uncovered, for about 45 minutes or until thickened and fairly smooth. Taste and adjust seasoning. Makes about 7 cups (1.75 L).

# Baked Three-Cheese and Mushroom Pasta

The nutty flavor of Fontina cheese complements the Gorgonzola and underlines this dish's rich mushroom taste. Ordinary white mushrooms are delicious, but if you can find shiitake, brown, portobello or any of the so-called "wild" mushrooms available in supermarkets now, they'll provide an extra meatiness to this vegetarian dish. Do try to find fresh rosemary for this one. Serve with bread sticks and a green salad.

| | | |
|---|---|---|
| 8 cups | tubular pasta (rigatoni, large penne or pennoni rigati) | 2 L |
| ⅓ cup | butter | 75 mL |
| 1 lb | mushrooms, sliced (6 cups/1.5 L) | 500 g |
| 2 | cloves garlic, minced | 2 |
| ¼ cup | all-purpose flour | 50 mL |
| 2 tbsp | chopped fresh rosemary (or 1 tsp/5 mL crushed dried) | 25 mL |
| ¼ tsp | hot pepper flakes | 1 mL |
| ½ cup | dry white wine | 125 mL |
| 4 cups | milk | 1 L |
| | Salt and pepper | |
| 6 oz | Fontina cheese, diced (about 1¼ cups/300 mL) | 175 g |
| ¼ lb | Gorgonzola cheese, crumbled (about 1 cup/250 mL) | 125 g |
| ½ cup | grated Asiago or Parmesan cheese | 125 mL |

In large pot of boiling salted water, cook pasta just until al dente, about 8 minutes. Pour in 2 cups (500 mL) cold water; drain well and cool.

Meanwhile, in large deep skillet, melt butter over medium-high heat; cook mushrooms and garlic, stirring often, for 7 minutes. Reduce heat to medium. Stir in flour, rosemary and hot pepper flakes; cook, stirring, for 3 minutes. Gradually stir in wine, then milk, stirring until smooth. Season with salt and pepper to taste. Cook over low heat for 5 minutes, stirring often.

Arrange half of the pasta in greased 12-cup (3 L) shallow baking dish. Top with half of the mushroom mixture, then half of the Fontina and half of the Gorgonzola. Repeat layers. Sprinkle Asiago on top. (Casserole can be prepared to this point, covered and refrigerated for up to 1 day, or frozen for up to 2 months. Thaw in refrigerator. Bring to room temperature before heating.)

Bake, covered, in 350°F (180°C) oven for 20 minutes. Uncover and bake for 20 minutes or until golden and bubbly. Makes about 6 servings.

# Baked Shells with Spinach and Prosciutto

This simple make-ahead casserole is at its delicious best when made with home-made sauce, but you can still enjoy a version with the equivalent amount of bought meatless spaghetti sauce. I've served it to several people who say they like it even better than popular lasagna.

| | | |
|---|---|---|
| ½ lb | jumbo pasta shells (about 32) | 250 g |
| 1 tbsp | olive oil | 15 mL |
| 1 | onion, chopped | 1 |
| 1 | pkg (10 oz/284 g) fresh spinach, cooked, squeezed dry and chopped | 1 |
| ¼ lb | prosciutto, diced | 125 g |
| 1½ cups | shredded Fontina cheese (about 6 oz/175 g) | 375 mL |
| 1 cup | ricotta cheese | 250 mL |
| 1 tbsp | chopped fresh basil (or 1 tsp/5 mL dried) | 15 mL |
| ¼ tsp | EACH nutmeg and pepper | 1 mL |
| 1 | egg, beaten | 1 |
| 3½ cups | All-Purpose Cooked Tomato Sauce (see recipe, page 52) | 875 mL |
| ½ cup | freshly grated Parmesan cheese | 125 mL |

In large pot of boiling salted water, cook pasta for 7 to 8 minutes or until al dente. Drain and rinse under cold water.

Meanwhile, in large deep skillet, heat oil over medium heat; cook onion for 5 minutes. Stir in spinach, prosciutto, half of the Fontina cheese, the ricotta, basil, nutmeg, pepper and egg.

Spread 1 cup (250 mL) of the All-Purpose Cooked Tomato Sauce in greased 13- x 9-inch (3 L) glass baking dish. Fill each pasta shell with about 1 tbsp (15 mL) of the spinach mixture; place in single layer in dish. Spoon remaining sauce over top. Sprinkle with remaining Fontina cheese and Parmesan cheese. (Recipe can be prepared to this point, covered and refrigerated for up to 1 day. Remove from refrigerator 30 minutes before heating.)

Bake, covered with foil, in 350°F (180°C) oven for about 30 minutes or until bubbly. Makes 6 servings.

# Elizabeth Baird's Pastitsio

My good friend the Food Director at *Canadian Living* magazine shared this wonderful make-ahead recipe with me. Elizabeth describes it as "a delicious variation on lasagna—a savory meat sauce sandwiched between layers of creamy, cheesy pasta custard—perfect for a buffet supper or family reunion."

| | | |
|---|---|---|
| 2 tbsp | vegetable oil | 25 mL |
| 3 | onions, finely chopped | 3 |
| 3 | large cloves garlic, minced | 3 |
| 3 lb | ground beef | 1.5 kg |
| 2 tsp | EACH dried oregano and basil | 10 mL |
| 1½ tsp | cinnamon | 7 mL |
| 1 tsp | EACH salt, pepper, granulated sugar and dried thyme | 5 mL |
| 1 cup | dry white wine or chicken stock | 250 mL |
| 1 | can (5½ oz/156 mL) tomato paste | 1 |
| 1 | can (28 oz/796 mL) tomatoes | 1 |
| ½ cup | minced fresh parsley | 125 mL |
| | *Pasta Custard Layers:* | |
| 5 cups | medium pasta shells | 1.25 L |
| ¾ cup | butter | 175 mL |
| ⅔ cup | all-purpose flour | 150 mL |
| 7 cups | milk | 1.75 L |
| 1 tsp | salt | 5 mL |
| ½ tsp | nutmeg | 2 mL |
| ¼ tsp | pepper | 1 mL |
| 4 | eggs | 4 |
| 2 cups | creamed cottage cheese | 500 mL |
| 2 cups | shredded mozzarella or Swiss cheese | 500 mL |
| ½ cup | freshly grated Parmesan cheese | 125 mL |

In large heavy saucepan or Dutch oven, heat oil over medium heat; cook onions and garlic until softened, about 5 minutes. Increase heat to high. Add beef; cook, stirring to break up, for about 3 minutes or until meat is no longer pink. Drain off any fat. Stir in oregano, basil, cinnamon, salt, pepper, sugar and thyme; cook for 3 minutes.

Pour in wine, tomato paste and tomatoes, mashing tomatoes with fork; bring to boil. Reduce heat and simmer, uncovered, for 20 minutes. Taste and adjust seasoning. Add parsley.

Pasta Custard Layers: In large pot of boiling salted water, cook pasta until al dente, about 8 minutes. Drain and transfer to very large bowl. Toss with 2 tbsp (25 mL) of the butter. Set aside.

In large heavy saucepan, melt remaining butter over medium heat; stir in flour and cook, without browning, for 3 minutes, stirring constantly. Gradually add milk, whisking until smooth; bring to simmer and cook for about 5 minutes or until thickened. Season with salt, nutmeg and pepper.

In large bowl, whisk eggs; whisk in about 1 cup (250 mL) of the hot sauce. Return mixture to saucepan; cook for 2 minutes, stirring. Remove from heat; blend in cottage cheese and mozzarella. Stir into pasta.

In each of two greased 13- x 9-inch (3.5 L) baking dishes, spread one-quarter of the pasta mixture. Spread meat filling over each. Spread remaining pasta mixture evenly over meat. Sprinkle with Parmesan. Bake in 375°F (190°C) oven for 50 to 60 minutes or until heated through, bubbly and top is lightly browned. Let stand for 10 minutes. Makes about 12 servings.

# Quick Tuna-Corn Casserole

I always keep items like a jar of salsa, tuna and frozen corn on hand for quick and easy suppers like this one. A crisp green salad makes a perfect partner.

| | | |
|---|---|---|
| 1 cup | penne pasta | 250 mL |
| ¼ lb | cream cheese, softened | 125 g |
| 1 cup | shredded Monterey Jack, Havarti or mild Cheddar cheese | 250 mL |
| ¼ cup | chopped onion | 50 mL |
| ¼ tsp | EACH dried oregano and pepper | 1 mL |
| 1 | can (6.5 oz/184 g) tuna, drained | 1 |
| 1 cup | drained canned or frozen corn | 250 mL |
| 1 cup | bottled salsa (mild or hot) | 250 mL |
| ¼ cup | coarsely chopped fresh coriander | 50 mL |
| 1 cup | corn flakes, crushed | 250 mL |
| 1 tbsp | butter, cut in bits | 15 mL |

In large saucepan of boiling salted water, cook pasta until al dente, about 8 minutes; drain well.

Meanwhile, in small bowl, combine cream cheese, Monterey Jack cheese, onion, oregano and pepper. In another bowl, combine tuna, corn, salsa and coriander.

Arrange half of the pasta in greased 6-cup (1.5 L) casserole. Dot with half of the cheese mixture, then half of the tuna mixture. Repeat layers. Sprinkle with corn flakes. Dot with butter. (Casserole can be prepared to this point, covered and refrigerated for up to 6 hours. When ready to bake, remove from refrigerator for 30 minutes.)

Bake, uncovered, in 350°F (180°C) oven for 45 minutes or until bubbly. Makes 2 or 3 servings.

# New-Style Tuna Casserole

The tuna noodle casserole of the '50s goes formal with bow ties, wild mushrooms and fresh rosemary. Quick and easy to make, it would be just right to serve to unexpected company with a green salad. You can, of course, use ordinary white mushrooms if wild are not available.

| | | |
|---|---|---|
| 3 cups | bow-tie pasta (farfalle) | 750 mL |
| 3 tbsp | butter | 45 mL |
| ¼ lb | wild mushrooms (crimini, portobello or shiitake), coarsely chopped | 125 g |
| 3 | cloves garlic, minced | 3 |
| 1 tbsp | chopped fresh rosemary (or 1 tsp/5 mL crumbled dried) | 15 mL |
| 1½ cups | milk | 375 mL |
| ¼ lb | unripened goat cheese or cream cheese, in bits | 125 g |
| ½ cup | sour cream | 125 mL |
| 1 | can (6 oz/170 g) tuna, drained | 1 |
| 1 cup | fresh bread crumbs | 250 mL |
| 2 tbsp | chopped fresh parsley | 25 mL |
| 1 tsp | grated lemon rind | 5 mL |

In large pot of boiling salted water, cook pasta until al dente, 8 to 10 minutes; drain well and return to pot.

Meanwhile, melt butter in large skillet; transfer 1 tbsp (15 mL) to medium bowl and set aside.

Add mushrooms and two-thirds of the garlic to pan; cook over medium-high heat for 7 minutes. Stir in rosemary. Reduce heat to low. Stir in milk, then add cheese, stirring until melted. Stir in sour cream. Add to drained pasta. Gently stir in tuna. Transfer to greased 6-cup (1.5 L) casserole.

To reserved butter, add bread crumbs, parsley, lemon rind and remaining garlic; spread evenly over pasta mixture. Bake in 350°F (180°C) oven for 20 to 30 minutes or until bubbly and top is golden brown. Makes 4 servings.

# Quick Smoked Sausage Stew with Pasta

If you have any kind of smoked sausage on hand and a good supply of canned ingredients in your cupboard, you can make this flavorful and comforting stew in minutes. Accompany with crusty Italian bread or rolls.

| | | |
|---|---|---|
| 1 tbsp | olive oil | 15 mL |
| ½ lb | smoked sausage, thinly sliced | 250 g |
| 2 | cloves garlic, minced | 2 |
| 2 | carrots, chopped | 2 |
| 1 tsp | EACH dried oregano and basil | 5 mL |
| ¼ tsp | hot pepper flakes | 1 mL |
| 1 | can (14 oz/398 mL) stewed tomatoes | 1 |
| 2 cups | chicken stock | 500 mL |
| 1 cup | macaroni | 250 mL |
| 1 | can (19 oz/540 mL) white pea (navy) beans, drained and rinsed | 1 |
| 2 tbsp | chopped fresh parsley | 25 mL |

In medium saucepan, heat oil over medium-high heat; cook sausage, garlic, carrots, oregano, basil and hot pepper flakes for 5 minutes, stirring often.

Stir in tomatoes, chicken stock, macaroni and beans; cover and bring to boil. Reduce heat and simmer for 8 to 10 minutes or until pasta is tender. Stir in parsley. Makes 4 servings.

# Chicken and Shrimp Pad Thai

Thailand's famous whole-meal noodle dish has been around for more than 200 years, but fits right into our modern lifestyle because it's quick to make, low in fat and full of flavor. If you have tamarind paste on hand, use it instead of ketchup.

| | | |
|---|---|---|
| ½ lb | rice noodles (fettuccine width) | 250 g |
| 3 tbsp | EACH ketchup and fresh lime juice | 45 mL |
| 2 tbsp | fish sauce* | 25 mL |
| 1 tbsp | rice vinegar | 15 mL |
| 1 tsp | hot chili paste or ½ tsp (2 mL) hot pepper flakes | 5 mL |
| ½ lb | boneless skinless chicken breasts | 250 g |
| 2 tsp | cornstarch | 10 mL |
| 2 tbsp | vegetable oil | 25 mL |
| 1 tsp | sesame oil | 5 mL |
| 3 | cloves garlic, minced | 3 |
| ½ lb | medium shrimp, cleaned (with tails on) | 250 g |
| ½ cup | firm tofu, cut in ½-inch (1 cm) cubes | 125 mL |
| 1 | egg | 1 |
| 1 cup | bean sprouts | 250 mL |
| 4 | green onions, cut in 1-inch (2.5 cm) pieces | 4 |
| ½ cup | chopped fresh coriander | 125 mL |
| 2 tbsp | coarsely chopped dry roasted peanuts | 25 mL |
| | Lime wedges | |
| | Sweet red pepper slices | |

In large bowl, soak noodles in warm water for about 10 minutes or until softened but still firm. Drain well.

In small bowl, combine ketchup, lime juice, fish sauce, vinegar and chili paste; set aside. Cut chicken into thin strips; toss with cornstarch and set aside.

In large wok or skillet, heat vegetable and sesame oils over medium-high heat; stir-fry garlic and chicken for 3 minutes. Add shrimp and tofu; stir-fry for 2 to 3 minutes or until shrimp are pink. Push to side of wok. Break egg into centre of wok; let set slightly before combining with chicken mixture.

Reduce heat to medium. Add noodles and ketchup mixture; bring to boil. Add bean sprouts, onions, half of the coriander and half of the peanuts. Transfer to large warm platter; sprinkle with remaining peanuts and coriander. Garnish with lime wedges and red pepper around edges. Makes 3 servings.

---

**\*Don't substitute anything else for fish sauce. When buying it in Oriental grocery stores, look for the brand with a squid on the label and store in refrigerator after opening.**

**Hint: To break rice noodles a bit before soaking, put them into a big bag so they won't scatter all over your kitchen.**

# Chicken and Turkey

# Baked Chicken and Sausage with Mixed Dried Fruit

I love combining chicken and sausage, and because they both go so well with fruit, here is a winning combination. This is one casserole I particularly like to do a day ahead so that I can remove any extra fat that comes to the top before reheating. Serve with bread and a salad of greens, cooked slivered beets and garlic croutons.

| | | |
|---|---|---|
| 1 lb | farmer's garlic sausage | 500 g |
| 4 | chicken legs | 4 |
| | Salt and pepper | |
| 2 | onions, sliced | 2 |
| ¼ cup | cider vinegar | 50 mL |
| 12 | cloves garlic, halved | 12 |
| 1 cup | EACH chicken stock and dry white wine (or all stock) | 250 mL |
| 2 tbsp | Dijon mustard | 25 mL |
| ½ tsp | EACH dried thyme, sage and rosemary | 2 mL |
| 1½ cups | mixed dried fruit (apricots, prunes, pears, apples, etc., halved if large) Chopped fresh parsley | 375 mL |

In large skillet, cook sausage over medium-high heat, turning often to brown all sides, about 10 minutes. Remove to drain well on paper towels. Cut into bite-size pieces.

Cut chicken legs into drumsticks and thighs. Add to skillet and brown, in batches, sprinkling with salt and pepper to taste. Transfer to shallow 12-cup (3 L) baking dish.

Pour off all but 1 tbsp (15 mL) drippings from skillet. Add onions; cook over medium heat for 5 minutes. Stir in vinegar; bring to boil, scraping up any brown bits from bottom of pan. Add garlic; stir in stock, wine, mustard, thyme, sage and rosemary. Simmer for 5 minutes, stirring often.

Arrange sausage and fruit around chicken in baking dish. Pour sauce over top. Cover and bake in 350°F (180°C) oven for 45 to 60 minutes or until juices run clear when chicken is pierced. (Casserole can be cooled, covered and refrigerated for up to 2 days; bring to room temperature to reheat in 350°F/180°C oven for about 30 minutes or until bubbly.) Serve garnished with parsley. Makes 4 servings.

# Chicken Shepherd's Pie

Ground chicken or turkey, now available in most supermarkets, makes a lean, delicious version of an old favorite. If necessary, cover the skillet's handle with foil to make it ovenproof.

| | | |
|---|---|---|
| 1 tsp | vegetable oil | 5 mL |
| 1 | onion, chopped | 1 |
| 1 lb | ground chicken | 500 g |
| 1 tbsp | all-purpose flour | 15 mL |
| 1 cup | chicken stock | 250 mL |
| 2 cups | frozen mixed vegetables | 500 mL |
| ¼ cup | chopped fresh parsley | 50 mL |
| 1 tbsp | ketchup | 15 mL |
| 1 tsp | Worcestershire sauce | 5 mL |
| ¼ tsp | dried sage | 1 mL |
| | Salt and pepper | |
| 6 | potatoes, peeled | 6 |
| 1 | egg | 1 |
| ⅓ cup | light cottage cheese | 75 mL |

In deep 10-inch (25 cm) ovenproof skillet, heat oil over medium heat; cook onion, stirring occasionally, for 3 minutes or until softened. Add chicken; cook, breaking up with back of spoon, for 5 to 7 minutes or until no longer pink. Sprinkle with flour; cook, stirring, for 1 minute. Gradually stir in stock; cook, stirring, until thickened.

Stir in vegetables, parsley, ketchup, Worcestershire sauce and sage; bring to boil. Reduce heat and simmer for 5 minutes. Season with salt and pepper to taste.

Meanwhile, in saucepan of boiling water, cook potatoes, covered, over medium-high heat for 15 to 20 minutes or until tender; drain and return to pot. Using potato masher, mash until smooth. Beat in egg and cottage cheese; season with salt and pepper to taste. Spoon over chicken mixture. Place pan in bottom third of oven and broil for 7 to 8 minutes or until potatoes are golden. Makes 4 servings.

# Easy Skillet Chicken and Rice

This easy stove-top casserole for two makes a hearty nutrient-packed meal. Just add a green salad or coleslaw.

| | | |
|---|---|---|
| 1 tbsp | vegetable oil | 15 mL |
| 2 | chicken legs | 2 |
| | Salt and pepper | |
| ⅔ cup | long-grain rice | 150 mL |
| 1 | onion, chopped | 1 |
| 1 | clove garlic, minced | 1 |
| ¼ tsp | EACH dried oregano and thyme | 1 mL |
| 1 | can (19 oz/540 mL) kidney beans, drained and rinsed | 1 |
| 1 | can (10 oz/284 mL) mushrooms, drained | 1 |
| 1⅓ cups | water | 325 mL |
| | Paprika | |

In skillet, heat oil over medium-high heat; add chicken and brown all over, about 10 minutes, sprinkling with salt and pepper to taste. Remove chicken and set aside. Pour off all but 1 tbsp (15 mL) drippings from pan. Add rice, onion, garlic, oregano and thyme; cook, stirring, over medium heat until rice is browned, about 3 minutes.

Stir in beans, mushrooms and water. Arrange chicken on top. Sprinkle with paprika. Bring to boil, cover, reduce heat to low and simmer for 30 to 40 minutes or until juices run clear when chicken is pierced and rice is tender. Makes 2 servings.

# Honey-Curried Chicken and Apricots

Nothing could be quicker to put together than this flavorful chicken casserole. Serve with rice or baked potatoes and broccoli.

| | | |
|---|---|---|
| 2 | onions, thinly sliced | 2 |
| 1 cup | halved dried apricots | 250 mL |
| 4 | chicken breast halves | 4 |
| | Salt and pepper | |
| ¼ cup | liquid honey | 50 mL |
| 2 tbsp | fresh lemon juice | 25 mL |
| 1 tbsp | curry powder | 15 mL |
| 1 tsp | ground cumin | 5 mL |

Arrange onions and apricots in greased shallow baking dish just big enough to hold chicken breasts in single layer. Arrange chicken, skin side up, on top. Sprinkle with salt and pepper.

Combine honey, lemon juice, curry powder and cumin; drizzle over chicken. (Recipe can be prepared to this point, covered and refrigerated for up to 8 hours; let stand at room temperature for 30 minutes before baking.)

Bake, uncovered, in 375°F (190°C) oven for about 45 minutes or until chicken is no longer pink inside, basting once or twice. Makes 4 servings.

# Chicken Niçoise

The thin sauce from this colorful dish is delicious on rice. Along with the rice, add a crisp green salad to your menu.

| | | |
|---|---|---|
| 8 | chicken thighs | 8 |
| ⅓ cup | fresh lemon juice | 75 mL |
| 2 | cloves garlic, minced | 2 |
| ½ tsp | EACH dried basil and thyme | 2 mL |
| 1 | bay leaf | 1 |
| 4 tsp | olive oil | 20 mL |
| 4 | small onions, quartered | 4 |
| ½ lb | mushrooms, quartered (2 cups/500 mL) | 250 g |
| 1 | can (19 oz/540 mL) tomatoes, drained and chopped | 1 |
| 1 | can (14 oz/398 mL) large pitted black olives, halved | 1 |
| 1½ cups | frozen cut green beans | 375 mL |
| | Salt and pepper | |

In shallow glass dish, sprinkle chicken with lemon juice, garlic, basil and thyme; add bay leaf. Let stand for 10 minutes. Remove chicken from marinade, reserving marinade.

In large deep skillet or shallow casserole, heat oil over medium-high heat; cook chicken, turning once, for 5 to 7 minutes or until golden brown. Remove chicken and set aside.

Add onions and mushrooms to skillet; cook, stirring, for 2 minutes. Add marinade and tomatoes, stirring to scrape up brown bits from bottom of pan.

Return chicken to pan along with olives; bring to boil. Reduce heat, cover and simmer for 40 minutes. (Recipe can be prepared to this point, cooled, covered and refrigerated for up to 24 hours. Reheat slowly.)

Increase heat to medium-low. Add green beans, pushing down into liquid. Cook, uncovered, for 5 minutes or until beans are tender-crisp. Skim off any fat; discard bay leaf. Season with salt and pepper to taste. Makes 4 to 6 servings.

# Chicken and Sausage Puttanesca

This is a wonderful make-ahead casserole everyone, young and old, will love. It's great for carrying to the cottage or chalet where you can easily serve it with crusty bread and a green salad. If you're feeling adventuresome and have saffron on hand, add a pinch to some hot buttered orzo for a delicious accompaniment.

| | | |
|---|---|---|
| 8 | chicken legs | 8 |
| | Salt and pepper | |
| 2 tbsp | olive oil | 25 mL |
| 1½ lb | Italian sausage (hot or mild), sliced | 750 g |
| 12 | cloves garlic, halved | 12 |
| 1 | onion, thinly sliced | 1 |
| 2 | sweet yellow peppers, thinly sliced | 2 |
| 1 | can (28 oz/796 mL) Italian plum tomatoes | 1 |
| 1 tbsp | anchovy paste | 15 mL |
| ½ cup | pitted black olives | 125 mL |
| ½ cup | chopped fresh parsley (approx) | 125 mL |
| ⅓ cup | drained capers | 75 mL |
| 3 tbsp | chopped drained oil-packed sun-dried tomatoes | 45 mL |
| 1 tbsp | mixed Italian herbs | 15 mL |
| Pinch | hot pepper flakes | Pinch |

Cut chicken legs into drumsticks and thighs. Sprinkle with salt and pepper. Set aside.

In large skillet, heat oil over medium-high heat; brown sausage well, about 10 minutes. With slotted spoon, remove to drain on paper towels. Pour off all but 2 tbsp (25 mL) drippings from pan; add chicken and brown, in batches. Transfer to large shallow casserole.

Pour off all but 2 tbsp (25 mL) drippings from pan; cook garlic and onion for 5 minutes. Add yellow peppers; cook for 2 minutes. Arrange vegetables and sausage around chicken.

Add tomatoes to skillet; bring to boil, scraping up any brown bits from bottom of pan. Stir in anchovy paste. Add olives, parsley, capers, sun-dried tomatoes, herbs and hot pepper flakes; pour over chicken mixture.

Bake in 400°F (200°C) oven, covered and basting often with pan juices, for 45 to 50 minutes or until juices run clear when chicken is pierced. (Casserole can be cooled, covered and refrigerated for up to 2 days; reheat in 350°F/180°C oven for 30 to 40 minutes.) Serve sprinkled with parsley. Makes 8 to 10 servings.

# Herb-Roasted Chicken Breasts with Garlic, Potatoes and Carrots

A cinch to put together, this delicious one-dish supper is great with creamy coleslaw for a family or company meal.

| | | |
|---|---|---|
| 2 tbsp | EACH fresh lemon juice and olive oil | 25 mL |
| ½ tsp | EACH salt, dried rosemary and thyme | 2 mL |
| ¼ tsp | pepper | 1 mL |
| 12 | cloves garlic | 12 |
| 1½ lb | small red potatoes, halved | 750 g |
| 4 | carrots, cut in 1-inch (2.5 cm) pieces | 4 |
| ½ lb | small mushrooms | 250 g |
| 4 | chicken breast halves | 4 |
| 1 cup | chicken stock | 250 mL |

Stir together lemon juice, oil, salt, rosemary, thyme and pepper; set aside.

In large shallow baking dish, toss together garlic, potatoes, carrots, mushrooms and 2 tbsp (25 mL) of the herb mixture; spread out in pan. Arrange chicken, skin-side-up, on vegetables. Sprinkle with remaining herb mixture. (Recipe can be prepared to this point, covered and refrigerated for up to 1 day. Let stand at room temperature for 30 minutes before proceeding.)

Bake, uncovered, in upper third of 450°F (230°C) oven for 20 minutes. Reduce temperature to 375°F (190°C). Bake for 25 minutes longer or until chicken is no longer pink inside and vegetables are tender. Transfer chicken and vegetables to heated platter.

Add stock to pan and bring to boil, scraping up any brown bits from bottom of pan. Boil until syrupy, about 5 minutes. Pour over chicken and vegetables. Makes 4 servings.

# Chicken Basque

This easy chicken bistro dish with its Spanish flavors is one of my favorite ways of incorporating rice into a dish. Serve the comforting stew with crisp steamed broccoli.

| | | |
|---|---|---|
| 4 | chicken legs | 4 |
| 1 tbsp | olive oil | 15 mL |
| | Salt and pepper | |
| 2 | onions, coarsely chopped | 2 |
| 1 | sweet red pepper, sliced | 1 |
| ¼ tsp | hot pepper flakes | 1 mL |
| 12 | cloves garlic, thinly sliced | 12 |
| ½ lb | prosciutto, coarsely chopped | 250 g |
| 2 tbsp | chopped sun-dried tomatoes* | 25 mL |
| 1 cup | parboiled rice | 250 mL |
| 1 | can (19 oz/540 mL) tomatoes | 1 |
| 1 cup | dry white wine or chicken stock | 250 mL |
| 1 | orange, peeled, halved crosswise and cut into wedges | 1 |
| 2 tbsp | black olives, pitted and halved | 25 mL |

Cut chicken legs into drumsticks and thighs. In large deep skillet or shallow ovenproof casserole, heat oil over medium-high heat; brown chicken, in batches, sprinkling lightly with salt and pepper. Remove and set aside.

Drain off all but 2 tbsp (25 mL) drippings from pan. Add onions, red pepper, hot pepper flakes, and salt and pepper to taste; cook over medium heat for 5 minutes.

Add garlic, prosciutto and sun-dried tomatoes; cook, stirring, for 2 minutes. Add rice and stir well to coat. Add tomatoes and wine; bring to boil, scraping up any brown bits from bottom of pan. Top with chicken; tuck orange wedges and olives around pieces. Cover and bake in 350°F (180°C) oven for 1 hour or until juices run clear when chicken is pierced. Makes 4 servings.

---

**\*It's not necessary to rehydrate tomatoes for this dish.**

# Oven-Baked Chicken with Red Onions and Mushrooms

Serve this easy chicken casserole with rice and green peas for a fast family supper. For company, you might like to make a wild rice pilaf.

| | | |
|---|---|---|
| 4 | chicken legs | 4 |
| 3 tbsp | butter | 45 mL |
| | Salt and pepper | |
| 1 lb | mushrooms, thinly sliced | 500 g |
| ½ tsp | EACH dried marjoram and thyme | 2 mL |
| Pinch | grated nutmeg | Pinch |
| 2 | large red onions, chopped | 2 |
| ½ cup | chicken stock | 125 mL |
| | Chopped fresh parsley | |

Cut chicken legs into drumsticks and thighs. In large skillet, heat 1 tbsp (15 mL) of the butter over medium-high heat; brown chicken lightly in batches, sprinkling with salt and pepper to taste. Remove and set aside.

Add mushrooms to skillet; stir in marjoram, thyme, nutmeg, and salt and pepper to taste; cook over medium heat, stirring occasionally, for 10 minutes. Transfer to bowl.

Add remaining butter to skillet; cook onions for 5 minutes. Season with salt and pepper. Spread half of the onions, then one-quarter of the mushrooms in shallow baking dish just big enough to hold chicken in single layer. Lay chicken on top. Cover with remaining mushrooms and onions. Pour in stock.

Bake, uncovered, in 350°F (180°C) oven for 40 to 45 minutes or until juices run clear when chicken is pierced. (Recipe can be prepared to this point, covered and refrigerated for up to 4 hours. Let stand at room temperature for 30 minutes.) Serve sprinkled with parsley. Makes 4 servings.

# Chicken Stew with Sage Dumplings

Nothing is more comforting than a steaming pan of chicken stew topped with fluffy dumplings. . .my husband's favorite supper. Try the dumplings on other stews, varying the selection of herbs to suit the stew.

| | | |
|---|---|---|
| 1 | chicken (3 lb/1.5 kg) | 1 |
| ½ cup | all-purpose flour | 125 mL |
| ¼ tsp | EACH salt, pepper, nutmeg and paprika | 1 mL |
| 1 tbsp | EACH butter and vegetable oil | 15 mL |
| 1 | small onion, chopped | 1 |
| ½ lb | mushrooms, quartered | 250 g |
| 2 | EACH carrots, parsnips and celery stalks, thinly sliced on diagonal | 2 |
| 2½ cups | chicken stock | 625 mL |
| ½ tsp | crumbled dried sage | 2 mL |
| ¼ tsp | dried thyme | 1 mL |
| ½ cup | whipping cream | 125 mL |
| ½ cup | frozen peas | 125 mL |
| ¼ cup | chopped fresh parsley | 50 mL |
| | *Dumplings:* | |
| 2 cups | sifted cake-and-pastry flour | 500 mL |
| 4 tsp | baking powder | 20 mL |
| 1 tsp | crumbled dried sage | 5 mL |
| ½ tsp | salt | 2 mL |
| 2 tbsp | lard or shortening | 25 mL |
| ⅔ cup | milk (approx) | 150 mL |

Cut chicken into pieces, cutting breast into 4 and back into 2. Wipe with paper towels.

In sturdy plastic bag, combine flour, salt, pepper, nutmeg and paprika. Add chicken, in batches, and shake to coat. Reserve remaining flour mixture.

In large saucepan, melt butter with oil over medium-high heat; brown chicken, in batches. Remove to large bowl.

Pour off all but 2 tbsp (25 mL) drippings from pan, reserving remaining drippings. Add onion and mushrooms; cook over medium heat, stirring often, for 5 minutes. With slotted spoon, add to chicken.

Add more drippings to pan if necessary. Stir in carrots, parsnips and celery; cook, stirring, for 5 minutes. With slotted spoon, add to bowl.

Stir reserved flour into pan; cook, stirring, for 1 minute. Add stock, sage and thyme; bring to boil, scraping up brown bits from bottom of pan. Return chicken, vegetables and any juices to pan; cover, reduce heat and simmer for about 45 minutes or until juices run clear when chicken is pierced. (Recipe can be prepared to this point, cooled, covered and refrigerated for up to 24 hours. Bring to simmer before proceeding.) Stir in cream, peas and parsley.

Dumplings: Have stew boiling gently in pan with about 3 inches (8 cm) headspace for dumplings to rise. In large bowl, combine flour, baking powder, sage and salt; cut in lard until like oatmeal. Stir in milk just until sticky dough forms, adding more milk if necessary. Cut out dumplings with tablespoon; drop onto floured plate. Gather up dumplings and drop quickly into stew, spacing evenly; cover pan and boil gently for 15 minutes without lifting lid. Serve immediately. Makes 4 to 6 servings.

# Chicken and Shrimp Jambalaya

This quick and easy version of the classic Creole stew is perfect for a casual Friday night supper with good friends. Accompany with crusty bread and an avocado salad.

| | | |
|---|---|---|
| 2 tbsp | vegetable oil | 25 mL |
| ½ lb | Black Forest ham, cubed | 250 g |
| 12 | chicken thighs (about 3 lb/1.5 kg) | 12 |
| 3 | onions, chopped | 3 |
| 2 | sweet green peppers, chopped | 2 |
| 2 cups | chopped celery | 500 mL |
| 4 | cloves garlic, minced | 4 |
| 1½ tsp | ground cumin | 7 mL |
| 1 tsp | EACH dried thyme and pepper | 5 mL |
| ½ tsp | EACH salt and dried oregano | 2 mL |
| ¼ tsp | cayenne pepper | 1 mL |
| Pinch | ground allspice | Pinch |
| 2 | bay leaves | 2 |
| 1 | can (28 oz/796 mL) tomatoes | 1 |
| 2 cups | beef stock | 500 mL |
| 2 cups | parboiled long-grain rice | 500 mL |
| ¼ cup | chopped fresh parsley | 50 mL |
| 6 | green onions, chopped | 6 |
| 12 | raw shrimp, cleaned (with tails on) | 12 |

In large wide saucepan, heat oil over medium-high heat; brown ham for 2 to 3 minutes. Using slotted spoon, transfer to large bowl. Add chicken to pan; brown, in batches and turning often with tongs. Add to bowl.

Pour off all but 2 tbsp (25 mL) fat from pan. Add onions, green peppers, celery and garlic; cook over medium heat for 3 to 5 minutes or until softened. Stir in ½ tsp (2 mL) of the cumin, the thyme, pepper, salt, oregano, cayenne, allspice and bay leaves; cook, stirring, for 2 minutes.

Return ham, chicken and any juices to pan. Stir in tomatoes and stock; bring to boil, stirring and breaking up tomatoes with spoon. Reduce heat to medium-low; cover and simmer, stirring occasionally, for 35 to 45 minutes or until juices run clear when chicken is pierced. Taste and adjust seasoning. Remove bay leaves.

Meanwhile, in large pot of lightly salted boiling water, cook rice for 6 minutes. (Rice will not be tender.) Drain in fine sieve. Place in 16-cup (4 L) Dutch oven or casserole dish; fluff with fork. Stir in remaining cumin and parsley.

Stir green onions into jambalaya mixture; spread over rice. Cover and bake in 350°F (180°C) oven for 25 minutes. Stick shrimp down into jambalaya mixture; bake for 10 to 15 minutes longer or until shrimp are pink and casserole is bubbly. Makes about 8 servings.

# Moroccan Chicken Tagine with Chick-Peas and Zucchini

A tagine is a classical Moroccan stew of meat, poultry, fish or just vegetables with assorted spices and sometimes fruit, cooked in a large covered clay pot of the same name. I actually was very tempted to carry home from Morocco one of these conical pots, but since I resisted, I cooked this chicken stew in a large Dutch oven. Serve over couscous and garnish with wedges of hard-cooked eggs if you like. Accompany with a salad of romaine, orange slices and black olives.

| | | |
|---|---|---|
| 2 tbsp | olive oil | 25 mL |
| 12 | chicken thighs (about 4 lb/2 kg) | 12 |
| | Salt and pepper | |
| 2 | onions, thinly sliced | 2 |
| 4 | cloves garlic, coarsely chopped | 4 |
| ½ cup | chopped fresh coriander | 125 mL |
| 1 tsp | EACH ground cumin, ginger and paprika | 5 mL |
| ½ tsp | EACH cinnamon and hot pepper flakes | 2 mL |
| ½ cup | water | 125 mL |
| 2 lb | tomatoes (6 medium), peeled, seeded and chopped (or two 28 oz/796 mL cans tomatoes, drained and chopped) | 1 kg |
| 2 cups | cooked chick-peas, rinsed and drained (or one 19 oz/540 mL can) | 500 mL |
| 3 | small zucchini, cut in ½-inch (1 cm) slices | 3 |

In Dutch oven, heat oil over medium-high heat; brown chicken, in batches, sprinkling with salt and pepper. Transfer to plate.

Pour off all but 2 tbsp (25 mL) drippings from pan. Reduce heat to medium. Add onions, garlic, 2 tbsp (25 mL) of the coriander, cumin, ginger, paprika, cinnamon and hot pepper flakes; cook, covered, for 5 minutes. Stir in water and tomatoes; bring to boil.

Return chicken to pan. Add chick-peas; cover and simmer for 45 minutes. (Stew can be prepared to this point, cooled, covered and refrigerated for up to 2 days; reheat gently.) Add zucchini; cook for 15 minutes or until just tender.

Stir in ¼ cup (50 mL) of the remaining coriander. Taste and adjust seasoning. Serve sprinkled with remaining coriander. Makes 6 servings.

# Make-Ahead Mediterranean Chicken

The sunny flavors of this easy casserole will be even better if you prepare it a day in advance. Serve with crusty bread or rice seasoned with a pinch of saffron if you wish and a crisp green salad.

| | | |
|---|---|---|
| 12 | boneless chicken breast halves (with skin) | 12 |
| | Salt and pepper | |
| ¼ cup | all-purpose flour | 50 mL |
| 3 tbsp | olive oil (approx) | 45 mL |
| 1 | onion, chopped | 1 |
| 12 | cloves garlic, halved | 12 |
| 1 cup | dry white wine or chicken stock | 250 mL |
| 1 | can (28 oz/796 mL) plum tomatoes, chopped | 1 |
| ½ cup | sun-dried tomatoes, slivered | 125 mL |
| ⅓ cup | chopped fresh parsley | 75 mL |
| 1 tbsp | balsamic vinegar | 15 mL |
| 1 tbsp | anchovy paste | 15 mL |
| ½ tsp | EACH dried thyme, oregano, rosemary and sage | 2 mL |
| Pinch | cayenne pepper | Pinch |
| 2 | strips (3- x 1-inch/8 x 2.5 cm) orange zest | 2 |
| 24 | pitted black olives | 24 |

Season chicken with salt and pepper; dredge lightly in flour.

In heavy casserole or saucepan, heat 1 tbsp (15 mL) of the oil over medium-high heat; brown chicken, in batches, adding more oil as needed. Transfer to plate.

In pan drippings, cook onion and garlic over medium heat for 3 to 4 minutes or until onion is softened. Do not let garlic brown. Stir in wine and bring to boil, scraping up any brown bits from bottom of pan. Stir in tomatoes, sun-dried tomatoes, half of the parsley, vinegar, anchovy paste, thyme, oregano, rosemary, sage, cayenne and orange zest; bring to boil.

Return chicken and any juices to pan; cover and simmer for about 20 minutes or until chicken is no longer pink inside. Discard orange zest. Stir in olives. Taste and adjust seasoning. (Recipe can be cooled, covered and refrigerated for up to 24 hours; reheat gently.) Serve garnished with remaining parsley. Makes 8 to 10 servings.

# Lemon-Rosemary Chicken with Gremolata Garnish

Almost everyone loves chicken, and this is the easy kind of make-ahead dish I like to serve for company with steamed rice and a salad of greens and sliced mushrooms.

| | | |
|---|---|---|
| 2 tbsp | EACH unsalted butter and olive oil | 25 mL |
| 2 | chickens (3 lb/1.5 kg each), cut up | 2 |
| | Salt and pepper | |
| 1 lb | shallots or pearl onions | 500 g |
| 1 lb | mini carrots | 500 g |
| 1 cup | EACH dry white vermouth and chicken stock | 250 mL |
| 2 tbsp | fresh lemon juice | 25 mL |
| 2 tbsp | chopped fresh rosemary (or 2 tsp/10 mL crumbled dried) | 25 mL |
| 2 | cans (each 14 oz/398 mL) artichoke hearts, drained and quartered | 2 |
| | | |
| | *Gremolata Garnish:* | |
| 2 | cloves garlic, minced | 2 |
| 3 tbsp | chopped fresh parsley | 45 mL |
| 1 tbsp | coarsely grated lemon rind | 15 mL |

In large skillet, melt butter with oil over medium-high heat; brown chicken, in batches, sprinkling lightly with salt and pepper. Arrange in single layer in large shallow baking dish or pan.

Pour off all but 2 tbsp (25 mL) drippings from pan. Add shallots and carrots; cook for 7 minutes, stirring often. Arrange around chicken pieces.

Add vermouth, stock and lemon juice to skillet; bring to boil, scraping up brown bits from bottom of pan. Stir in rosemary; boil for 3 to 5 minutes or until slightly reduced. Add artichoke hearts; toss to coat well. Pour over chicken mixture. (Recipe can be prepared to this point, covered and refrigerated for up to 4 hours. Let stand at room temperature for 30 minutes.)

Bake, covered, in 350°F (180°C) oven for 1 to 1½ hours or until juices run clear when thigh is pierced.

Gremolata Garnish: Stir together garlic, parsley and lemon rind. (Gremolata can be covered and refrigerated for up to 4 hours.) Sprinkle over stew to serve. Makes 8 to 10 servings.

# Roasted Pepper and Chicken Pot Pie with Phyllo Crust

Both chicken and peppers are roasted, then combined in a delicious make-ahead pie just right for entertaining. If you wish, top with puff pastry instead of the phyllo. See Old-Fashioned Turkey Pot Pie (page 97) for instructions.

| | | |
|---|---|---|
| 1 | chicken (about 3 lb/1.5 kg) | 1 |
| 3 | sweet peppers (red or yellow or combination) | 3 |
| 1 lb | shallots, halved (about 16) | 500 g |
| ½ lb | mushrooms, quartered | 250 g |
| 3 tbsp | all-purpose flour | 45 mL |
| 1 cup | EACH dry white wine and chicken stock | 250 mL |
| ½ cup | whipping cream | 125 mL |
| ½ tsp | EACH dried thyme and marjoram | 2 mL |
| | Salt and pepper | |
| 2 | small zucchini, thinly sliced | 2 |
| ¼ cup | chopped fresh parsley | 50 mL |
| 8 | sheets phyllo pastry | 8 |
| 3 tbsp | butter, melted | 45 mL |

Place chicken and peppers in roasting pan; roast in 450°F (230°C) oven for 40 minutes or until peppers are charred, turning once. Remove peppers and place in small covered saucepan.

Roast chicken for 5 to 10 minutes longer or until meat thermometer registers 185°F (85°C). Cool and shred meat, discarding skin and bones, but retaining pan juices.

Retaining any juices, peel cooled peppers; seed and cut into 1-inch (2.5 cm) wide strips. (Chicken and peppers can be covered and refrigerated for up to 24 hours.)

Remove any fat from juices in pan. Measure 2 tbsp (25 mL) juices into skillet. Add shallots and mushrooms; cook over medium heat, stirring occasionally, for 10 to 15 minutes or until shallots are tender. Sprinkle with flour; cook for 1 minute. Stir in wine, stock, cream, thyme, marjoram, and salt and pepper to taste; bring to boil and cook, stirring until thickened. Stir in zucchini; cook for 2 minutes. Stir in chicken, peppers and juices and parsley. Spoon into shallow 8-cup (2 L) baking dish. Cool.

Place 1 phyllo sheet over chicken mixture, folding under excess pastry around edges to fit inside dish. Lightly brush sheet with butter. Repeat with remaining sheets and butter, making sure to brush top sheet. (Recipe can be prepared to this point, covered and refrigerated for up to 12 hours. Let stand at room temperature for 30 minutes.) Bake uncovered in 375°F (190°C) oven for about 30 minutes or until pastry is golden and filling bubbly. Makes 6 servings.

Hint: Buy phyllo at a store where there's a fast turnover; stale phyllo crumbles easily and is difficult to work with. If frozen, thaw in refrigerator and unwrap just before using. Work quickly and keep sheets covered with waxed paper and a damp tea towel to prevent drying out until needed.

# Individual Chicken Pot Pies

This is the perfect big-batch recipe to make and freeze on a weekend. If you wish, fill foil pans with chicken mixture, top with your own pastry (see recipe for Never-Fail Big-Batch Pastry, page 142), and freeze all ready to bake. Bake, frozen, in 450°F (230°C) oven for 40 to 45 minutes or until golden brown.

| | | |
|---|---|---|
| 1½ lb | boneless skinless chicken breasts | 750 g |
| 2 tbsp | butter | 25 mL |
| 1 lb | mushrooms, quartered | 500 g |
| 2 | carrots, diced | 2 |
| 1 | stalk celery, sliced | 1 |
| ⅓ cup | sliced leek | 75 mL |
| 1 | clove garlic, minced | 1 |
| 1¼ cups | chicken stock | 300 mL |
| 2 tbsp | cornstarch | 25 mL |
| ½ cup | plain yogurt | 125 mL |
| ½ tsp | salt | 2 mL |
| ¼ tsp | EACH pepper, dried rosemary and thyme | 1 mL |
| 1 cup | frozen green peas | 250 mL |
| 2 tbsp | chopped fresh parsley | 25 mL |
| 1 | pkg (411 g) frozen puff pastry, thawed | 1 |
| 1 | egg yolk | 1 |
| 2 tbsp | cream or milk | 25 mL |

Cut chicken into 1-inch (2.5 cm) pieces. In large saucepan, melt butter over medium heat; cook chicken for about 4 minutes or until no longer pink. With slotted spoon, remove chicken to plate.

In same saucepan, cook mushrooms, carrots, celery, leek and garlic for 3 minutes or until softened. Stir in 1 cup (250 mL) of the stock.

In small bowl, combine remaining stock with cornstarch until smooth; stir in yogurt. Add to saucepan. Add chicken, salt, pepper, rosemary and thyme. Bring to simmer; cook, covered, over low heat for 20 minutes. Stir in peas and parsley. (Recipe can be prepared to this point, cooled, covered and refrigerated for up to 24 hours, or frozen up to 1 month. Thaw in refrigerator.) Spoon into eight 1-cup (250 mL) ovenproof soup bowls or 4-½ by 1¼-inch (11 x 3 cm) foil tart pans.

On lightly floured surface, roll out pastry to 1/8-inch (3 mm) thickness. Cut out 8 circles slightly larger than circumference of bowls.

Stir together egg yolk and cream; brush over edges of bowls. Top each with pastry, pressing gently to seal. Cut slit in top of each for steam to escape.

Cut leaf shapes from pastry scraps and use to decorate tops of pies. Brush pies with egg mixture. Place on baking sheet and bake in 400°F (200°C) oven for 35 to 40 minutes or until puffed and golden. Makes 8 servings.

# Hungarian Chicken Skillet Stew

Serve this comforting stew with egg noodles along with a cabbage salad.

| | | |
|---|---|---|
| 4 | chicken legs (about 2 lb/1 kg) | 4 |
| 4 | slices side bacon, diced | 4 |
| 2 | stalks celery, diced | 2 |
| 2 | carrots, thinly sliced | 2 |
| 1 | onion, chopped | 1 |
| 1 | sweet green pepper, diced | 1 |
| 1 tbsp | EACH paprika and tomato paste | 15 mL |
| 1 cup | chicken stock | 250 mL |
| ½ cup | sour cream | 125 mL |
| 2 tbsp | all-purpose flour | 25 mL |
| | Salt and pepper | |
| 2 tbsp | chopped fresh parsley | 25 mL |

Cut chicken legs into drumsticks and thighs. In large skillet, cook bacon over medium-high heat for 2 to 4 minutes or until crisp; remove and set aside. Add chicken to skillet; brown, in batches. Add to bacon.

Drain off all but 1 tsp (5 mL) fat from pan. Cook celery, carrots, onion and green pepper for about 3 minutes or until softened. Stir in paprika and tomato paste; stir in stock and bring to boil.

Return chicken and bacon to pan; reduce heat to low, cover and simmer for about 1 hour or until juices run clear when chicken is pierced. Remove chicken to warmed platter; cover to keep warm.

Skim off any fat from pan drippings. Whisk sour cream with flour until smooth; whisk into pan juices and cook over low heat, stirring, for about 2 minutes or until thickened. Season with salt and pepper to taste. Pour over chicken; sprinkle with parsley. Makes 4 servings.

# Chick-Pea Chicken Skillet Stew

Follow the easy directions on the box to prepare couscous. Mound onto two heated plates and spoon this interesting chicken stew on top. Toss a green salad to go alongside. If you wish three servings, just add another chicken leg.

| | | |
|---|---|---|
| 1 tbsp | vegetable oil | 15 mL |
| 2 | chicken legs | 2 |
| | Salt and pepper | |
| 2 | EACH carrots and stalks celery, sliced | 2 |
| 1 | EACH onion and clove garlic, chopped | 1 |
| 1 tsp | ground cumin | 5 mL |
| ½ tsp | EACH dried oregano, ginger and curry powder | 2 mL |
| Pinch | cinnamon | Pinch |
| 1 | can (19 oz/540 mL) chick-peas, drained and rinsed | 1 |
| 1 cup | chicken stock | 250 mL |
| 2 tbsp | chopped fresh coriander or parsley | 25 mL |

In large skillet, heat oil over medium-high heat; brown chicken all over, 7 to 10 minutes, sprinkling lightly with salt and pepper. Remove chicken to plate.

Drain off all but 1 tbsp (15 mL) fat from pan. Add carrots, celery, onion, garlic, cumin, oregano, ginger, curry powder and cinnamon; cook, stirring, for 2 minutes. Add chick-peas and stock, stirring to scrape up brown bits from bottom of pan.

Arrange chicken on top; cover and cook over medium-low heat for about 30 minutes or until juices run clear when chicken is pierced. Serve garnished with coriander. Makes 2 servings.

# Tropical Chicken Breasts

Chicken is combined with ripe, juicy mango in this company casserole from Isabel Campabadal's cooking school in Costa Rica, where I spent an extremely enjoyable week. Serve with rice and this time, have your green salad feature hearts of palm, one of Costa Rica's great delicacies.

| | | |
|---|---|---|
| 8 | boneless skinless chicken breasts (about 6 oz/175 g each) | 8 |
| 4 | cloves garlic, minced | 4 |
| 1 tbsp | Worcestershire sauce | 15 mL |
| 1 tsp | salt | 5 mL |
| ½ tsp | pepper | 2 mL |
| 4 | slices Black Forest ham | 4 |
| 1 | large ripe mango | 1 |
| ½ cup | all-purpose flour | 125 mL |
| ½ tsp | dried thyme | 2 mL |
| ¼ cup | unsalted butter | 50 mL |
| ¼ cup | brandy | 50 mL |
| 2 | onions, sliced | 2 |
| 1 cup | EACH dry white wine and chicken stock | 250 mL |
| 1 tsp | curry powder | 5 mL |
| 2 tbsp | chopped fresh parsley | 25 mL |

Place chicken breasts between 2 large pieces of waxed paper; pound with mallet or rolling pin to flatten.

In small bowl and using back of spoon, blend together garlic, Worcestershire sauce and half each of the salt and pepper until well combined. Spread over 1 side of each chicken breast. Cut ham slices in half; place each on chicken breast.

Peel mango. Cut half away from pit in 1 piece; cut into 8 wedges and place each near edge of each chicken breast. Beginning at mango side, roll up breasts; secure with bamboo skewers or tie with string.

In small shallow bowl, combine flour, thyme and remaining salt and pepper; roll chicken in mixture to coat. (Rolls can be covered and refrigerated for up to 4 hours.)

In large skillet, melt butter over medium-high heat; cook chicken rolls, turning, for 5 to 7 minutes or until browned on all sides. Add brandy to skillet. Immediately ignite with lighted match at inside edge of skillet. When flame goes out, remove chicken rolls to plate; set aside.

Add onions to skillet; cook over medium heat, stirring often, for 5 minutes or until softened. Stir in wine and stock; bring to boil over medium-high heat, scraping up any brown bits from bottom of pan.

Cut remaining mango away from pit; cut into small pieces and add to pan along with curry powder. Stir well; return chicken rolls to skillet. Bring to boil. Reduce heat to medium; simmer, covered, for 30 minutes or until chicken is no longer pink inside, turning chicken once and stirring sauce occasionally.

Stir in parsley. Taste sauce and adjust seasonings. Remove skewers or string from chicken rolls. Serve with sauce spooned over top. Makes 8 servings.

# Chicken-Prosciutto Rolls in Tomato Sauce

The sauce in this lovely company dish takes on a slightly creamy appearance as some of the cheese oozes out into it. Serve with lots of crusty bread and a mixed green salad. Bocconcini is a fresh unripened cheese usually sold in tubs of liquid; if unavailable, use 1½-inch (4 cm) cubes of a really fresh mozzarella cheese.

| | | |
|---|---|---|
| 8 | chicken thighs (about 2 lb/1 kg) | 8 |
| ¼ cup | freshly grated Parmesan cheese | 50 mL |
| 3 tbsp | chopped fresh parsley | 45 mL |
| 1 tbsp | EACH chopped fresh basil and oregano (or 1 tsp/5 mL dried) | 15 mL |
| 8 | slices prosciutto | 8 |
| 4 | bocconcini cheese, halved | 4 |
| 1 tbsp | olive oil | 15 mL |
| 1 | onion, chopped | 1 |
| 2 | cloves garlic, minced | 2 |
| 1 | can (28 oz/796 mL) diced tomatoes | 1 |
| Pinch | hot pepper flakes | Pinch |
| 1 tbsp | balsamic vinegar | 15 mL |
| | Hot cooked fettuccine | |

Remove bone from chicken thighs by scraping off meat with small sharp knife. Place between 2 pieces of waxed paper and lightly pound with meat mallet or rolling pin. Lay skin side down on work surface.

In small bowl, combine Parmesan cheese, 2 tbsp (25 mL) of the parsley, basil and oregano; spread evenly over chicken. Top with prosciutto slice; place bocconcini cheese near 1 end. Starting at cheese end, roll up chicken; tie with string in 1 or 2 places.

In large deep skillet, heat oil; brown chicken rolls, in batches. Remove to plate. Add onion and garlic to skillet; cook over medium heat for 5 minutes, stirring often. Stir in tomatoes, hot pepper flakes and vinegar; bring to boil, scraping up brown bits from bottom of pan. Cook, uncovered, for 10 minutes.

Return chicken and any juices to pan, spooning sauce over top. Cover, reduce heat and simmer for about 20 minutes or until juices run clear when chicken is pierced. (Recipe can be prepared to this point, cooled, covered and refrigerated for up to 24 hours. Gently reheat, stirring sauce often.) Stir in remaining parsley. Serve over fettuccine. Makes 4 to 6 servings.

# Cardamom Chicken Curry

There are many wonderful spicy overtones to this easy chicken stew, with a small amount of coconut milk (found in most supermarkets) giving a nice hint of the exotic. Serve on hot basmati rice with a salad of mixed lettuces or shredded red and green cabbage for a perfect company dish. Accompany with your favorite curry condiments—mango chutney, toasted coconut, cashews or peanuts, banana chips.

| | | |
|---|---|---|
| 16 | boneless skinless chicken breast halves (about 4½ lb/2.1 kg) | 16 |
| ¼ cup | all-purpose flour | 50 mL |
| 2 tbsp | ground cardamom | 25 mL |
| 1 tsp | salt | 5 mL |
| ½ tsp | pepper | 2 mL |
| 2 tbsp | EACH olive oil and butter | 25 mL |
| 3 | onions, chopped | 3 |
| 6 | cloves garlic, minced | 6 |
| 1 tbsp | EACH minced fresh ginger and minced fresh red or green chilies | 15 mL |
| 1 tbsp | EACH ground cumin and coriander | 15 mL |
| 1 tsp | turmeric | 5 mL |
| ½ tsp | cayenne pepper | 2 mL |
| 1 cup | chicken stock | 250 mL |
| 1 | can (28 oz/796 mL) tomatoes | 1 |
| 1 | can (14 oz/400 mL) coconut milk | 1 |
| 2 cups | plain yogurt | 500 mL |
| ⅓ cup | packed brown sugar | 75 mL |
| ½ tsp | saffron | 2 mL |
| ¼ tsp | EACH ground cloves, nutmeg and cinnamon | 1 mL |
| | Sprigs fresh coriander | |

Score top of chicken breasts with sharp knife. Combine flour, cardamom, salt and pepper; rub all over chicken to coat well.

In large skillet, heat half each of the oil and butter over medium-high heat; brown chicken, in batches and adding more oil and butter as needed. Remove to large flameproof casserole or Dutch oven.

Pour off all but 2 tbsp (25 mL) fat from pan. Add onions; cook over medium heat for 5 minutes. Add garlic, ginger, chilies, cumin, coriander, turmeric and cayenne; cook, stirring, for 2 minutes. Add chicken stock; bring to boil, scraping up any brown bits from bottom of pan. Add to chicken.

Coarsely crush tomatoes with liquid; add to chicken along with coconut milk. Bring to boil; reduce heat and simmer for 10 minutes. Stir in yogurt, brown sugar, saffron, cloves, nutmeg and cinnamon; cover and cook over low heat for 20 minutes.

Uncover and cook, stirring occasionally, for about 30 minutes or until sauce is slightly thickened. Taste and adjust seasoning. (Curry can be cooled, covered and refrigerated for up to 2 days or frozen for up to 1 month. Thaw in refrigerator. Rewarm over low heat, stirring occasionally.) Garnish with fresh coriander. Makes 8 to 12 servings.

# "Jerk" Chicken Stew

This spicy Caribbean-style chicken skillet supper uses many of the seasonings the Arawak Indians of Jamaica used when they cooked animals over a fire. It's a quick and easy treatment for chicken thighs. If you like your food hotter, use two Scotch bonnet peppers—those wrinkled little multi-colored chilies that look a bit like a squashed hat. Serve with hot white rice.

| | | |
|---|---|---|
| 1½ tsp | ground allspice | 7 mL |
| 1 tsp | EACH cinnamon and dried thyme | 5 mL |
| ¼ tsp | EACH nutmeg and salt | 1 mL |
| 6 | chicken thighs | 6 |
| 1 tbsp | vegetable oil | 15 mL |
| 2 | onions, sliced | 2 |
| 2 | cloves garlic, minced | 2 |
| 1 | Scotch bonnet pepper, minced | 1 |
| 1 tbsp | minced fresh ginger | 15 mL |
| 1 | can (14 oz/398 mL) diced tomatoes | 1 |
| 2 tbsp | EACH packed brown sugar and soy sauce | 25 mL |
| 2 tsp | grated orange rind | 10 mL |
| 2 | sweet potatoes, peeled and coarsely cubed | 2 |
| 1 tbsp | cornstarch | 15 mL |
| 1 | pkg (10 oz/284 g) fresh spinach, shredded | 1 |

In large bowl, combine allspice, cinnamon, thyme, nutmeg and salt; add chicken and roll to coat well.

In deep skillet or shallow saucepan, heat oil over medium-high heat; brown chicken, in batches. Remove and set aside.

Pour off all but 2 tbsp (25 mL) drippings from pan. Add onions, garlic, pepper, ginger and any remaining spices in bowl; cook, stirring, over medium heat for 5 minutes. Stir in tomatoes, ½ cup (125 mL) water, sugar, soy sauce and rind; bring to boil, scraping up any brown bits from bottom of pan.

Return chicken to pan. Add sweet potatoes; reduce heat, cover and simmer for about 30 minutes or until potatoes are tender and juices run clear when chicken is pierced.

Dissolve cornstarch in 2 tbsp (25 mL) cold water; stir into pan juices and cook, stirring, until boiling and somewhat thickened. (Recipe can be prepared to this point, covered and refrigerated for up to 24 hours. Heat over low heat, stirring often.) Add spinach, poking down into juices; cover and cook for about 4 minutes or just until spinach is wilted. Makes about 4 servings.

**Hint: When handling hot peppers, wear rubber gloves to protect your hands from burns. If you don't have gloves, wash your hands immediately in hot soapy water after mincing the pepper.**

# Anne Lindsay's Szechuan Orange-Ginger Chicken

My good friend Anne Lindsay passes along a popular recipe from her best-seller, *The Lighthearted Cookbook.* It's quick, easy and delicious served with rice.

| | | |
|---|---|---|
| 1 lb | boneless skinless chicken breasts | 500 g |
| 1 | EACH sweet green and red pepper | 1 |
| 1 | orange | 1 |
| 2 tbsp | dry sherry | 25 mL |
| 1 tsp | bottled chili paste* | 5 mL |
| 1 tsp | EACH granulated sugar and cornstarch | 5 mL |
| 2 tbsp | vegetable oil | 25 mL |
| 1 tbsp | minced fresh ginger | 15 mL |
| 1 tsp | minced garlic | 5 mL |

Cut chicken into 1-inch (2.5 cm) cubes; set aside. Cut peppers into 1-inch (2.5 cm) squares.

Using vegetable peeler, remove rind from orange (orange part only, no white). Cut rind into thin julienne strips about 1½ inches (4 cm) long; set aside. Squeeze orange and reserve ¼ cup (50 mL) juice.

In small bowl, combine reserved orange juice, sherry, chili paste, sugar and cornstarch until smooth.

In wok or skillet, heat oil over high heat; stir-fry chicken for 2 to 3 minutes or until no longer pink inside. Remove chicken and set aside.

Add orange rind, ginger and garlic; stir-fry for 10 seconds. Add peppers; stir-fry for 1 minute. Add chili paste mixture and bring to boil. Return chicken to wok; stir until heated through. Serve immediately. Makes 4 servings.

---

**\*Bottled chili or hot red pepper paste is available in some supermarkets and most Oriental grocery stores. You can substitute about ½ tsp (2 mL) hot pepper flakes if you wish. Use more or less chili paste if you want a hotter or milder dish.**

# Garden Vegetable and Chicken Paella

Traditionally made with a variety of meats, seafood and vegetables cooked in a saffron-flavored rice (see Summer Party Paella, page 181), paella simply made with chicken and vegetables can still be exciting and absolutely delicious.

| | | |
|---|---|---|
| 4 | chicken legs | 4 |
| 2 tbsp | olive oil | 25 mL |
| | Salt and pepper | |
| 1 | Spanish onion, chopped | 1 |
| 1 | EACH sweet red and yellow pepper, cut in strips | 1 |
| 1 | jalapeño or other hot pepper, minced | 1 |
| 2 | small zucchini, diced | 2 |
| 2 | cloves garlic, minced | 2 |
| 2 | tomatoes, peeled, seeded and chopped | 2 |
| 1 tbsp | chopped fresh thyme (or 1 tsp/5 mL dried) | 15 mL |
| 1¼ cups | parboiled rice | 300 mL |
| Pinch | saffron | Pinch |
| 2 cups | chicken stock | 500 mL |

Cut chicken legs into drumsticks and thighs. In large skillet, heat oil over medium-high heat; brown chicken, in batches, sprinkling with salt and pepper. Transfer to large shallow casserole (at least 14-cup/3.5 L).

Drain off all but 2 tbsp (25 mL) drippings from pan. Add onion, sweet peppers and jalapeño; cook over medium heat for 10 minutes, stirring often. Add zucchini, garlic, tomatoes, thyme, and salt and pepper to taste; cook, stirring often, for 10 minutes or until thickened. Stir in rice and saffron until rice is coated.

Stir in stock and bring to boil, stirring to scrape up brown bits from bottom of pan. Add to chicken; cover and bake in 375°F (190°C) oven for about 50 minutes or until most of the liquid has been absorbed and juices run clear when chicken is pierced. Let stand, covered, for 5 minutes before serving. Makes 4 to 6 servings.

# Herbed Chicken Breasts in a Loaf of Bread

Although you could easily enjoy this simple chicken stew if it were served in a bowl, it's great fun to present it in a big, round crusty loaf of bread. Toss a green salad with a mustard vinaigrette to go alongside.

| | | |
|---|---|---|
| 2 lb | boneless skinless chicken breasts | 1 kg |
| ¼ cup | all-purpose flour | 50 mL |
| 2 tsp | chopped fresh rosemary (or ½ tsp/2 mL dried) | 10 mL |
| 1 tsp | EACH chopped fresh sage and marjoram (or ¼ tsp/1 mL dried) | 5 mL |
| ¼ tsp | EACH salt, pepper and paprika | 1 mL |
| ¼ cup | butter | 50 mL |
| 2 tbsp | olive oil | 25 mL |
| ½ lb | mushrooms, quartered | 250 g |
| 1 | sweet red pepper, diced | 1 |
| 6 | shallots, halved | 6 |
| 1¼ cups | dry white wine | 300 mL |
| 3 tbsp | chopped fresh parsley | 45 mL |
| 1 tbsp | Dijon mustard | 15 mL |
| 3 | cloves garlic | 3 |
| 1 cup | frozen peas, thawed | 250 mL |
| 1 | round loaf (2 lb/1 kg, 10 inches/ 25 cm across and about 3 inches/ 8 cm high) crusty Italian bread | 1 |

Cut chicken into 1½-inch (4 cm) cubes. In plastic bag or bowl, combine flour, rosemary, sage, marjoram, salt, pepper and paprika; add chicken and shake to coat well.

In deep skillet or shallow casserole, melt 1 tbsp (15 mL) of the butter with half of the oil over medium heat; cook mushrooms, red pepper and shallots for 5 minutes. Remove with slotted spoon to bowl.

Add 1 tbsp (15 mL) butter and remaining oil to skillet; brown chicken, in batches. Add to bowl. Stir wine into skillet and bring to boil, scraping up any brown bits from bottom of pan. Stir in parsley, mustard and 2 of the garlic cloves, crushed. Return chicken and vegetables to pan; bring to boil. Cover, reduce heat and simmer for about 15 minutes or until chicken is no longer pink inside. (Stew can be cooled, covered and refrigerated for up to 1 day. Reheat gently.) Taste and adjust seasoning. Stir in peas and heat through.

With bread knife, carefully cut lid from top of bread. Cut and scoop out interior, leaving about 1-inch (2.5 cm) thick shell and reserving bread for another use. Melt remaining 2 tbsp (25 mL) butter; brush over inside of shell and lid. Cut remaining garlic clove in half; rub over buttered surface. Place lid on top and heat in 350°F (180°C) oven for 10 minutes. Place on round platter or board and spoon in warm chicken mixture. Replace lid to present at table. Serve by spooning out stew, then cutting bread into wedges to go with it. Makes 6 to 8 servings.

# White-Hot Chicken Chili

In Texas, where I discovered chili of every description, there was much talk of white chili made with chicken and white beans. When I came home to recreate this quick version, I discovered I still liked to add some chili powder, which does render the dish less than white. This is a good one to serve in taco shells or rolled up in flour tortillas.

| | | |
|---|---|---|
| 2 tbsp | vegetable oil | 25 mL |
| 1 | EACH onion and stalk celery, chopped | 1 |
| 1¼ lb | boneless skinless chicken breasts, cubed | 625 g |
| 2 | cloves garlic, minced | 2 |
| 2 | jalapeño peppers, chopped | 2 |
| 1 tbsp | chili powder | 15 mL |
| 1 tsp | EACH ground cumin and dried oregano | 5 mL |
| Pinch | EACH salt and cayenne pepper | Pinch |
| 2 cups | chicken stock | 500 mL |
| 1 | can (19 oz/540 mL) white kidney beans, drained and rinsed | 1 |
| ¼ cup | chopped fresh coriander or parsley | 50 mL |

In large saucepan, heat half of the oil over medium heat; cook onion and celery for 5 minutes. Push to one side. Heat remaining oil on other side of pan over high heat; brown chicken on all sides, about 5 minutes.

Stir in garlic, jalapeño peppers, chili powder, cumin, oregano, salt and cayenne; cook, stirring, for 1 minute. Stir in stock; bring to boil. Cover and reduce heat; simmer for 15 minutes. Uncover and simmer for 10 minutes. Stir in beans; cook for 5 minutes, stirring occasionally.

Taste and adjust seasoning if necessary. Serve sprinkled with coriander. Makes about 4 servings.

# Maple-Glazed Cornish Hens on Braised Cabbage

The sweetness of maple syrup is an excellent complement to both the cabbage and the little game hens in this easy but elegant company dish. Add some slices of baked sweet potatoes to the platter.

| | | |
|---|---|---|
| 2 | Cornish hens | 2 |
| 1 tbsp | EACH unsalted butter and vegetable oil | 15 mL |
| | Salt and pepper | |
| ¼ cup | maple syrup | 50 mL |
| 4 | shallots, minced | 4 |
| 2 | cloves garlic, minced | 2 |
| 8 cups | thinly sliced green cabbage | 2 L |
| ¼ cup | red wine vinegar | 50 mL |
| 1 tbsp | grainy Dijon mustard | 15 mL |
| ¼ tsp | cayenne pepper | 1 mL |
| ¼ cup | dried currants | 50 mL |

Cut hens in half, removing backbone by cutting on either side. Dry hens well. In large skillet, heat butter with oil over medium heat; brown hen halves on both sides, about 5 minutes, sprinkling lightly with salt and pepper.

Place halves, skin side up, on rack in small roasting pan; brush with half of the maple syrup. (Hens can be prepared to this point, covered and refrigerated for up to 3 hours.) Roast, uncovered, in 375°F (190°C) oven for 30 minutes or until juices run clear when thigh is pierced and breast is no longer pink inside, basting occasionally with pan juices.

Meanwhile, discard all but 2 tbsp (25 mL) drippings from skillet. Add shallots and garlic; cook over medium-low heat for 5 minutes, stirring. Add cabbage, vinegar, remaining maple syrup, mustard and cayenne; bring to boil. Reduce heat and simmer, covered, for 10 minutes or until cabbage is tender. (Cabbage can be prepared to this point and set aside at room temperature for up to 2 hours. Reheat gently.)

Stir in currants and heat through. Mound on warm serving platter. Arrange hen halves on top and drizzle any pan juices over hens. Makes 2 to 4 servings.

# Do-Ahead Stir-Fried Turkey

Stir-frying is one of the quickest cooking methods, but you can get bogged down preparing the ingredients. If you want dinner in less than 10 minutes, slice the vegetables and meat the night before, then wrap individually in plastic wrap or sandwich bags and refrigerate. Serve with Oriental noodles which cook in just a few minutes, or the steamed kind that just need reheating.

| | | |
|---|---|---|
| ½ cup | chicken stock | 125 mL |
| 1 tbsp | EACH granulated sugar, soy sauce and rice wine or dry sherry | 15 mL |
| 2 tsp | rice vinegar | 10 mL |
| ¼ tsp | EACH salt and pepper | 1 mL |
| Dash | hot pepper sauce | Dash |
| 1 tsp | sesame oil | 5 mL |
| 1 tbsp | minced fresh ginger | 15 mL |
| 1 | clove garlic, minced | 1 |
| 1½ tsp | cornstarch | 7 mL |
| ½ cup | whole blanched almonds | 125 mL |
| 1 lb | boneless skinless turkey or chicken breast | 500 g |
| ½ lb | snow peas | 250 g |
| ¼ lb | mushrooms | 125 g |
| 1 | stalk celery | 1 |
| 1 | sweet red pepper | 1 |
| 2 tbsp | peanut or vegetable oil | 25 mL |

In measuring cup, stir together stock, sugar, soy sauce, wine, vinegar, salt, pepper and hot pepper sauce until sugar dissolves.

In small stainless steel saucepan, heat sesame oil over medium heat; stir-fry ginger and garlic for a few seconds. Stir in stock mixture; bring to boil, stirring. Dissolve cornstarch in 2 tsp (10 mL) cold water; whisk into sauce and cook, stirring, until thickened. Cook for 30 seconds; remove from heat. Let cool, cover and refrigerate.

In pie plate, toast almonds in 350°F (180°C) oven for 5 minutes or until golden. (Alternatively, microwave at High for 1 to 2 minutes.) Let cool, wrap and set aside.

Cut turkey into 2- x ½-inch (5 x 1 cm) strips; wrap in plastic wrap. Trim snow peas and wrap. Slice mushrooms and wrap. Slice celery diagonally and wrap. Cut red pepper into strips and wrap. Refrigerate overnight.

Just before serving, reheat sauce over low heat, stirring often. In wok or large skillet, heat peanut oil over high heat; stir-fry turkey for 1 to 2 minutes or until no longer pink. Add mushrooms, celery and red pepper; stir-fry for 1 minute. Add snow peas; stir-fry for 1 minute or until vegetables are tender-crisp. Add almonds. Stir in sauce. Serve immediately. Makes about 4 servings.

# Old-Fashioned Turkey Pot Pie

This is one of my favorite ways to enjoy roast turkey the next day. It's so delicious that you can even serve the pie to guests without the stigma of "leftovers." If you have no cooked turkey, poach turkey (or chicken) parts in the stock about half an hour and remove before adding vegetables.

| | | |
|---|---|---|
| 6 cups | chicken or turkey stock | 1.5 L |
| 4 | red potatoes, cut in 1-inch (2.5 cm) cubes | 4 |
| 4 | stalks celery, diced | 4 |
| 3 | carrots, diced | 3 |
| ¼ cup | butter | 50 mL |
| 6 | green onions, sliced | 6 |
| ½ lb | mushrooms, quartered | 250 g |
| ½ cup | all-purpose flour | 125 mL |
| ¼ cup | whipping cream | 50 mL |
| 6 cups | diced cooked turkey | 1.5 L |
| 2 cups | frozen peas | 500 mL |
| ½ cup | chopped fresh parsley | 125 mL |
| 1 tsp | EACH crumbled dried sage and marjoram | 5 mL |
| | Salt and pepper | |
| Half | pkg (397 g) frozen puff pastry, thawed | Half |
| 1 | egg | 1 |

In medium saucepan, bring stock to simmer; cook potatoes, celery and carrots for 15 to 20 minutes or until tender-crisp. Reserving liquid, drain vegetables in colander and set aside.

In same pot, melt butter over medium heat; cook onions for 3 minutes. Add mushrooms and cook for 3 minutes. Sprinkle with flour; cook, stirring, for 2 minutes. Gradually stir in reserved stock, whisking constantly; cook, whisking, until thickened. Stir in cream.

Add cooked vegetables, turkey, peas, parsley, sage, marjoram, and salt and pepper to taste. Spoon into greased 12-cup (3 L) shallow baking dish. Cool.

Roll out puff pastry to fit top of dish. With fork, beat together egg and 1 tsp (5 mL) water to make glaze; brush onto rim of dish and place pastry on top, pressing onto rim. If desired, make decoration of any leftover pastry and place on top. Make small hole in middle of pastry. (Pie can be prepared to this point and refrigerated for up to 6 hours. Refrigerate glaze.) Brush pastry all over with glaze.

Bake in 425°F (220°C) oven for 25 to 30 minutes or until puffed, browned and bubbly. Makes about 8 servings.

# Turkey and Corn Enchiladas

If turkey is unavailable for this colorful casserole, substitute chicken and serve the results with red onion and spinach salad.

| | | |
|---|---|---|
| 2 tbsp | butter | 25 mL |
| 6 | green onions, minced | 6 |
| 1 | sweet red pepper, finely diced | 1 |
| 3 cups | corn kernels (fresh or frozen) | 750 mL |
| 1 tsp | ground cumin | 5 mL |
| ¼ tsp | cayenne pepper | 1 mL |
| 3 cups | shredded Monterey Jack or mild Cheddar cheese | 750 mL |
| 2 oz | light cream cheese | 50 g |
| ½ cup | sour cream | 125 mL |
| 3 cups | cubed cooked turkey | 750 mL |
| 1¾ cups | bottled mild chunky salsa | 425 mL |
| 12 | large flour tortillas | 12 |

In large skillet, heat butter over medium heat; cook half each of the green onions and red pepper, stirring often, for 3 to 5 minutes or until softened. Stir in corn, cumin and cayenne. Add ¼ cup (50 mL) water; cover and cook until water is evaporated, about 5 minutes. Remove from heat. Stir in half of the cheese, all the cream cheese and sour cream. Stir in turkey.

Spread one-third of the salsa in 13- x 9-inch (3.5 L) baking dish. Dividing evenly, spread filling down centre of each tortilla; roll up, folding in ends. Place seam side down in dish. Spread remaining salsa over top; sprinkle with remaining cheese, onions and red pepper. (Recipe can be prepared to this point, covered and refrigerated for up to 8 hours. Let stand at room temperature for 30 minutes before baking.)

Bake, covered, in 350°F (180°C) oven for about 20 minutes or until heated through. Makes 6 to 8 servings.

# Turkey and Wild Rice Casserole

Lindsay Reid of Lindsay's Food Shop in Stratford, Ontario, keeps a constant supply of staples just suited to casserole making because, as he says, "Customers ask for this type of food as it travels well and stands reheating." I've adapted this recipe from one of Lindsay's popular casseroles. I think it would be perfect for a Boxing Day luncheon or any other time when you have leftover turkey and company coming.

| | | |
|---|---|---|
| 2 tbsp | olive oil | 25 mL |
| 1 | large onion, diced | 1 |
| 1 | clove garlic, crushed | 1 |
| 2 cups | sliced mushrooms | 500 mL |
| 2 tbsp | all-purpose flour | 25 mL |
| 2½ cups | turkey or chicken stock | 625 mL |
| ½ cup | dry white wine | 125 mL |
| 4 cups | cooked basmati rice | 1 L |
| 1 cup | cooked wild rice | 250 mL |
| ½ cup | dried cranberries | 125 mL |
| 3 tbsp | chopped fresh parsley (preferably Italian) | 45 mL |
| 1 tsp | EACH chopped fresh rosemary and thyme (or ¼ tsp/1 mL dried) | 5 mL |
| ½ tsp | salt | 2 mL |
| Pinch | pepper | Pinch |
| 1 | bunch broccoli | 1 |
| 2 cups | shredded or diced cooked turkey | 500 mL |

*Topping:*

| | | |
|---|---|---|
| 1½ cups | fresh bread crumbs | 375 mL |
| ½ cup | freshly grated Parmesan cheese | 125 mL |
| ¼ cup | chopped fresh parsley | 50 mL |
| 2 tbsp | butter, melted | 25 mL |
| | Salt and pepper | |

In large skillet, heat oil over medium heat; cook onion, garlic and mushrooms for 7 minutes, stirring often.

Sprinkle with flour; cook for 2 minutes, stirring. Gradually stir in stock and wine; cook, stirring, until thickened. Stir in basmati rice, wild rice, cranberries, parsley, rosemary, thyme, salt and pepper. (Mixture will be soupy, but rice will absorb moisture.) Taste and adjust seasoning.

Trim and peel broccoli stalks; separate into florets and chop stalks. In large pot of boiling salted water, blanch broccoli for 2 minutes. Drain and refresh under cold running water.

In 13- x 9-inch (3.5 L) baking dish, layer half of the rice mixture, then all of the broccoli, then turkey. Top with remaining rice mixture.

Topping: Combine crumbs, cheese, parsley, butter, and salt and pepper to taste; sprinkle over casserole. Bake, uncovered, in 375°F (190°C) oven for about 35 minutes or until bubbly and top is golden brown. Makes 6 to 8 servings.

---

Hint: For 4 cups (1 L) cooked basmati rice, pick over 1 cup (250 mL) raw rice, discarding any foreign matter; rinse well. Add rice to 2 cups (500 mL) boiling salted water; cover, reduce heat to low and cook for about 15 minutes or until grains are tender and water has been absorbed. Let stand for 5 minutes; fluff with a fork.

For 1 cup (250 mL) cooked wild rice, rinse ¼ cup (50 mL) wild rice and add to large quantity of boiling water; cover and boil for about 45 minutes or until grains are tender but not splayed. Drain and fluff with a fork.

# Beef and Veal

# Meat Loaf and Oven-Roasted Vegetable Supper

For a very inexpensive meal-in-one dish, cook all the vegetables around tonight's meat loaf just as you would with a roast. If you like, accompany with butter for the vegetables, chili sauce for the meat and a cabbage slaw.

| | | |
|---|---|---|
| 1 | egg | 1 |
| ¼ cup | EACH dry bread crumbs, milk and ketchup | 50 mL |
| 1 tbsp | Worcestershire sauce | 15 mL |
| ½ tsp | dried sage | 2 mL |
| | Salt and pepper | |
| 1 lb | lean ground beef | 500 g |
| 2 | slices side bacon | 2 |
| 3 | potatoes | 3 |
| 2 | onions | 2 |
| 1 | small acorn squash (unpeeled) | 1 |
| | Vegetable oil | |

In large bowl, beat egg lightly. Stir in bread crumbs, milk, ketchup, Worcestershire sauce, sage, ½ tsp (2 mL) salt and ¼ tsp (1 mL) pepper. Gently mix in beef. Transfer to large greased baking pan (like broiler pan); pat into free-form loaf, about 6 x 4 inches (15 x 10 cm). Arrange bacon strips lengthwise over top, tucking in ends at ends of meat. (Loaf can be prepared to this point, covered and refrigerated for up to 8 hours.)

Cut each potato into 8 wedges. Peel and cut each onion into 6 wedges. Seed and cut squash into 8 wedges. Brush vegetables all over with oil; arrange around meat loaf and sprinkle vegetables with salt and pepper to taste.

Bake, uncovered, in 350°F (180°C) oven for about 1 hour and 15 minutes, turning vegetables occasionally, until meat thermometer in loaf registers 170°F (75°C). Makes 4 servings.

# Dark and Delicious Texas Chili

When I did television appearances for Mike Farmer, a former producer for Global News, he told me about his mother's delicious chili. One day, I was very pleased to receive a fax of Betty Farmer's chili recipe, thanks to Mike, and I've adapted it for this great chili. A secret ingredient, cocoa, makes it rich, dark and delicious. This one does have beans.

| | | |
|---|---|---|
| 1½ lb | lean ground beef | 750 g |
| 1 | onion, chopped | 1 |
| 1 | clove garlic, minced | 1 |
| 2 tbsp | unsweetened cocoa powder | 25 mL |
| 1 tbsp | EACH all-purpose flour and chili powder | 15 mL |
| 1 tsp | EACH dried oregano, granulated sugar, salt, ground coriander and ground cumin | 5 mL |
| Pinch | hot pepper flakes | Pinch |
| 2 | cans (each 28 oz/796 mL) tomatoes (preferably one regular and one crushed) | 2 |
| 1 | sweet green pepper, diced | 1 |
| 2 | stalks celery, diced | 2 |
| 2 | cans (each 19 oz/540 mL) red kidney beans (undrained) | 2 |

In large saucepan over medium-high heat, cook beef, onion and garlic, breaking up meat, until beef is no longer pink.

Stir together cocoa, flour, chili powder, oregano, sugar, salt, coriander, cumin and hot pepper flakes; stir into beef mixture.

Add tomatoes, green pepper and celery; bring to boil. Reduce heat, cover and simmer for 45 minutes, stirring occasionally. Stir in kidney beans; simmer for 10 minutes. Makes 6 servings.

# Texas Red

Texan-style chili traditionally contains no beans, but is hearty enough to satisfy the biggest appetite. If you like less heat, just reduce the jalapeños in this spicy chili.

| | | |
|---|---|---|
| 2 lb | boneless beef (blade roast or round steak) | 1 kg |
| 3 tbsp | vegetable oil | 45 mL |
| ¼ cup | chili powder | 50 mL |
| 3 | onions, chopped | 3 |
| 4 | cloves garlic, minced | 4 |
| 1 | can (28 oz/796 mL) crushed tomatoes in purée or diced tomatoes | 1 |
| 1 tbsp | EACH packed brown sugar and red wine vinegar | 15 mL |
| 2 tsp | ground cumin | 10 mL |
| 1 tsp | EACH dried oregano, paprika and salt | 5 mL |
| 2 | jalapeño peppers, seeded and minced | 2 |

Trim beef well and cut into ¾-inch (2 cm) cubes. In skillet, heat oil over medium-high heat; brown beef, in batches. Transfer to large saucepan with slotted spoon. Add chili powder and set aside.

Add onions and garlic to skillet; cook over medium heat for 5 minutes. Stir into meat along with tomatoes. Bring to boil; reduce heat, cover and cook 20 minutes.

Stir in brown sugar, vinegar, cumin, oregano, paprika and salt; cook for 2 hours, covered.

Stir in jalapeño peppers; cook, uncovered, for 10 minutes. Taste and adjust seasoning. Makes 4 to 6 servings.

# Classic Cabbage Rolls

A few years ago, Ontario's Ministry of Culture sponsored a food show at the Ontario Science Centre in Toronto. Part of the show was a series of ongoing food demonstrations by Ontario authors and cooks, and this was the recipe I demonstrated at the show. This makes a good number, so that you can freeze batches for future flavorful meals. Or, it's a great big-batch recipe to cook with a friend and divide the results.

| | | |
|---|---|---|
| 1 | large cabbage or 2 small cabbages, cored | 1 |
| | *Filling:* | |
| 1 cup | long-grain rice | 250 mL |
| 1½ cups | boiling water | 375 mL |
| 2 lb | lean ground beef | 1 kg |
| 1 | onion, minced | 1 |
| 2 | cloves garlic, minced | 2 |
| 1 | can (10 oz/284 mL) condensed beef consommé | 1 |
| 1 | egg, beaten | 1 |
| 1 tsp | EACH Worcestershire sauce and salt | 5 mL |
| ½ tsp | pepper | 2 mL |
| | *Sauce:* | |
| ¼ cup | butter | 50 mL |
| ½ cup | packed brown sugar | 125 mL |
| 2 tbsp | all-purpose flour | 25 mL |
| 2 | onions, sliced | 2 |
| 1 | can (28 oz/796 mL) tomatoes | 1 |
| 1 | can (14 oz/398 mL) tomato sauce | 1 |
| ¾ cup | cider vinegar | 175 mL |
| 2 tsp | Worcestershire sauce | 10 mL |
| | Salt and pepper | |

In large pot of boiling water, blanch cabbage for 2 minutes. Remove outer leaves. Place any torn leaves in bottoms of two 13- x 9-inch (3.5 L) shallow baking dishes. If it becomes too difficult to remove leaves from cabbage, blanch again. Without cutting through leaf, trim thick rib from outside of each leaf for easier rolling.

Filling: In medium saucepan, add rice to boiling water; cook for 1 minute. Cover, turn off heat and let stand for about 10 minutes or until water is absorbed.

Meanwhile, in large bowl, stir together beef, onion, garlic, ½ cup (125 mL) undiluted consommé, egg, Worcestershire sauce, salt and pepper. Stir in prepared rice.

Place about ⅓ cup (75 mL) filling in centre of each cabbage leaf. Fold sides over filling and roll up from stem. Secure with toothpicks.

Sauce: In large skillet, melt half of the butter over medium heat; stir in 2 tbsp (25 mL) of the brown sugar. Working in batches and adding remaining butter and sugar as needed, add cabbage rolls and cook until glazed on all sides, about 5 minutes. Remove toothpicks and arrange rolls close together and seam side down over cabbage in baking dishes.

Combine flour with remaining consommé until smooth; stir into skillet. Add onions, tomatoes, tomato sauce, vinegar, Worcestershire sauce, and salt and pepper to taste; bring to boil. Cook, stirring, until slightly thickened, 3 to 5 minutes. Pour over cabbage rolls. Bake, covered, in 325°F (160°C) oven for about 2½ hours or until cabbage is tender. Makes about 30 rolls.

# Quick Sauerkraut "Cabbage Roll" Casserole

In the markets around the Waterloo region of Ontario, soured heads of cabbage are often available for making cabbage rolls. I've incorporated the flavors of these delicious rolls into a quick and easy casserole. Serve with pickled beets and whole wheat bread or rolls.

| | | |
|---|---|---|
| ½ cup | parboiled rice | 125 mL |
| 1 lb | lean ground beef | 500 g |
| ½ lb | mushrooms, sliced | 250 g |
| | (2½ cups/625 mL) | |
| 1 | onion, chopped | 1 |
| 2 | cloves garlic, minced | 2 |
| 1 tsp | Worcestershire sauce | 5 mL |
| | Pepper | |
| 1 | can (7½ oz/213 mL) | 1 |
| | tomato sauce | |
| ½ cup | sour cream | 125 mL |
| 2 cups | sauerkraut, drained and rinsed | 500 mL |
| 1 cup | fresh bread crumbs | 250 mL |
| 1 tbsp | butter, melted | 15 mL |

Cook rice in 2 cups (500 mL) boiling salted water for 5 minutes. Drain well.

Meanwhile, in large skillet, cook beef, breaking up meat, mushrooms, onion and garlic over medium heat for about 8 minutes or until beef is no longer pink and vegetables are softened, stirring often. Drain off any fat. Season with Worcestershire sauce, and pepper to taste. Stir in rice, tomato sauce and sour cream.

In deep 6-cup (1.5 L) casserole, alternately layer 3 layers of sauerkraut and 2 of beef mixture. Stir together crumbs and butter; sprinkle evenly on top. (Casserole can be prepared to this point, covered and refrigerated for up to 8 hours. Let stand at room temperature for 30 minutes.)

Bake, covered, in 350°F (180°C) oven for about 45 minutes or until rice is tender and topping is golden brown. Makes 4 servings.

---

**Variation: Substitute 3 cups (750 mL) chopped cabbage for sauerkraut and cook in 1 tbsp (15 mL) butter just until wilted, about 5 minutes.**

# Mexican Beef Pie

A crunchy cornmeal mixture provides an easy crust for this spicy beef pie. It's perfect for a family supper, served with a crisp green salad.

| | | |
|---|---|---|
| 1 lb | lean ground beef | 500 g |
| 3 | cloves garlic, minced | 3 |
| 1 | onion, chopped | 1 |
| 2 tsp | chili powder | 10 mL |
| 1 tsp | dry mustard | 5 mL |
| ¼ tsp | EACH ground cumin, hot pepper flakes, dried oregano and salt | 1 mL |
| 1 | can (14 oz/398 mL) tomatoes | 1 |
| Half | sweet green pepper, diced | Half |
| 1 | can (14 oz/398 mL) kidney beans (undrained) | 1 |
| | *Cornmeal Topping:* | |
| ¾ cup | coarse cornmeal | 175 mL |
| ½ cup | all-purpose flour | 125 mL |
| ½ tsp | EACH baking soda, salt and granulated sugar | 2 mL |
| 1 cup | shredded Cheddar cheese | 250 mL |
| ¾ cup | buttermilk | 175 mL |
| 1 | egg | 1 |
| 2 tbsp | vegetable oil | 25 mL |

In large skillet, cook beef, garlic, onion, chili powder, mustard, cumin, hot pepper flakes, oregano and salt over medium heat for 5 minutes, breaking up beef with spoon. Stir in tomatoes, breaking up with spoon; cook, uncovered, for 20 minutes, stirring occasionally. Stir in green pepper. Arrange half in shallow 8-cup (2 L) casserole; top with half of the kidney beans. Repeat layers; set aside.

Cornmeal Topping: In large bowl, combine cornmeal, flour, baking soda, salt and sugar; stir in cheese. Stir together buttermilk, egg and oil; stir into dry ingredients just until combined. Spread evenly over casserole. Bake in 450°F (230°C) oven for about 15 minutes or until set and lightly browned. Makes 6 servings.

# Saucy Beef Stew

Brown the meat while the rest of the stew comes to a boil, then let them simmer together in a slow oven. If desired, stir in extra cooked vegetables (potato cubes, turnip slices, parsnip pieces) before serving with lots of crusty bread to capture the sauce.

| | | |
|---|---|---|
| 2 lb | stew beef | 1 kg |
| ¼ cup | all-purpose flour | 50 mL |
| ½ tsp | salt | 2 mL |
| ¼ tsp | pepper | 1 mL |
| 2 cups | beef stock | 500 mL |
| 1 | can (14 oz/398 mL) tomatoes | 1 |
| 5 | carrots, sliced | 5 |
| 2 | onions, sliced | 2 |
| ½ lb | mushrooms, sliced (2½ cups/625 mL) | 250 g |
| ½ tsp | EACH crushed dried rosemary and thyme | 2 mL |
| ½ cup | dry red wine or additional stock | 125 mL |

Cut beef into 1½-inch (4 cm) cubes. In bag, toss beef with flour, salt and pepper. Spread beef on large shallow baking pan; bake in 500°F (260°C) oven for 10 to 15 minutes or until lightly browned.

Meanwhile, in large flameproof casserole or Dutch oven, combine beef stock, tomatoes, carrots, onions, mushrooms, rosemary and thyme, breaking up tomatoes with fork; bring to boil. Add browned beef.

Stir wine into beef browning pan; bring to boil, scraping up any brown bits from bottom of pan. Add to meat mixture; cover and bake in 300°F (150°C) oven for 2 hours or until beef is tender. Makes about 6 servings.

# Oven Beef Stew with Beer and Squash

Squash is often overlooked as a stew vegetable, but in fact, it adds lots of color and flavor to this beef-and-beer braised dish that's low in fat.

| | | |
|---|---|---|
| 2 lb | stew beef | 1 kg |
| ¼ cup | all-purpose flour | 50 mL |
| ¼ tsp | EACH salt and pepper | 1 mL |
| 2 tsp | vegetable oil | 10 mL |
| ½ lb | small mushrooms | 250 g |
| 2 | onions, chopped | 2 |
| 2 tbsp | brown sugar | 25 mL |
| 2½ cups | beef stock | 625 mL |
| 1 | bottle (12 oz/341 mL) dark beer | 1 |
| 1 tsp | dried thyme | 5 mL |
| 1 lb | butternut squash | 500 g |
| 3 | potatoes | 3 |
| | Chopped fresh parsley | |

Cut beef into 1½-inch (4 cm) cubes. In bag, toss beef with flour and sprinkle lightly with salt and pepper. Spread beef on large shallow baking pan; bake in 500°F (260°C) oven for 10 to 15 minutes or until slightly browned. Reduce temperature to 325°F (160°C).

Meanwhile, in large Dutch oven or flameproof casserole, heat oil over medium heat; cook mushrooms, onions and brown sugar, stirring often, for about 10 minutes or until mushroom liquid has evaporated. Stir in stock, beer, thyme, and salt and pepper to taste; bring to boil. Stir in browned beef and any flour; cover tightly and transfer to oven. Bake for 1 hour and 15 minutes.

Peel, seed and cut squash into thin 1½-inch (4 cm) long rectangular pieces. Peel potatoes and cut into 1½-inch (4 cm) chunks. Stir into stew and bake, covered, for 45 minutes or until vegetables and beef are very tender. Serve sprinkled with parsley. Makes about 6 servings.

# Argentinian Autumn Stew

This great party dish (stew baked in a pumpkin) is a favorite recipe from Genie Berger, a good Cambridge, Ontario, cook who passes along this sage advice: "You might want to get your oven's interior dimensions first and take them along when choosing a pumpkin!" Of course, if you want to make the stew when pumpkins are not in season, just bake it in a big casserole or ovenproof pot.

| | | |
|---|---|---|
| 4 lb | stew beef | 2 kg |
| 2 tbsp | olive oil | 25 mL |
| 4 | onions, chopped | 4 |
| 3 | cloves garlic, minced | 3 |
| 2 | large sweet green peppers, diced | 2 |
| 2½ cups | beef stock | 625 mL |
| ¾ cup | Madeira wine | 175 mL |
| 2 | large tomatoes, peeled and chopped | 2 |
| 2 tsp | EACH granulated sugar and salt | 10 mL |
| ½ tsp | pepper | 2 mL |
| 24 | dried pitted prunes | 24 |
| 1 lb | dried apricots | 500 g |
| 6 | sweet potatoes, peeled and cubed | 6 |
| 1 | pkg (2 lb/1 kg) frozen corn kernels | 1 |
| 5 tbsp | cornstarch | 75 mL |
| 1 | large pumpkin (to hold 32 cups/8 L) | 1 |

Cut beef into 1-inch (2.5 cm) cubes. In large skillet, heat oil over medium-high heat; brown beef, in batches. Transfer with slotted spoon to 32-cup (8 L) Dutch oven.

Add onions, garlic and green peppers to skillet; cook over medium heat for about 5 minutes or until softened, stirring often. Add to meat.

Add beef stock and Madeira to skillet; bring to boil, scraping up any brown bits from bottom of pan. Stir into meat mixture along with tomatoes, sugar, salt, pepper, prunes, apricots, sweet potatoes and corn. Bring to boil; reduce heat, cover and simmer for 1¼ hours, stirring occasionally.

Dissolve cornstarch in a little of the pan liquid; blend into stew and cook until thickened. (Recipe can be prepared to this point, cooled, covered and refrigerated for up to 1 day. Bring to simmer over low heat, stirring often, before proceeding.)

Cut top off pumpkin to form lid. Remove seeds and membranes. Fill pumpkin with stew; replace top. Bake in 325°F (160°C) oven for 1 hour or until beef is tender and pumpkin is tender enough to be scooped out, but not mushy. Place pumpkin on large platter and serve from it. Makes about 12 servings.

# Easy Beef and Leek Stew in Chive Popovers

I quickly put together this stew one evening before I left the house for a meeting, leaving my husband and son home to stir and eventually enjoy it for dinner. I arrived home to find all kinds of notes on my scribbled recipe, including "Really tasted good" and "Gravy was nice and rich," but alas there was no stew. The two of them had eaten every bit of it and I had to test it again. It goes very well in the popovers (like having gravy on Yorkshire Pudding), but you can enjoy it with crusty bread instead if you like.

| | | |
|---|---|---|
| 1¼ lb | stew beef | 625 g |
| 2 tbsp | olive oil | 25 mL |
| 4 | small leeks, thickly sliced | 4 |
| 4 | carrots, cut in 1-inch (2.5 cm) chunks | 4 |
| 2 tbsp | all-purpose flour | 25 mL |
| | Salt and pepper | |
| 2 tbsp | balsamic vinegar | 25 mL |
| 2½ cups | beef stock | 625 mL |
| ⅓ cup | sun-dried tomato strips | 75 mL |
| 1 tsp | dried thyme | 5 mL |
| Pinch | hot pepper flakes | Pinch |
| | Chive Popovers (recipe follows) | |

Cut beef into 2-inch (5 cm) cubes. In large saucepan, heat oil over medium-high heat; brown beef all over, about 10 minutes.

Add leeks and carrots; cook for 5 minutes, stirring often. Sprinkle with flour, and salt and pepper to taste; cook for 3 minutes, stirring constantly.

Stir in vinegar, then stock, 1 cup (250 mL) water, sun-dried tomatoes, thyme and hot pepper flakes; bring to boil, scraping up any brown bits from bottom of pan. Reduce heat, cover and simmer for 2 hours, stirring occasionally and adding a bit more water if necessary. Taste and adjust seasoning. Split open popovers and serve stew on top. Makes 4 servings.

# Chive Popovers

Popovers are really easy to make. I remember my daughter, Anne, making them often for breakfast when she was a child. You can, of course, substitute other herbs for the chives, or leave them out altogether.

| 2 | eggs | 2 |
|---|---|---|
| 1 cup | milk | 250 mL |
| 1 cup | all-purpose flour | 250 mL |
| 2 tbsp | snipped fresh chives or green onions | 25 mL |
| ½ tsp | salt | 2 mL |

In large bowl, beat eggs; stir in milk, flour, chives and salt until blended. (Don't overmix; ignore a few lumps.) Fill 12 well-greased muffin cups three-quarters full with batter.

Place in cold oven. Turn oven to 450°F (230°C); bake for 25 minutes. Remove and prick each popover with point of sharp knife to release steam. Bake for 5 to 10 minutes or until golden brown and puffed. (Popovers can be cooled, placed on cookie sheet, covered with clean towel and set aside at room temperature for up to 8 hours. Reheat in 350°F/180°C oven for 5 to 10 minutes.) Makes 12 popovers.

# Winter Braised Short Ribs and Vegetables

Tender ribs with hot corn bread or crusty rolls and coleslaw make a hearty meal for a cold winter night.

| | | |
|---|---|---|
| 2 lb | beef short ribs | 1 kg |
| 1 | clove garlic, halved | 1 |
| ¼ cup | all-purpose flour | 50 mL |
| 1 tsp | paprika | 5 mL |
| ½ tsp | salt | 2 mL |
| ¼ tsp | pepper | 1 mL |
| 2 tbsp | vegetable oil (approx) | 25 mL |
| 2 | onions, sliced | 2 |
| 1 cup | hot water | 250 mL |
| 1 | can (7½ oz/213 mL) tomato sauce | 1 |
| 1 | bay leaf | 1 |
| 3 | EACH carrots and potatoes, peeled and quartered | 3 |
| 1 cup | cubed peeled winter squash | 250 mL |
| 1 cup | frozen corn kernels | 250 mL |
| ½ cup | chopped sweet green pepper | 125 mL |

Cut ribs into pieces and trim off excess fat. Rub all surfaces of meat with cut side of garlic. In plastic bag, toss ribs with flour, paprika, salt and pepper. Meanwhile, in large flameproof casserole, heat half of the oil over medium heat; cook onions, stirring often, for 5 minutes or until softened but not browned. Remove with slotted spoon and set aside.

Add ribs to casserole; brown in batches, adding more oil if necessary. Remove and set aside.

Add any remaining flour mixture to casserole; cook, stirring, for 2 minutes. Gradually stir in water, tomato sauce and bay leaf; bring to boil. Return meat and onions to pan; cover, reduce heat and simmer for 1½ hours.

Add carrots, potatoes and squash; simmer for 20 minutes or until vegetables are tender. Skim off fat. Discard bay leaf. (Recipe can be prepared to this point, cooled, covered and refrigerated for up to 3 days. Lift fat from surface. Reheat gently.)

Stir in corn and green pepper; simmer for 5 minutes. Taste and adjust seasoning. Makes 4 servings.

# Baked Curried Beef and Sweet Potatoes

Mashed sweet potatoes contrast nicely with lightly curried ground beef in this comforting supper dish. If you are freezing it, do not add almonds; sprinkle them over top just before serving.

| | | |
|---|---|---|
| 4 | small sweet potatoes | 4 |
| 1 tbsp | butter | 15 mL |
| | Salt and pepper | |
| 2 tbsp | chopped fresh parsley | 25 mL |
| 1 tbsp | vegetable oil | 15 mL |
| 1 | onion, chopped | 1 |
| 1 tbsp | minced fresh ginger | 15 mL |
| 1 lb | lean ground beef | 500 g |
| 2 tbsp | curry powder | 25 mL |
| 1 tsp | EACH ground cumin and coriander | 5 mL |
| 2 cups | beef stock | 500 mL |
| 2 tbsp | tomato paste | 25 mL |
| ⅓ cup | EACH raisins and slivered almonds | 75 mL |

Pierce sweet potatoes several times with fork. Bake in 400°F (200°C) oven for about 1 hour or until tender. (Or peel and cut in large chunks; boil in water for 20 minutes or microwave on High for 7 to 15 minutes.) Peel and mash with butter, and salt and pepper to taste. Stir in parsley. Transfer to 4-cup (1 L) casserole. (Potatoes can be covered and refrigerated for up to 1 day or frozen for up to 2 months. Thaw in refrigerator and bring to room temperature for 30 minutes before proceeding.)

Meanwhile, in large skillet, heat oil over medium heat; cook onion and ginger for 5 minutes. Add beef, breaking up with spoon; cook until no longer pink, about 7 minutes. Drain off fat.

Stir in curry powder, cumin and coriander. Add stock and tomato paste; bring to boil. Reduce heat and simmer for 20 to 25 minutes or until most of the liquid has evaporated. Stir in raisins and almonds. Taste and adjust seasoning. Transfer to 4-cup (1 L) casserole. (Beef mixture can be covered and refrigerated for up to 2 days, or frozen for up to 2 months; thaw in refrigerator and bring to room temperature for 30 minutes before proceeding.)

Reheat both casseroles, covered, in 350°F (180°C) oven for about 30 minutes or until bubbly. To serve, spoon sweet potatoes onto heated platter; make a well in centre and spoon in curried beef. Makes 4 servings.

# Indian Corn Stew

This old recipe from Nova Scotia is like a Canadian chili con carne using corn instead of kidney beans. It's quick and economical when late-summer vegetables are plentiful, but you could use frozen corn out of season. For a hotter version, use a small hot pepper and half a sweet green pepper instead of one whole sweet green pepper.

| | | |
|---|---|---|
| 2 tbsp | vegetable oil | 25 mL |
| 1 lb | lean ground beef | 500 g |
| 1 | onion, finely chopped | 1 |
| 1 | large clove garlic, minced | 1 |
| 3 cups | uncooked corn kernels (4 to 6 ears) | 750 mL |
| 3 | tomatoes, peeled and chopped | 3 |
| 1 tbsp | Worcestershire sauce | 15 mL |
| ½ tsp | salt | 2 mL |
| ½ tsp | granulated sugar | 2 mL |
| ¼ tsp | pepper | 1 mL |
| 1 | large sweet green pepper, chopped | 1 |

In large heavy skillet, heat oil over high heat; cook beef, breaking up with spoon, until no longer pink. Stir in onion and garlic; cook for 5 minutes.

Stir in corn, tomatoes, Worcestershire sauce, salt, sugar and pepper; cover and cook over low heat for 15 minutes. Stir in green pepper; cook for 15 minutes. Makes 4 to 6 servings.

---

**Hint: Buy ground beef when it's on special, flatten each pound (500 g) into a thin disk, close tightly in freezer bag and freeze to have on hand for spur-of-the-moment casseroles like Edna's Easy Noodle Stroganoff (page 117). The thin disk will thaw much more easily right in the pan than a thick clump of beef.**

# Edna's Easy Noodle Stroganoff

My dear friend Edna Staebler finds food one of the great pleasures in life. She has written about it to the enjoyment of hundreds of thousands of readers in her "Schmecks" series of cookbooks, *Food that Really Schmecks, More Food that Really Schmecks* and *Schmecks Appeal*. From the last one, this easy one-pot supper is typical of the kind of impromptu meal Edna would make for friends who drop in around suppertime.

| | | |
|---|---|---|
| 1 lb | ground beef | 500 g |
| 1 | large onion, chopped or sliced | 1 |
| 1 | can (28 oz/796 mL) tomatoes or 7 fresh tomatoes, peeled, seeded and chopped | 1 |
| 2 tsp | Worcestershire sauce | 10 mL |
| ½ tsp | salt | 2 mL |
| ¼ tsp | pepper | 1 mL |
| ½ lb | egg noodles | 250 g |
| 1 cup | sour cream | 250 mL |
| | Chopped fresh parsley | |

In large heavy saucepan, cook beef and onion over medium-high heat, breaking up meat with spoon, for about 5 minutes or until meat is no longer pink. Pour off fat.

Stir in tomatoes (add 1 cup/250 mL water if using fresh tomatoes), Worcestershire sauce, salt and pepper; bring to boil. Stir in noodles, a few at a time, so mixture keeps boiling.

Reduce heat to low; cover and simmer, stirring often, for 8 to 10 minutes or until noodles are tender. Stir in sour cream and heat through but do not boil. Taste and adjust seasoning if necessary. Serve garnished with parsley. Makes 4 servings.

# Tex-Mex Potato-Beef Casserole

This easy one-dish family supper is great with a romaine lettuce and orange salad. Serve with sour cream if you wish.

| | | |
|---|---|---|
| 1 lb | lean ground beef | 500 g |
| 1 | onion, chopped | 1 |
| 2 | cloves garlic, minced | 2 |
| 1 tbsp | chili powder | 15 mL |
| ¼ tsp | EACH ground cumin, hot pepper flakes, dried oregano and salt | 1 mL |
| 1 | can (19 oz/540 mL) stewed tomatoes | 1 |
| 1 | sweet green pepper, diced | 1 |
| ⅓ cup | coarsely chopped pitted black olives | 75 mL |
| 4 | potatoes (unpeeled), thinly sliced | 4 |
| 1 tbsp | all-purpose flour | 15 mL |
| 1 tbsp | vegetable oil | 15 mL |
| 1 cup | shredded Cheddar cheese | 250 mL |
| 2 | green onions, sliced | 2 |

In large skillet, cook beef, onion and garlic over medium heat, breaking up meat with spoon, for about 5 minutes or until meat is no longer pink. Drain off any fat.

Stir in chili powder, cumin, hot pepper flakes, oregano and salt; cook, stirring, for 1 minute. Stir in tomatoes; cook, stirring occasionally, for about 15 minutes or until thickened slightly. Stir in green pepper and olives.

Meanwhile, in shallow 8-cup (2 L) baking dish, toss potatoes with flour and oil; spread evenly in dish. Spoon meat mixture over top. Bake, covered, in 350°F (180°C) oven for about 45 minutes or until potatoes are tender when tip of sharp knife is inserted down through meat.

Sprinkle with cheese; bake, uncovered, for 5 minutes or until melted. Sprinkle green onions around edge and serve. Makes 4 servings.

# Spicy Shepherd's Pie with Feta-Potato Topping

This is just as comforting as the original leftover beef-potato-gravy combination.

| | | |
|---|---|---|
| 2 | medium eggplants, peeled | 2 |
| | Salt and pepper | |
| 1½ lb | lean ground beef | 750 g |
| 1 | onion, chopped | 1 |
| 4 | cloves garlic, minced | 4 |
| 1 cup | chopped drained canned tomatoes | 250 mL |
| 1 tsp | EACH ground cumin, oregano, cinnamon and allspice | 5 mL |
| 1 tbsp | olive oil | 15 mL |
| ½ lb | mushrooms, quartered | 250 g |
| 2 | carrots, diced | 2 |
| Pinch | hot pepper flakes | Pinch |
| ½ cup | chopped fresh parsley | 125 mL |
| 6 | potatoes, peeled and quartered | 6 |
| 2 cups | crumbled feta cheese (about ½ lb/250 g) | 500 mL |
| ½ cup | freshly grated Parmesan cheese | 125 mL |
| 1 | egg | 1 |

Cut eggplants into 1-inch (2.5 cm) cubes. Place in sieve and sprinkle lightly with salt; set aside.

In large nonstick skillet, cook beef, onion and half of the garlic over medium-high heat, breaking up beef with spoon, for 5 minutes or until beef is no longer pink. Drain off any fat. Stir in tomatoes, cumin, oregano, cinnamon, allspice, and salt and pepper to taste. Transfer to 12-cup (3 L) casserole.

Rinse and pat eggplant dry. In same skillet, heat oil over medium heat; cook eggplant, mushrooms, carrots, hot pepper flakes and remaining garlic for 10 minutes, stirring often. Stir in parsley. Spoon evenly over meat mixture.

Meanwhile, in saucepan of boiling salted water, cook potatoes for 20 minutes or until tender. Reserving water, drain well. Return potatoes to saucepan and dry out slightly over low heat. Remove from heat. Add feta cheese, Parmesan cheese, egg, and salt and pepper to taste; beat until smooth, adding about 2 tbsp (25 mL) cooking water to make fluffy. Spread over vegetables. (Casserole can be prepared to this point, cooled, covered and refrigerated for up to 6 hours. Remove from refrigerator 30 minutes before heating.)

Bake, uncovered, in 400°F (200°C) oven for 45 to 60 minutes or until bubbly, covering top with foil if it gets too brown. Makes 6 servings.

# Daube of Beef with Orange

A wonderful dish to serve company, this layered stew from southern France is truly no-tend as it simmers away in the oven, sending forth the most enticing of aromas. Serve with lots of crusty bread or mashed potatoes and a green salad. If you wish, substitute 1 cup (250 mL) beef stock and ¼ cup (50 mL) each orange juice and red wine vinegar for the wine.

| | | |
|---|---|---|
| 1 | large orange | 1 |
| 3 lb | stew beef, cut in 2-inch (5 cm) cubes | 1.5 kg |
| 1½ cups | dry red wine | 375 mL |
| 2 tbsp | olive oil | 25 mL |
| 1 tsp | EACH salt and dried thyme | 5 mL |
| ½ tsp | pepper | 2 mL |
| 1 | bay leaf | 1 |
| 3 | cloves garlic, crushed | 3 |
| ½ lb | slices side bacon, cut in 2-inch (5 cm) pieces | 250 g |
| ½ lb | small mushrooms | 250 g |
| 8 | carrots, sliced | 8 |
| 16 | peeled blanched pearl onions (or 4 small onions, quartered) | 16 |
| ½ cup | all-purpose flour | 125 mL |
| 2½ cups | beef stock | 625 mL |
| 2 tbsp | tomato paste | 25 mL |

Cut long ½-inch (1 cm) wide strip of rind (without white part) from orange. In large bowl, combine beef, orange rind strip, wine, oil, salt, thyme, pepper, bay leaf and garlic. Cover and marinate in refrigerator for at least 6 hours or overnight.

Arrange one-third of the bacon over bottom of 20- or 24-cup (5 or 6 L) casserole; cover with half of the mushrooms, then half of the carrots, then half of the onions. Reserving marinade, toss beef with flour to coat completely; arrange half over vegetables. Repeat layers once. Cover with remaining bacon.

Stir stock and tomato paste into marinade; pour over casserole. Cover and bake in 325°F (160°C) oven for 3½ to 4 hours or until beef is very tender. Discard bay leaf and orange rind. (Stew can be cooled, covered and refrigerated for up to 2 days. Let stand at room temperature for 30 minutes before reheating in 325°F/160°C oven for 30 to 45 minutes.) Makes 8 to 10 servings.

# Polenta "Lasagna"

Accompany with a crisp green salad and crusty Italian bread.

| | | |
|---|---|---|
| 2 tbsp | olive oil | 25 mL |
| ½ lb | mushrooms, sliced | 250 g |
| | Salt and pepper | |
| 1 lb | lean ground beef | 500 g |
| ½ lb | hot Italian sausage, casings removed | 250 g |
| 1 | onion, finely chopped | 1 |
| 1 | clove garlic, minced | 1 |
| 1 | can (14 oz/398 mL) tomato sauce (preferably low salt) | 1 |
| ¼ cup | chopped fresh parsley | 50 mL |
| 1 tsp | dried basil | 5 mL |
| ½ tsp | dried oregano | 2 mL |
| ¼ tsp | hot pepper flakes | 1 mL |
| ⅓ cup | fresh bread crumbs | 75 mL |
| 2 | eggs | 2 |
| | Polenta (recipe follows) | |
| ¼ cup | freshly grated Parmesan cheese | 50 mL |

In large deep skillet, heat oil over high heat; cook mushrooms until golden brown, about 3 minutes, stirring often. With slotted spoon, remove to plate; sprinkle lightly with salt and pepper to taste.

In same pan, cook beef, sausage, onion and garlic over medium-high heat, breaking up meat with spoon, until beef is no longer pink, about 5 minutes. Drain off any fat.

Stir in tomato sauce, parsley, basil, oregano and hot pepper flakes; bring to boil. Reduce heat and simmer, partially covered, for 30 minutes, stirring often. Cool slightly. Taste and adjust seasoning, remembering cheese will be salty. Stir in mushrooms, bread crumbs and eggs.

Spread half of the Polenta in greased 13- x 9-inch (3 L) glass baking dish. Top with meat mixture, smoothing top. Spread with remaining Polenta, smoothing top. Sprinkle with cheese. (Casserole can be prepared to this point, covered and refrigerated for up to 8 hours. Let stand at room temperature for 30 minutes before baking.)

Cover loosely with foil; bake in 350°F (180°C) oven for 30 minutes. Uncover and broil for about 5 minutes or until golden brown. Makes 4 to 6 servings.

# Polenta

| 4 cups | water | 1 L |
| 1 tsp | salt | 5 mL |
| 1 cup | yellow cornmeal | 250 mL |
| ¼ cup | freshly grated Parmesan cheese | 50 mL |
| 2 tbsp | butter | 25 mL |
| ¼ tsp | pepper | 1 mL |

In saucepan, bring water and salt to boil. Gradually add cornmeal in slow, steady stream, whisking constantly until slightly thickened. Reduce heat to low and cool, stirring often with wooden spoon, for 15 to 20 minutes or until mixture comes away from side of pan. Remove from heat; stir in cheese, butter and pepper.

# Updated Sloppy Joes

Made with the same beef mixture used in chili (minus the beans), Sloppy Joes were popular in the 1950s. I've spiced these up and served them on Kaisers instead of the usual hamburger buns. But for a change of pace, try the mixture on cut baked potatoes to make an easy comforting meal accompanied by a crisp green salad. I hate to admit it, but on a cold January night when my son and I tested this recipe for supper, it tasted so good that the two of us pretty well polished off what should have been four servings.

| | | |
|---|---|---|
| 1 lb | lean ground beef | 500 g |
| 1 | small onion, chopped | 1 |
| 1 | clove garlic, minced | 1 |
| 1 | EACH sweet green and yellow pepper, diced | 1 |
| 1 | can (14 oz/398 mL) tomato sauce | 1 |
| 1 tbsp | EACH red wine vinegar, fresh lemon juice, Worcestershire sauce and packed brown sugar | 15 mL |
| 1 tsp | EACH Dijon mustard, paprika and Tabasco sauce | 5 mL |
| | Salt and pepper | |
| 4 | Kaiser buns, split and toasted | 4 |

In medium saucepan or large skillet, cook beef, onion, garlic and sweet peppers over medium-high heat, breaking up meat with spoon, until meat is no longer pink, about 10 minutes. Drain off any fat. Stir in tomato sauce, vinegar, lemon juice, Worcestershire sauce, brown sugar, mustard, paprika, Tabasco sauce, and salt and pepper to taste; bring to boil. Reduce heat and simmer, uncovered and stirring occasionally, until thickened, about 20 minutes. Spoon over buns. Makes 4 servings.

# Make-Ahead Meatball Meals

Versatile and economical, meatballs continue to be a popular way of serving ground meat. And somehow, I like the texture of them in casseroles and soups better than loose ground meat. You can make Basic Meatballs on a weekend and freeze them for the start of several meals. Simply pop the frozen meatballs into other simmering ingredients and they'll be ready to enjoy in about 15 minutes—a true homemade convenience food.

## Basic Meatballs

Packaged in airtight containers, meatballs will keep for up to four months in the freezer. Remember, when forming meatballs, handle the meat mixture lightly for more tender texture.

| | | |
|---|---|---|
| 4 | eggs | 4 |
| 1 cup | fine dry bread crumbs | 250 mL |
| 1 cup | milk | 250 mL |
| ½ cup | finely chopped onion | 125 mL |
| ¼ cup | finely chopped fresh parsley | 50 mL |
| 2 tsp | salt | 10 mL |
| 1½ tsp | dry mustard | 7 mL |
| 4 lb | ground beef | 2 kg |

In large bowl, beat eggs; stir in bread crumbs until well combined. Stir in milk, onion, parsley, salt and mustard. Add meat and knead with wet hands until well blended.

Pat meat into 15- x 10-inch (40 x 25 cm) jelly roll pan or into rectangle about 1 inch (2.5 cm) thick. Cut into 1-inch (2.5 cm) squares. With wet hands, form each square into ball.

Place meatballs in large shallow baking pans; bake in 400°F (200°C) oven for about 25 minutes or until browned and no longer pink inside. With slotted spoon, transfer meatballs to trays or baking sheets, leaving space between each. Let cool, then freeze until firm. Transfer to heavy plastic bags and store in freezer for up to 4 months. Makes 150 meatballs.

# Italian Pot Pie with Parmesan Mashed Potatoes

Instead of being teamed up with pasta, these meatballs are topped with creamy mashed potatoes.

| | | |
|---|---|---|
| 1 tbsp | olive oil | 15 mL |
| 1 | small onion, chopped | 1 |
| 1 | clove garlic, minced | 1 |
| 1 | can (14 oz/398 mL) tomatoes | 1 |
| ½ tsp | EACH dried basil and oregano | 2 mL |
| 36 | frozen Basic Meatballs (recipe, page 124) | 36 |
| 1½ lb | baking potatoes, peeled and quartered (3 or 4 large) | 750 g |
| 1 | egg, beaten | 1 |
| 1 cup | freshly grated Parmesan cheese | 250 mL |
| | Salt and pepper | |
| 2 tbsp | chopped fresh parsley | 25 mL |

In skillet, heat oil over medium heat; cook onion and garlic for 5 minutes. Stir in tomatoes, basil, oregano and Basic Meatballs; simmer, uncovered and stirring often, for 15 minutes. Spoon into 8-inch (2 L) baking dish.

Meanwhile, in saucepan of boiling water, cook potatoes for 20 minutes or until tender. Drain well; mash until smooth. Stir in egg, ¾ cup (175 mL) of the Parmesan cheese, and salt and pepper to taste. Stir in parsley. Spoon over meatball mixture. Sprinkle with remaining Parmesan. (Casserole can be prepared to this point, covered and refrigerated for up to 1 day. Let stand at room temperature for 30 minutes.)

Bake in 350°F (180°C) oven, covered, for 30 to 45 minutes. Uncover and bake for 10 minutes or until heated through. Broil for 1 minute or until cheese is golden. Makes 4 servings.

# Hungarian Goulash Meatballs

Crusty bread is all you need to accompany this easy supper.

| | | |
|---|---|---|
| 1 tbsp | vegetable oil | 15 mL |
| 2 | onions, sliced | 2 |
| ½ lb | mushrooms, sliced | 250 g |
| 1 tbsp | caraway seeds, crushed* | 15 mL |
| 1 tbsp | paprika | 15 mL |
| | Salt | |
| 2 cups | beef stock | 500 mL |
| 1 | can (14 oz/398 mL) tomatoes, chopped | 1 |
| 1 tsp | dried basil | 5 mL |
| 1 | sweet green pepper, diced | 1 |
| 36 | frozen Basic Meatballs (recipe, page 124) | 36 |
| 1 tsp | dried marjoram | 5 mL |
| | Pepper | |
| ¼ lb | egg noodles, broken up | 125 g |

In large saucepan, heat oil over medium-high; cook onions and mushrooms for 5 minutes, stirring often. Stir in caraway seeds, paprika, and salt to taste; cook for 1 minute, stirring.

Stir in stock, tomatoes, basil, green pepper and Basic Meatballs; bring to boil. Reduce heat, cover and simmer, stirring often, for 15 minutes.

Stir in marjoram, and salt and pepper to taste. Add noodles, pushing down into liquid; cover and cook for 5 to 7 minutes or until tender and meatballs are heated through. Makes 4 to 6 servings.

---

*Hint: Crush caraway seeds with a mortar and pestle or place in sturdy plastic bag and roll firmly with rolling pin.

# Meatball Stroganoff

Enjoy this low-cost version of a favorite classic with a crisp green vegetable on the side.

| | | |
|---|---|---|
| 1 tbsp | vegetable oil | 15 mL |
| 2 | onions, thinly sliced | 2 |
| ½ lb | mushrooms, thinly sliced | 250 g |
| 1 tbsp | granulated sugar | 15 mL |
| 1 tbsp | prepared mustard (preferably hot) | 15 mL |
| 36 | frozen Basic Meatballs (recipe, page 124) | 36 |
| 2 cups | sour cream (regular or light) | 500 mL |
| | Salt and pepper | |
| | Hot buttered noodles | |

In large skillet, heat oil over medium-high heat; stir in onions and mushrooms to coat with oil. Stir in sugar, mustard and Basic Meatballs; cover, reduce heat to low and simmer, stirring often, for about 20 minutes or until vegetables are softened and meatballs are heated through.

Gradually stir in sour cream; cover and simmer for 2 to 3 minutes or until heated through but not boiling. Season with salt and pepper to taste. Serve on hot buttered noodles. Makes 4 to 6 servings.

# Meatball Subs

Enjoy this fun main course with a nice selection of raw vegetable sticks and pickles as a light supper or hearty lunch—great for serving the gang while they watch a game. The vegetable-packed sauce and meatball mixture would also make a flavorful addition to cooked pasta. If you can't find crushed tomatoes in a supermarket, purée canned whole tomatoes in a blender or food processor.

| | | |
|---|---|---|
| 1 tbsp | olive oil | 15 mL |
| 2 | onions, chopped | 2 |
| 2 | sweet peppers (red or green), diced | 2 |
| 1 | can (28 oz/796 mL) crushed tomatoes | 1 |
| 1 tsp | dried oregano | 5 mL |
| ½ tsp | dried thyme | 2 mL |
| Pinch | hot pepper flakes | Pinch |
| | Salt and pepper | |
| 4 | cloves garlic, minced | 4 |
| 1 tsp | fennel seeds | 5 mL |
| 36 | frozen Basic Meatballs (recipe, page 124) | 36 |
| ½ cup | chopped fresh parsley | 125 mL |
| 6 | submarine rolls, split lengthwise and toasted | 6 |
| | Freshly grated Parmesan cheese | |

In medium saucepan, heat oil over low heat; cook onions, covered and stirring occasionally, for 20 minutes. Add sweet peppers; cook over medium heat, uncovered, for 5 minutes.

Stir in tomatoes, oregano, thyme, hot pepper flakes, and salt and pepper to taste; bring to boil. Reduce heat and simmer, partially covered, for 15 minutes. Stir in garlic and fennel seeds. (Sauce can be prepared to this point, cooled, covered and refrigerated for up to 2 days or frozen for up to 2 months. Bring to simmer before proceeding.)

Stir in Basic Meatballs; simmer, covered, for 15 minutes. Stir in parsley; simmer for about 5 minutes or until meatballs are heated through.

Arrange 6 meatballs in each bun; spoon some of the sauce over top. Sprinkle with Parmesan cheese to taste. Pass extra sauce and cheese. Makes 6 servings.

# Eggplant Beef Skillet

This easy one-skillet supper with its Middle Eastern flavors is a wonderful way of cooking eggplant without having to use much fat. If you wish, use low-fat mozzarella and lamb for an even lighter dish. Serve with warm pita bread and a salad of lettuce, orange slices and black olives.

| | | |
|---|---|---|
| 1 | eggplant (about 1 lb/500 g) | 1 |
| | Salt | |
| 1 lb | lean ground beef or lamb | 500 g |
| 1 | small onion, chopped | 1 |
| 1 | clove garlic, minced | 1 |
| 1 | can (7½ oz/213 mL) tomato sauce | 1 |
| ½ cup | dry red wine or water | 125 mL |
| 2 tbsp | chopped fresh parsley | 25 mL |
| ¾ tsp | dried oregano | 4 mL |
| ½ tsp | cinnamon | 2 mL |
| ¼ tsp | pepper | 1 mL |
| ¼ lb | mozzarella cheese, shredded | 125 g |
| | Paprika | |
| | Freshly grated Parmesan cheese | |

Peel eggplant and cut into ½-inch (1 cm) thick slices. Lay out in single layer and sprinkle lightly with salt; set aside.

Meanwhile, in large skillet, cook beef, onion and garlic over medium-high heat, breaking up meat with spoon, until meat is no longer pink, about 5 minutes. Drain off any fat. Stir in tomato sauce, wine, parsley, oregano, cinnamon and pepper; bring to simmer.

Pat eggplant dry with paper towels; overlap slices on top of meat mixture. Cover and reduce heat to low; cook for 20 minutes or until eggplant is tender, turning slices once. Top with mozzarella and sprinkle with paprika to taste. Serve immediately with Parmesan cheese to sprinkle on each serving. Makes 4 servings.

# Cheeseburger Pizza

You don't need any accompaniments to this filling main-course family pizza. If you like, you can cheat by using purchased dough or even a purchased baked crust.

| | | |
|---|---|---|
| ¾ lb | lean ground beef | 375 g |
| ½ lb | mushrooms, sliced | 250 g |
| 1 | clove garlic, minced | 1 |
| 1 tsp | dried oregano | 5 mL |
| Pinch | hot pepper flakes | Pinch |
| | Salt and pepper | |
| 1 | can (7½ oz/213 mL) tomato or pizza sauce | 1 |
| 1 lb | Easy Pizza Dough (recipe, page 220) | 500 g |
| Half | sweet green pepper, cut in rings | Half |
| 2 tbsp | coarsely chopped black olives (optional) | 25 mL |
| ½ lb | Cheddar or mozzarella cheese, thinly sliced | 250 g |

In large skillet, cook beef, mushrooms and garlic over medium-high heat, breaking up meat with spoon, for about 5 minutes or until beef is no longer pink. Drain off any fat. Stir in oregano, hot pepper flakes, and salt and pepper to taste. Stir in tomato sauce; cook, uncovered, for 3 minutes or until thickened.

Place dough on greased 12-inch (30 cm) pizza pan. Sprinkle evenly with meat mixture; garnish with pepper rings, and black olives if using. Slightly overlap cheese slices on top; bake in 450°F (230°C) oven for about 15 minutes or until crust is golden brown. Makes 3 or 4 servings.

# Beef and Vegetable Stir-Fry with Noodles

Stir-fries are a quick and easy way to serve up a dramatic one-pot meal. Although they don't fit into my book's mainly make-ahead theme, I've included this one because it is so fast, simple and truly one-pot with the ready-to-use noodles. Look for these vacuum-packed steamed noodles in the produce department; if you can't find them, you can substitute cooked spaghetti. Oriental-style vegetables are readily available.

| | | |
|---|---|---|
| 3 tbsp | EACH wine vinegar and soy sauce | 45 mL |
| 2 tbsp | packed brown sugar | 25 mL |
| 1 tbsp | cornstarch | 15 mL |
| 1 lb | round steak | 500 g |
| 2 tbsp | vegetable oil | 25 mL |
| 1 | pkg (750 g) frozen Oriental-style mixed vegetables (8 cups/2 L) | 1 |
| 1 | pkg (350 or 400 g) steamed Chinese noodles, broken up | 1 |

In small bowl, combine vinegar, soy sauce, sugar, cornstarch and 2 tbsp (25 mL) water; stir until cornstarch is dissolved. Set aside.

Trim fat from steak; cut meat into thin slices across the grain diagonally. In nonstick skillet or large wok, heat half of the oil over medium-high heat; cook meat, stirring, for 2 to 3 minutes or until well browned. Remove and set aside.

Add remaining oil to pan; stir-fry vegetables for 5 to 6 minutes or until tender. Stir cornstarch mixture; stir into pan along with meat. Cook, stirring, until sauce is boiling and thickened. Add noodles; cook until heated through. Makes 4 servings.

# Oven-Braised Steak with Mustard and Wild Mushrooms

An old favorite combination—steak and mushrooms—gets a modern twist with some wild mushrooms now available in most supermarkets. You could, of course, use ordinary white mushrooms if wild are unavailable. Like a small pot roast, this is perfect when a large piece of beef is too much to handle. This is great on creamy mashed potatoes or noodles.

| | | |
|---|---|---|
| 1½ lb | blade steak | 750 g |
| 1 tbsp | olive oil | 15 mL |
| 4 | shallots or small onions, halved | 4 |
| 1 tbsp | all-purpose flour | 15 mL |
| ⅓ cup | brandy or additional stock | 75 mL |
| 1½ cups | beef stock | 375 mL |
| 3 tbsp | Dijon mustard | 45 mL |
| 3 | cloves garlic, thinly sliced | 3 |
| 1 | bay leaf | 1 |
| ½ tsp | dried thyme | 2 mL |
| ¼ lb | crimini (brown) or portobello mushrooms, coarsely chopped | 125 g |
| 2 tbsp | butter | 25 mL |
| ¼ lb | EACH oyster and shiitake mushrooms, sliced | 125 g |
| | Salt and pepper | |

Trim beef and cut into 4 pieces; set aside. In Dutch oven or deep skillet, heat oil over medium heat; brown shallots and remove to plate. Add meat to pan in batches and brown on both sides; remove to plate.

Add flour to pan; cook, stirring, for 1 minute. Stir in brandy and bring to boil, scraping up any brown bits from bottom of pan. Cook, stirring, until thickened.

Stir in stock, mustard, two-thirds of the garlic, bay leaf and thyme; bring to boil. Return meat and shallots to pan; cover and bake in 325°F (160°C) oven for 1 hour. Turn steak over and add crimini mushrooms; cover and cook for 1 hour or until steak is tender.

In large skillet, melt butter over medium-high heat; cook oyster and shiitake mushrooms, remaining garlic, and salt and pepper to taste, stirring, for 3 minutes.

Place steak on hot platter. Discard bay leaf. Taste and adjust sauce for seasoning; spoon over steak. Spoon sautéed mushrooms over top. Makes 4 servings.

# Two-Onion Pot-Roasted Beef

You may remember your grandmother's pot roast; this one will be the best of what you recall and more. It's better made ahead and reheated. If you wish, serve with creamy mashed potatoes or buttered noodles and a green vegetable or cabbage salad.

| | | |
|---|---|---|
| ⅓ cup | all-purpose flour | 75 mL |
| ½ tsp | EACH salt, pepper and dried thyme | 2 mL |
| 4 lb | boneless blade or rump roast | 2 kg |
| 2 tbsp | olive oil | 25 mL |
| 2 | onions, chopped | 2 |
| 3 | red onions, cut in thin wedges | 3 |
| ½ lb | mushrooms, quartered | 250 g |
| 1 | stalk celery, thinly sliced | 1 |
| 4 | cloves garlic, minced | 4 |
| 2 cups | dry red wine | 500 mL |
| 1 cup | beef stock | 250 mL |
| 2 tbsp | EACH tomato paste and balsamic vinegar | 25 mL |
| 2 tsp | anchovy paste | 10 mL |
| 2 | bay leaves | 2 |
| ¾ lb | mini carrots | 375 g |
| | Chopped fresh parsley | |

In large bowl, combine flour, salt, pepper and thyme; add roast and roll to coat well.

In large flameproof casserole or roasting pan, heat 1 tbsp (15 mL) of the oil over medium heat; brown beef well on all sides, about 5 minutes, turning with 2 wooden spoons. Pack chopped onions on top of meat and sprinkle with any remaining flour; roast, uncovered, in 300°F (150°C) oven for 1 hour.

Meanwhile, in large skillet, heat remaining oil over medium heat; cook red onions, mushrooms and celery, stirring often, for 5 minutes. Stir in garlic; cook for 2 minutes.

Stir in wine, stock, tomato paste, balsamic vinegar, anchovy paste and bay leaves; bring to boil, scraping up any brown bits from bottom of pan.

Turn roast over, pushing chopped onions underneath. Pour vegetable mixture over top. Cover and roast for 2 hours, basting occasionally with pan liquid.

Add carrots; roast for 1 to 1½ hours or until meat is very tender, basting occasionally. Discard bay leaves. Let cool, cover and refrigerate overnight.

Transfer roast to cutting board, scraping off vegetables. Thinly slice and overlap slices in large baking dish; arrange vegetables around meat. Skim fat from sauce and spoon sauce over top. (Recipe can be prepared to this point, covered and refrigerated for up to 4 hours.) Cover with foil and reheat in 350°F (180°C) oven for about 30 minutes or until meat is heated through. Serve sprinkled with parsley. Makes 8 servings.

**Hint: Tomato paste is now available in tubes in many supermarkets and delis. It keeps for months in the refrigerator.**

# Pot-au-Feu

## (French Boiled Beef and Root Vegetables)

Nigel Didcock, a talented young chef who has worked around the world in such prestigious kitchens as The Connaught Hotel in London, Troisgros in France and Langdon Hall near Cambridge, Ontario, is now executive chef at The Sutton Place in Toronto. On his Sundays off, he loves to cook wonderful meals for friends in his own great kitchen. Pot-au-Feu is one of his favorites which he describes as an "event" when you "passionately want to partake in a two- or three-hour feast." The pot-au-feu is simplicity itself, but Nigel likes to make a production out of its presentation. He puts the condiments—coarse salt, cracked pepper and a variety of mustards and gherkins—around the edge of each plate "like an artist's palette," he says. He ladles some of the broth into bowls, places vegetables on top and passes lots of crusty French bread, gherkins and great wine. You can serve the broth as a separate course, or with the meat and vegetables or save it for another soup.

| | | |
|---|---|---|
| 2 lb | EACH beef short ribs, cut in serving pieces, beef blade roast and beef shanks | 1 kg |
| | Bouquet garni* | |
| 1 tsp | salt (approx) | 5 mL |
| 8 | small marrow bones | 8 |
| 8 | small onions | 8 |
| 4 | whole cloves, stuck into 1 onion | 4 |
| 4 | leeks, cleaned and tied | 4 |
| 4 | carrots, quartered | 4 |
| 3 | EACH white turnips and parsnips, peeled and quartered | 3 |
| 1 | EACH small rutabaga and celery root, peeled and cut in 2-inch (5 cm) pieces | 1 |

Place ribs, roast and shanks in large stockpot. Add enough cold water to cover by 1 inch (2.5 cm); bring to boil. Reduce heat to low; cook for 15 minutes, skimming off any scum. Add bouquet garni and salt; simmer, partially covered, for 1½ hours, skimming occasionally.

Add marrow bones, onions, clove-studded onion, leeks, carrots, turnips, parsnips, rutabaga and celery root; bring to boil. Reduce heat and simmer, partially covered, for 1½ hours, adding more liquid if needed to keep meat covered. Remove meat, marrow bones and vegetables with slotted spoon. Discard bouquet garni.

Slice roast and arrange with other meat, marrow and vegetables on warm platter; cover with foil and keep warm.

If serving broth, skim off any fat and strain into clean saucepan. Bring to simmer and strain again. Season with salt to taste. Ladle into warm bowls and serve separately or place vegetables and meat on top. Makes about 10 servings.

---

**\*Bouquet garni: In cheesecloth bag, tie 2 tsp**
**(10 mL) dried thyme, 4 stems parsley,**
**6 peppercorns and 1 crushed bay leaf.**

# Veal Shanks Braised with Garlic and Orange

The traditional braising treatment for veal shanks is Osso Buco, a dish that's topped off with garlic, lemon and parsley to serve. Here, I've opted for an orange and parsley topping, and included lots of garlic that will become sweet and soft with long cooking right in the sauce. Enjoy with crusty bread, creamy mashed potatoes or polenta along with a mixed green salad.

| | | |
|---|---|---|
| ¼ cup | olive oil (approx) | 50 mL |
| 2 | onions, chopped | 2 |
| 2 | leeks, thickly sliced | 2 |
| 4 | carrots, cut in 1-inch (2.5 cm) pieces | 4 |
| 1 tbsp | EACH chopped fresh thyme and rosemary (or 1 tsp/5 mL dried) | 15 mL |
| 2 | bay leaves | 2 |
| 1 lb | mushrooms, sliced | 500 g |
| 4 | veal centre-cut shanks (1-inch/2.5 cm thick) | 4 |
| ¼ cup | all-purpose flour | 50 mL |
| | Salt and pepper | |
| 1 cup | dry red wine (preferably *Pinot Noir*) | 250 mL |
| 2 cups | beef stock | 500 mL |
| 2 tbsp | fresh orange juice | 25 mL |
| 12 | cloves garlic | 12 |
| 1 cup | frozen peas, thawed | 250 mL |
| ⅓ cup | chopped fresh parsley | 75 mL |
| ¼ cup | minced orange zest* | 50 mL |

In large Dutch oven, heat 2 tbsp (25 mL) of the oil over medium heat; cook onions, leeks, carrots, thyme, rosemary and bay leaves for 10 minutes, stirring often. Add mushrooms; cook for 4 minutes, stirring occasionally. With slotted spoon, remove to bowl.

Coat shanks with flour and salt and pepper to taste, shaking off excess. Heat 1 tbsp (15 mL) of the remaining oil in pan over high heat; brown shanks well, in batches if necessary and adding more oil as needed. Remove to bowl.

Sprinkle any remaining flour into pan; cook, stirring, for 1 minute. Gradually stir in wine; bring to boil, scraping up any brown bits from bottom of pan. Add stock, orange juice and garlic; bring to boil.

Return veal and vegetables with any juices to pan. Cover and bake in 350°F

(180°C) oven for about 1 hour and 15 minutes or until veal is tender. Discard bay leaves. (Shanks can be cooled, covered and refrigerated for up to 1 day. Reheat gently, stirring often.)

Mash some of the garlic into sauce. Add peas and heat through on top of stove. Taste and adjust seasoning. Combine parsley and orange zest. Serve with sauce spooned over each shank and sprinkled with parsley mixture. Makes 4 servings.

---

**\*Hint: With vegetable peeler, remove only dark orange part of rind from 1 large orange. Finely chop with sharp knife.**

# Osso Buco-Style Braised Veal

When our local Italian grocery store has stewing veal on sale, I use the classic treatment for veal shanks on more manageable veal cubes. Serve with pasta or creamy mashed potatoes and a salad of spinach and mushrooms.

| | | |
|---|---|---|
| 1 tbsp | butter | 15 mL |
| 1 | onion, chopped | 1 |
| 2 | EACH carrots and stalks celery, diced | 2 |
| 2 | cloves garlic, minced | 2 |
| 1 | strip (4 inches/10 cm) lemon rind | 1 |
| 2 lb | boneless stewing veal | 1 kg |
| ¼ cup | all-purpose flour | 50 mL |
| | Salt and pepper | |
| 2 tbsp | olive oil (approx) | 25 mL |
| ½ cup | dry vermouth | 125 mL |
| 1 cup | EACH chicken stock and coarsely chopped canned plum tomatoes with juice | 250 mL |
| 3 | sprigs fresh parsley | 3 |
| 1 | bay leaf | 1 |
| | *Gremolata:* | |
| 2 | cloves garlic, minced | 2 |
| 2 tbsp | chopped fresh parsley | 25 mL |
| 2 tsp | chopped lemon zest | 10 mL |

In large ovenproof saucepan or flameproof casserole, melt butter over medium heat; cook onion, carrots and celery for 10 minutes, stirring often. Add garlic and lemon rind. Remove from heat and set aside.

Cut veal into 2-inch (5 cm) cubes. Toss with flour and ¼ tsp (1 mL) each salt and pepper until coated. In large skillet, heat 1 tbsp (15 mL) of the oil over medium-high heat; brown veal, in batches and adding more oil as needed. Arrange over vegetables in pan.

Pour off any fat from skillet. Add vermouth and boil for 2 minutes, scraping up any brown bits from bottom of pan; pour over veal. Add stock to skillet and bring to simmer; add tomatoes, parsley, bay leaf, and salt and pepper to taste. Pour over veal.

Bring veal mixture to boil on top of stove. Cover tightly and bake in 350°F (180°C) oven for 2 hours. Discard lemon rind, parsley sprigs and bay leaf. (Veal can be cooled, covered and refrigerated for up to 2 days or frozen for up to 2 months. Thaw in refrigerator. Heat in 350°F/180°C oven for 30 to 40 minutes or slowly, on top of stove, stirring often.)

Gremolata: Combine garlic, parsley and lemon zest. Sprinkle over stew; bake for 5 to 10 minutes. Makes 4 to 6 servings.

# Veal and Mushroom Pies

When I'm having a number of house guests over the holidays (or any time), I love to have several meals tucked away in the freezer. These delicious meat pies are just right for instant suppers. They're great with chili sauce and Boston lettuce tossed with lemon juice and olive oil.

| | | |
|---|---|---|
| 2 tbsp | EACH butter and vegetable oil | 25 mL |
| 1½ lb | mushrooms, sliced (about 8 cups/2 L) | 750 g |
| 1 cup | chopped shallots or mild onion | 250 mL |
| 2½ lb | ground veal | 1.25 kg |
| 2½ cups | hot beef stock | 625 mL |
| 1 tbsp | Worcestershire sauce | 15 mL |
| ½ tsp | EACH dried marjoram, rosemary and salt | 2 mL |
| ¼ tsp | pepper | 1 mL |
| ½ cup | chopped fresh parsley | 125 mL |
| | Pastry for 2 deep double-crust 9-inch (23 cm) pies (see Never-Fail Big-Batch Pastry, page 142) | |
| 1 | egg yolk | 1 |
| 1 tbsp | cold water | 15 mL |

In large shallow saucepan or Dutch oven, heat butter with half of the oil over medium-high heat; cook mushrooms, stirring often, for 7 minutes. With slotted spoon, transfer to bowl; let cool, cover and refrigerate.

In same pan, heat remaining oil; cook shallots over medium-low heat for 3 minutes, stirring often. Add veal and increase heat to medium-high; cook, breaking up with back of spoon, for about 5 minutes or until no longer pink.

Stir in stock, Worcestershire sauce, marjoram, rosemary, salt and pepper; bring to boil. Reduce heat, cover and simmer for 1 hour, stirring occasionally. Remove from heat, uncover and let cool until steam stops; cover and refrigerate until chilled. (Mixture will be thick but moist.) Lift off and discard any fat from top; break up meat.

Drain mushrooms; stir into meat mixture along with parsley. Taste and adjust seasoning.

On lightly floured surface, roll out half of the pastry and line two deep 9-inch (23 cm) pie plates. Divide meat mixture between plates. Roll out remaining pastry. Wet edges of bottom pastry with cold water; place pastry over top and crimp or press with fork.

Beat together egg yolk and water; brush over pies. Cut large vent in tops to let steam escape. Bake in 425°F (220°C) oven for 10 minutes. Reduce temperature to 350°F (180°C); bake for 30 to 35 minutes or until golden brown.

(Pies can be cooled on racks, covered with foil and frozen in airtight containers for up to 2 months. Thaw in refrigerator overnight. Reheat, covered with foil, in 350°F/180°C oven for 30 minutes. Uncover and heat for 10 to 15 minutes longer or until bubbly.) Makes 2 pies, about 12 servings.

# Never-Fail Big-Batch Pastry

With a batch of this tender, flaky pastry stored in the freezer, meat pies will take just minutes to make. For best results, work the pastry gently and quickly.

| | | |
|---|---|---|
| 4 cups | cake-and-pastry flour | 1 L |
| 2 cups | all-purpose flour | 500 mL |
| 1½ tsp | salt | 7 mL |
| 1 lb | cold lard or shortening | 500 g |
| 1 | egg | 1 |
| 1 tsp | vinegar | 5 mL |
| | Ice water | |

In large bowl, combine flours and salt. In food processor, process one-third of the flour mixture with one-third of the lard until mixture resembles coarse rolled oats; transfer to large bowl. Repeat in 2 batches with remaining flour and lard. (Alternatively, in large bowl, cut lard into flour mixture with pastry blender or 2 knives.)

In 1-cup (250 mL) measure, beat egg with vinegar. Fill measure with ice water; stir well.

Gradually add liquid to flour mixture, tossing lightly with fork until dough just holds together, adding a few drops more water if necessary. Finish by combining mixture gently with hands. (The dough may crumble slightly at this point.) Form into 6 disks. Wrap each in waxed paper; seal in freezer bag and refrigerate for up to 1 day or freeze for up to 6 months. Makes enough for three double-crust 9-inch (23 cm) pies.

# Pork

# Skillet Pork Chops with Sauerkraut

With the interesting combination of sauerkraut and tomatoes, this easy skillet supper is full of flavor.

| | | |
|---|---|---|
| 2 tbsp | olive oil | 25 mL |
| 4 | pork chops | 4 |
| | Salt and pepper | |
| 4 | potatoes, peeled and sliced | 4 |
| 1 | onion, sliced | 1 |
| 2 | cloves garlic, minced | 2 |
| 1 | can (19 oz/540 mL) tomatoes | 1 |
| ½ tsp | EACH crushed caraway seeds and packed brown sugar | 2 mL |
| ½ lb | sauerkraut, preferably from bag or jar | 250 g |
| | Chopped fresh parsley | |

In large skillet, heat half of the oil over medium-high heat; brown chops on both sides, sprinkling with salt and pepper to taste. Remove to plate.

In same skillet, heat remaining oil over medium heat; cook potatoes, onion and garlic for 5 minutes, stirring often. Sprinkle with salt and pepper to taste.

Gently stir in tomatoes, breaking up with spoon; bring to boil, stirring up brown bits from bottom of pan. Stir in caraway seeds and sugar.

Return chops and any juices to pan; top with sauerkraut. Bring to simmer; cover, reduce heat and cook for 30 to 40 minutes or until pork and potatoes are tender, gently stirring occasionally to prevent sticking. Serve sprinkled with parsley. Makes 4 servings.

---

**Hint: Because dry meat browns better, be sure to pat chops dry.**

# Pork Chop and Creamed Cabbage Casserole

Economical and homey family fare, this dish is delicious enough for company on a cold blustery night. If you wish, pop some potatoes into the oven to bake before you start the casserole and serve with pickled beets and whole wheat rolls.

| | | |
|---|---|---|
| ¼ cup | butter | 50 mL |
| 1 | onion, chopped | 1 |
| 8 cups | shredded cabbage (1 small head) | 2 L |
| 1 cup | light cream | 250 mL |
| ½ tsp | crumbled dried sage | 2 mL |
| | Salt and pepper | |
| 4 | pork chops | 4 |
| ½ cup | dry white wine | 125 mL |
| ¼ cup | chopped fresh parsley | 50 mL |
| ¼ cup | freshly grated Parmesan cheese | 50 mL |

In large skillet, melt butter over medium heat; cook onion and cabbage, stirring often, until cabbage is wilted, about 7 minutes. Reduce heat to low; cover and cook for 5 minutes longer.

Stir in cream, sage, ½ tsp (2 mL) salt and ¼ tsp (1 mL) pepper; increase heat to medium. Simmer, uncovered, for 5 minutes or until cabbage is tender and sauce is thickened.

Meanwhile, trim fat from chops. Place separate skillet over medium-high heat; rub piece of fat over bottom until lightly greased. Discard fat. Cook chops until well browned on both sides, about 15 minutes, sprinkling lightly with salt and pepper to taste. Remove chops and set aside.

Discard any fat from skillet. Stir in wine and bring to boil over high heat, scraping up any brown bits from bottom of pan. Stir into cabbage mixture along with parsley.

In shallow casserole large enough to hold chops in single layer, spread half of the cabbage mixture. Arrange chops on top and cover with remaining cabbage mixture. Sprinkle with cheese. (Recipe can be prepared to this point, covered and refrigerated for up to 6 hours. Let stand at room temperature for 30 minutes before proceeding.)

Bake, uncovered, in 350°F (180°C) oven for 20 to 30 minutes or until golden brown and chops are tender. Makes 4 servings.

# Pork Chops Baked on Fruited Sauerkraut

For recipes like this, I buy wonderful homemade sauerkraut in the markets of Kitchener and Waterloo, Ontario. Since homemade is not always available, try to find bagged sauerkraut rather than the tinned kind. Add some potatoes to the oven to bake alongside and serve with pickled beets.

| | | |
|---|---|---|
| 1 tbsp | vegetable oil | 15 mL |
| 4 | pork chops | 4 |
| ½ tsp | dried thyme | 2 mL |
| | Salt and pepper | |
| 1 | bag (19 oz/540 mL) sauerkraut (or about 1 lb/500 g) | 1 |
| 1 cup | thick sweetened applesauce or 1 apple, chopped | 250 mL |
| ½ tsp | caraway seeds | 2 mL |
| 1 | bay leaf | 1 |
| | Red apple slices and parsley sprig | |

In large ovenproof skillet, heat oil over medium heat; cook pork chops for about 2 minutes per side or until just starting to brown, sprinkling lightly with thyme, and salt and pepper to taste. Transfer to plate.

Meanwhile, drain sauerkraut; rinse under cold running water and drain well again. In bowl, combine sauerkraut, applesauce, caraway seeds, bay leaf and ¼ tsp (1 mL) pepper.

Transfer sauerkraut to skillet; place chops on top. Bake, uncovered, in 350°F (180°C) oven for about 45 minutes or until chops are very tender. Garnish with apple and parsley to serve right from skillet. Makes 4 servings.

# Spareribs with Sauerkraut

When I was growing up on a farm, we made all our own sauerkraut, and no other will ever taste as good. If you do have to buy it, avoid cans and look for plastic bags or jars of sauerkraut. Serve this easy oven dish with rye bread and pickled beets for a heartwarming fall or winter supper.

| | | |
|---|---|---|
| 3 lb | pork spareribs | 1.5 kg |
| | Salt and pepper | |
| 1 | jar (32 oz/909 mL) wine-flavored sauerkraut (undrained) | 1 |
| 3 | large cooking apples, peeled and sliced | 3 |
| 1 tbsp | packed brown sugar | 15 mL |

Trim off fat and cut spareribs into serving-size pieces. Place, meaty side up, in roasting pan; sprinkle lightly with salt and pepper to taste. Bake, uncovered, in 400°F (200°C) oven for 30 minutes.

Reduce heat to 350°F (180°C). Remove ribs; drain off all but 1 tbsp (15 mL) pan drippings. Stir in sauerkraut, apples and sugar; top with spareribs. Cover tightly and bake for 1 hour or until spareribs are very tender. Makes 4 servings.

# Tex-Mex Pork Chops with Black Bean-Corn Salsa

Enjoy this quick skillet supper with corn bread and a green salad.

| | | |
|---|---|---|
| 4 | pork chops | 4 |
| 1 | clove garlic, minced | 1 |
| 2 tsp | chili powder | 10 mL |
| 1 tsp | EACH ground cumin and oregano | 5 mL |
| ¼ tsp | hot pepper flakes | 1 mL |
| | Salt and pepper | |
| 1 tbsp | vegetable oil | 15 mL |
| 1 | can (19 oz/540 mL) black beans, drained and rinsed | 1 |
| 1 cup | corn kernels (frozen or canned) | 250 mL |
| 1 cup | bottled salsa (preferably chunky) | 250 mL |
| ⅓ cup | chopped fresh coriander | 75 mL |

Trim any fat from chops. Combine garlic, chili powder, cumin, oregano, hot pepper flakes and ¼ tsp (1 mL) each of the salt and pepper; rub all over chops.

In large heavy skillet, heat oil over medium-high heat; cook chops for 5 minutes on each side, reducing heat if starting to stick. Remove to plate.

Remove any fat and burnt bits from pan. Return chops and any juices. Add beans, corn and salsa. (Recipe can be prepared to this point, covered and refrigerated for up to 8 hours. Bring to room temperature for 30 minutes before proceeding.)

Bring to boil, reduce heat and simmer for about 8 minutes or until sauce is hot. Taste and adjust seasoning if necessary. Serve sprinkled with coriander. Makes 4 servings.

# Lima Beans and Pork Chops with Potato Crust

Since I love lima beans so much, I just had to work them into this quick and easy casserole that's sure to be a family hit.

| | | |
|---|---|---|
| 2 cups | lima beans (fresh or frozen) | 500 mL |
| | Salt and pepper | |
| 2 tbsp | minced onion | 25 mL |
| 2 tbsp | chopped fresh parsley | 25 mL |
| 1 tbsp | packed brown sugar | 15 mL |
| 1 tsp | dry mustard | 5 mL |
| 4 | loin pork chops | 4 |
| 3 cups | frozen hash brown potatoes | 750 mL |
| ¾ cup | shredded Cheddar cheese | 175 mL |
| ½ cup | light sour cream | 125 mL |

In saucepan of boiling salted water, cook lima beans until almost tender. Reserving ½ cup (125 mL) cooking water, drain beans and transfer to 9-inch (2.5 L) square baking dish. Stir in salt and pepper to taste, onion, half of the parsley, the brown sugar, mustard and reserved cooking water; spread out in pan.

In greased skillet over medium-high heat, brown chops; sprinkle with salt and pepper to taste and arrange over beans. (Recipe can be prepared to this point, covered and refrigerated for up to 6 hours. Let stand at room temperature 30 minutes.)

Combine potatoes, cheese, sour cream and remaining parsley; spread over chops. Bake, covered, in 350°F (180°C) oven for 30 minutes. Uncover and bake 30 minutes longer. Broil for about 3 minutes or until topping is golden. Makes 4 servings.

# Pineapple Sweet-and-Sour Pork

My kids have always loved this easy, inexpensive dish for which I buy fresh picnic pork shoulder when it's on sale. By the way, it's easier to cube the meat if it is partially frozen. If you're freezing the cooked dish, add the peppers as you reheat it. Serve on lots of hot steamed rice.

| | | |
|---|---|---|
| 2 lb | boneless lean pork, cubed | 1 kg |
| ¼ cup | low-salt soy sauce | 50 mL |
| 4 tsp | cornstarch | 20 mL |
| 1 tsp | Oriental sesame oil | 5 mL |
| 1 | can (19 oz/540 mL) unsweetened pineapple tidbits | 1 |
| ½ cup | chicken stock or water | 125 mL |
| 3 tbsp | EACH ketchup, packed brown sugar and rice vinegar | 45 mL |
| 3 tbsp | vegetable oil | 45 mL |
| 2 | cloves garlic, minced | 2 |
| 1 tbsp | minced fresh ginger | 15 mL |
| 1 | onion, thinly sliced | 1 |
| 2 | sweet green peppers, cut in strips | 2 |

Toss pork with 2 tbsp (25 mL) of the soy sauce, 1 tsp (5 mL) of the cornstarch and sesame oil; let stand for 30 minutes.

Combine juice from pineapple, stock, remaining soy sauce, remaining cornstarch, ketchup, brown sugar and vinegar. Set aside.

Heat wok over high heat; add 2 tbsp (25 mL) of the vegetable oil. Stir-fry pork just until no longer pink. Remove to bowl. Wipe out pan with paper towel; reheat and add remaining oil. Stir-fry garlic and ginger for 15 seconds. Add onion; stir-fry for 1½ minutes. Add pineapple sauce; cook, stirring, until thickened.

Return pork to pan; cover and simmer for about 1 hour or until pork is very tender. Add pineapple and green peppers; cook for 3 minutes or until heated through. Makes 6 servings.

# Skillet Pork Stew

The apples in this super easy stew turn into a lovely sauce. Use pork shoulder, a leg steak, butt chops or a roast—whatever is on special.

| | | |
|---|---|---|
| 1 lb | lean pork | 500 g |
| 2 tbsp | all-purpose flour | 25 mL |
| ¼ tsp | EACH salt and pepper | 1 mL |
| 2 tbsp | vegetable oil (approx) | 25 mL |
| 1 | onion, coarsely chopped | 1 |
| 1 cup | apple juice or water | 250 mL |
| 2 tsp | EACH Dijon mustard and vinegar | 10 mL |
| ½ tsp | dried thyme | 2 mL |
| 4 | cloves garlic, halved | 4 |
| 2 | carrots, cut in 2-inch (5 cm) pieces | 2 |
| 2 | apples, peeled and quartered | 2 |
| 4 | small potatoes, quartered | 4 |
| 1 cup | frozen peas | 250 mL |

Cut pork into 1-inch (2.5 cm) cubes. In bag, combine flour, salt and pepper; add pork and shake to coat. Set aside.

In large skillet, heat half of the oil over low heat; cook onion for 5 minutes. Transfer to bowl.

Heat remaining oil over medium-high heat; brown pork, in batches if necessary and adding more oil if needed. Add to bowl.

Pour apple juice into skillet; bring to boil, scraping up brown bits from bottom of pan. Stir in mustard, vinegar and thyme. Return pork and onion to skillet. Add garlic, carrots and apples; cover and bring to boil. Reduce heat and cook for 15 minutes, stirring occasionally.

Add potatoes; cook for 15 to 20 minutes or until meat and vegetables are tender. Stir in peas; cook for 5 minutes. Makes 4 servings.

# Pork and Apple Stew

Apples and pork are always good companions, but never more so than in this rich and wonderful stew. Great with cabbage salad!

| | | |
|---|---|---|
| 2¼ lb | boneless pork shoulder or butt | 1 kg |
| ¼ cup | all-purpose flour | 50 mL |
| 1 tsp | salt | 5 mL |
| ¼ tsp | pepper | 1 mL |
| ¼ cup | vegetable oil (approx) | 50 mL |
| 2 | onions, sliced | 2 |
| 4 | cloves garlic, minced | 4 |
| 2 cups | apple juice or cider | 500 mL |
| 1 tbsp | EACH Dijon mustard and cider vinegar | 15 mL |
| 1½ tsp | crumbled dried rosemary | 7 mL |
| 5 | large apples, peeled and thickly sliced | 5 |
| 2 cups | diced (½-inch/1 cm) rutabaga | 500 mL |
| 1 | large tomato | 1 |
| ¼ cup | chopped fresh parsley | 50 mL |

Cut pork into 1-inch (2.5 cm) cubes. In bag, combine flour, half of the salt and the pepper; add pork, in batches, and shake to coat. Set aside.

In large Dutch oven or flameproof casserole, heat 1 tbsp (15 mL) of the oil over low heat; cook onions and garlic for 5 minutes. Remove with slotted spoon to large bowl.

Add pork to pan in batches and brown over medium-high heat, adding more oil as needed. Remove with slotted spoon and add to bowl.

Pour apple juice into pan; bring to boil, scraping up any brown bits from bottom of pan. Return pork and onion mixture with any juices to pan. Stir in remaining salt, mustard, vinegar, rosemary, two-thirds of the apples and the rutabaga. Cover tightly and bring to boil. Transfer to 350°F (180°C) oven; bake, stirring occasionally, for about 1½ hours or until pork is tender. (Stew can be prepared to this point, cooled, covered and refrigerated for up to 1 day; reheat gently before continuing.)

Meanwhile, in small heavy skillet, heat 2 tsp (10 mL) oil over medium-high heat; sauté remaining apples until tender-crisp, about 3 minutes. Peel, seed and chop tomato. Stir into cooked stew along with sautéed apple and parsley. Makes 6 to 8 servings.

# Variation:
# Pork and Apple Stew with Cheddar-Bacon Crust

Instead of stirring in sautéed apples, tomato and parsley to serve, top warm stew with this biscuit crust.

| | | |
|---|---|---|
| 1¼ cups | all-purpose flour | 300 mL |
| 2 tsp | baking powder | 10 mL |
| ¼ tsp | salt | 1 mL |
| 2 tbsp | cold butter, cut in bits | 25 mL |
| 1½ cups | shredded Cheddar cheese | 375 mL |
| 4 | slices cooked crisp bacon, crumbled | 4 |
| ⅔ cup | buttermilk (approx) | 150 mL |

In bowl, stir together flour, baking powder and salt; cut in butter until like oatmeal. Stir in cheese and bacon. Stir in enough buttermilk to make soft, sticky dough. Drop by large spoonfuls into rough rounds on top of stew. Bake in 425°F (220°C) oven for 20 to 25 minutes or until crust is golden brown.

# Basque Pork Stew

Steam broccoli while the stew reheats and serve on rice if you wish. I like just nice crusty bread to soak up all the sweet juice from this easy stew.

| | | |
|---|---|---|
| 2 lb | lean pork shoulder | 1 kg |
| 3 tbsp | olive oil (approx) | 45 mL |
| | Salt and pepper | |
| 2 | onions, thickly sliced lengthwise | 2 |
| 1 cup | chicken stock | 250 mL |
| 2 tbsp | tomato paste | 25 mL |
| 2 | sweet red peppers, cut in strips | 2 |
| ¼ lb | prosciutto or ham, coarsely chopped (about 1 cup/250 mL) | 125 g |
| 10 | cloves garlic, thinly sliced | 10 |
| 1 tsp | each paprika and dried thyme | 5 mL |
| ¼ tsp | hot pepper flakes | 1 mL |
| 1 | orange | 1 |

Cut pork into 1½-inch (4 cm) cubes. In deep skillet or shallow saucepan, heat 1 tbsp (15 mL) of the oil over medium-high heat; brown pork in batches, sprinkling with salt and pepper to taste and adding more oil as needed. Remove and set aside.

Add onions to pan; cook over medium heat for 5 minutes. Add stock and tomato paste; bring to boil, scraping up any brown bits from bottom of pan. Return pork to pan. Stir in red peppers, prosciutto, garlic, paprika, thyme and hot pepper flakes.

Grate rind (excluding white part) from orange and add to stew. Peel orange and coarsely chop; stir into stew. Reduce heat to low; cover and simmer for 1 to 1½ hours or until pork is tender, stirring occasionally. Taste and adjust seasoning. (Stew can be cooled, covered and refrigerated for up to 2 days or frozen for up to 2 months. Thaw in refrigerator. Reheat slowly.) Makes 4 servings.

# Orange Teriyaki Pork Roasted with Savoy Cabbage

Adding parboiled cabbage wedges to the roasting pan transforms an economical roast of pork into an interesting one-dish meal. Pop sweet potatoes into the oven to roast alongside.

| | | |
|---|---|---|
| 3 lb | pork butt roast | 1.5 kg |
| ¼ cup | EACH fresh orange juice and soy sauce | 50 mL |
| 1 tbsp | EACH granulated sugar, grated orange rind and minced fresh ginger | 15 mL |
| 2 | cloves garlic, minced | 2 |
| ½ tsp | pepper | 2 mL |
| 1 | small head savoy cabbage | 1 |

Place pork in sturdy plastic bag; set in bowl. Combine orange juice, soy sauce, sugar, orange rind, ginger, garlic and pepper; pour over roast. Seal and marinate in refrigerator for at least 2 hours or for up to 6 hours. Let stand at room temperature for 30 minutes.

Reserving marinade, place roast on rack in shallow roasting pan. Roast in 325°F (160°C) oven, basting occasionally with marinade, for 1½ hours.

Meanwhile, cut cabbage into wedges. In saucepan of boiling water, cook cabbage for 5 minutes; drain and arrange around roast on rack.

Roast, turning cabbage once and basting cabbage and roast, for 30 to 45 minutes longer or until meat thermometer inserted into pork registers 160°F (70°C) and cabbage is tender.

Keeping cabbage warm, remove roast to carving board and tent with foil; let stand for 10 minutes before carving. Serve warm with cabbage wedges. Makes 8 servings.

# Pork Pot Roast with Sweet Potatoes and Fruit

Drizzle crisply cooked green beans with a little cider vinegar or lemon juice as the perfect accompaniment to this simple pot roast, which would be welcome for Sunday dinner with or without company. Sweet potatoes, which sometimes have a rather dry texture when cooked alone, are a moist and delicious highlight of the dish.

| | | |
|---|---|---|
| 2½ lb | pork loin roast | 1.25 kg |
| 2 | cloves garlic, slivered | 2 |
| 1 tsp | EACH crumbled dried sage and dry mustard | 5 mL |
| ½ tsp | EACH dried thyme, salt and crumbled dried rosemary | 2 mL |
| Pinch | cayenne pepper | Pinch |
| 2 | onions, cut in wedges | 2 |
| 3 | large sweet potatoes, peeled and sliced 1 inch (2.5 cm) thick | 3 |
| | Pepper | |
| 2 cups | apple cider or apple juice | 500 mL |
| 1 cup | EACH dried pitted prunes and dried apricots | 250 mL |
| 2 tbsp | cornstarch | 25 mL |
| ½ cup | 2% evaporated milk or light cream | 125 mL |

With point of sharp knife, make slits in pork and insert garlic. Combine sage, mustard, thyme, salt, rosemary and cayenne; rub over pork.

Scatter onions in roasting pan; place pork on top. Arrange sweet potatoes around pork; sprinkle everything with pepper to taste. Roast in 350°F (180°C) oven for 1 hour.

Pour in cider; scatter prunes and apricots around pork. Cover and roast for 1 hour or until meat thermometer inserted in pork registers 160°F (70°C).

Remove pork, potatoes and fruit to warm platter and tent with foil. Bring pan juices to boil. Dissolve cornstarch in milk; stir into juices and bring to boil, stirring constantly until thickened and smooth. Taste and adjust seasoning. Slice meat and surround with potatoes and fruit; pass sauce in heated sauceboat. Makes 4 to 6 servings.

# Short-Cut Pork and Apple Pie

Be sure to use deep-dish pie shells for this hearty recipe. There is a generous amount of filling, and it may look as if it won't all go in the shell, but if you mound it with your hands, it will fit. You can, of course, make your own pastry (see Never-Fail Big-Batch Pastry, page 142) and use a very deep 10-inch (25 cm) pie plate for an even more delicious supper. A nice creamy cabbage salad and pickled beets would go nicely here.

| | | |
|---|---|---|
| 2 tbsp | all-purpose flour | 25 mL |
| ½ tsp | salt | 2 mL |
| ¼ tsp | pepper | 1 mL |
| 2 lb | lean pork, cut in ½-inch (1 cm) cubes | 1 kg |
| ¼ cup | vegetable oil (approx) | 50 mL |
| 2 | onions, chopped | 2 |
| 2 | cloves garlic, minced | 2 |
| ½ cup | water | 125 mL |
| 1 tsp | dried sage | 5 mL |
| ¼ tsp | EACH ground cloves and dried thyme | 1 mL |
| 3 | apples, peeled and sliced | 3 |
| 2 | potatoes, peeled and sliced | 2 |
| 1 tbsp | granulated sugar | 15 mL |
| 2 | frozen (9-inch/23 cm) deep-dish pie shells, thawed | 2 |
| 1 | egg | 1 |

In large bowl, combine flour, salt and pepper; add pork and toss to coat well.

In large saucepan, heat 2 tbsp (25 mL) of the oil over medium-high heat; brown pork in batches and adding more oil as needed. Remove to bowl.

Add onions and garlic to saucepan; cook, stirring, for 3 minutes or until softened. Return pork to saucepan. Add water, sage, cloves and thyme; bring to boil. Reduce heat to medium-low; simmer, uncovered, for 10 minutes.

Stir in apples, potatoes and sugar; simmer for 10 minutes. Remove from heat; let cool for 10 minutes. Mound pork filling into 1 pie shell (shell will be very full). Beat egg with 1 tbsp (15 mL) cold water; brush over edge of filled pie shell. With knife, gently loosen edge of second pie shell from foil plate. Place shell upside down over filling; remove foil plate. With floured fork, press edge of shells together. Brush top all over with egg mixture; cut holes for steam to escape.

Bake in 425°F (220°C) oven for 10 minutes. Reduce heat to 350°F (180°C); bake for 30 to 35 minutes or until golden brown. (Pie can be cooled, covered and refrigerated for up to 1 day or frozen for up to 2 months. Thaw in refrigerator. Reheat, covered with foil, in 350°F/180°C oven for 35 to 40 minutes or until bubbly.) Serve in wedges. Makes 8 servings.

# Stuffed Squash with Ham and Rice

Although cooking for one or two is a challenge, there are some simple tricks that make meal planning easier. Preparing more than enough rice for one meal and using the leftovers to make this easy one-dish supper is a delicious example.

| | | |
|---|---|---|
| 1 | acorn squash (about 2 lb/1 kg) | 1 |
| | Salt and pepper | |
| 1 cup | cooked rice | 250 mL |
| 2 | slices Black Forest ham, slivered (4 oz/125 g) | 2 |
| 1 | can (10 oz/284 mL) stewed tomatoes, drained | 1 |
| Pinch | EACH hot pepper flakes and dried oregano | Pinch |
| ½ cup | shredded mozzarella cheese | 125 mL |

Cut squash in half lengthwise; seed and place, cut side down, in microwaveable baking dish. Add 2 tbsp (25 mL) water; cover and microwave at High for 8 minutes or until almost tender. Season with salt and pepper to taste.

Meanwhile, in large bowl, toss together rice, ham, tomatoes, hot pepper flakes and oregano; mound in squash cavities. (Squash can be prepared to this point, covered and refrigerated for up to 8 hours.)

Microwave, uncovered, at High for 3 minutes or until heated through. Sprinkle with mozzarella; microwave for 45 seconds or until cheese melts. Makes 2 servings.

---

Note: To bake instead of microwave, place halved squash in baking dish; cover with foil and bake in 350°F (180°C) oven for 40 to 45 minutes or until almost tender. Mound rice mixture in cavities; bake for 15 minutes. Sprinkle with mozzarella; bake for 5 minutes.

# Portuguese Pork with Clams

In many restaurants like the one where I enjoyed this dish in the Algarve, the stew arrives at the table in a *cataplana,* a domed, hinged double pan that looks like a huge seashell. Enjoy this dish with crusty Portuguese bread and a green salad dressed with olive oil and lemon juice.

| | | |
|---|---|---|
| 3½ lb | lean boneless pork | 1.75 kg |
| 4 | cloves garlic, crushed | 4 |
| 1 tbsp | paprika | 15 mL |
| 1 | bay leaf | 1 |
| ½ tsp | salt | 2 mL |
| ¼ tsp | pepper | 1 mL |
| 1½ cups | dry white wine | 375 mL |
| 3 | tomatoes | 3 |
| 2 | EACH onions and sweet red peppers | 2 |
| 2 lb | small hard-shelled clams | 1 kg |
| 3 tbsp | olive oil (approx) | 45 mL |
| ¼ tsp | hot pepper flakes | 1 mL |
| ¼ cup | chopped fresh coriander | 50 mL |
| 1 | lemon, cut in wedges | 1 |

Trim pork and cut into 1-inch (2.5 cm) cubes. Place in sturdy plastic bag along with garlic, paprika, bay leaf, salt and pepper; shake to mix. Pour in wine; press out air and seal tightly. Place bag in bowl and refrigerate for 12 hours, turning bag occasionally.

Peel and seed tomatoes; chop finely. Slice onions thinly. Cut red peppers into thin strips. Wash and scrub clams, discarding any that are not tightly closed and scraping off any barnacles. Set vegetables and clams aside.

Drain pork in sieve set over bowl, reserving marinade. Discard garlic and bay leaf; pat pork cubes dry.

In large skillet, heat 2 tbsp (25 mL) of the oil over medium-high heat; brown pork, in batches and adding more oil if needed. With slotted spoon, transfer to large flameproof casserole.

Pour reserved marinade into skillet; bring to boil, scraping up any brown bits from bottom of pan. Boil over high heat until reduced to about ¾ cup (175 mL), about 5 minutes. Pour over pork; cover and set aside.

Wipe out skillet and heat remaining oil over medium heat; cook onions and red peppers, stirring often, for 5 minutes or until softened but not browned. Add tomatoes and hot pepper flakes; simmer for 4 minutes. Stir into pork mixture.

Arrange clams, hinged side down, over pork mixture. Cover tightly and cook over high heat for 5 to 10 minutes or until clams have opened. Discard any that do not open. Sprinkle with coriander. Garnish with lemon wedges. Makes about 8 servings.

# Roasted Vegetable and Sausage Ratatouille

Roasting the vegetables gives this classic stew extra flavor, and adding sausage turns it into a substantial main course. Sop up juices with crusty bread and add a salad of crisp greens.

| | | |
|---|---|---|
| 1 | eggplant, cut in ½-inch (1 cm) cubes | 1 |
| ½ lb | mushrooms, quartered | 250 g |
| 2 | zucchini (or 1 zucchini and 1 yellow summer squash), cut in ¾-inch (2 cm) cubes | 2 |
| 1 | EACH sweet red and yellow pepper, diced | 1 |
| 1 | small Spanish onion, diced | 1 |
| ½ tsp | EACH salt and pepper | 2 mL |
| 3 tbsp | olive oil | 45 mL |
| ⅓ cup | chopped fresh parsley | 75 mL |
| 2 tbsp | chopped fresh basil (or 2 tsp/10 mL dried) | 25 mL |
| 1 lb | hot Italian sausage | 500 g |
| 2 | cloves garlic, minced | 2 |
| 3 | large tomatoes, peeled, seeded and chopped (or one 19 oz/540 mL can) | 3 |
| 1 tbsp | EACH soy sauce and red wine vinegar | 15 mL |
| 1 tsp | granulated sugar | 5 mL |
| Pinch | hot pepper flakes | Pinch |

In large greased shallow roasting pan, combine eggplant, mushrooms, zucchini, sweet peppers and onion. Sprinkle with salt and pepper; drizzle with 2 tbsp (25 mL) of the oil. Roast in 400°F (200°C) oven for 30 minutes, stirring once. Stir in parsley and basil.

Meanwhile, in large skillet, bring sausage and 1 cup (250 mL) water to boil; cover and simmer for 8 minutes. Drain and cut into ½-inch (1 cm) thick slices. Heat remaining oil in skillet; brown sausage for 5 minutes. Remove with slotted spoon to drain on paper towel.

Add garlic to skillet; cook for 2 minutes over medium heat. Stir in tomatoes, soy sauce, vinegar, sugar and hot pepper flakes; cook, stirring often, for 5 minutes or until thickened. Stir tomato mixture and sausage into roasted vegetables. Roast for 15 minutes. (Ratatouille can be cooled, covered and refrigerated for up to 2 days. Reheat gently.) Makes 4 servings.

# Sausage Burrito Casserole

Be sure the tortillas are fresh for easier rolling when everyone helps make this fun supper. A green salad, then pineapple or banana slices broiled with butter, brown sugar and coconut complete the menu.

| | | |
|---|---|---|
| 1 lb | hot or mild Italian sausage | 500 g |
| 1 | small onion, chopped | 1 |
| 1 | sweet green pepper, chopped | 1 |
| 2 | cloves garlic, minced | 2 |
| ½ tsp | EACH dried marjoram and oregano | 2 mL |
| 1 | can (14 oz/398 mL) red kidney beans, drained and rinsed | 1 |
| 2 cups | bottled salsa | 500 mL |
| ¼ cup | freshly grated Parmesan cheese | 50 mL |
| 10 | flour tortillas (8 inches/20 cm) | 10 |
| 2 cups | shredded Monterey Jack or mild Cheddar cheese (about 8 oz/250 g) | 500 mL |
| ¼ cup | chopped green onions | 50 mL |
| | Light sour cream | |

Remove sausage from casings. In large nonstick skillet, cook meat over medium heat, breaking up with spoon, for 5 minutes or until no longer pink. Drain off any fat.

Add onion, green pepper, garlic, marjoram and oregano; cook for 3 minutes or until softened. Mix in beans; cook for 3 minutes, stirring occasionally and mashing beans slightly. Stir in 1 cup (250 mL) of the salsa and Parmesan cheese. Taste and adjust seasonings if necessary.

Spoon about ½ cup (125 mL) of the mixture onto bottom third of each tortilla. Fold bottom over filling and roll up to enclose filling.

Place, seam side down, in greased 13- x 9-inch (3 L) baking dish. Sprinkle cheese over top. Cover with greased foil. (Recipe can be prepared to this point, covered and refrigerated for up to 8 hours. Let stand at room temperature for 30 minutes before baking.)

Bake, covered, in 350°F (180°C) oven for 15 to 20 minutes or until heated through. Spoon remaining salsa over top; sprinkle with green onions. Serve with sour cream. Makes 4 servings.

# Sausage and Mushroom Pie

A marinated broccoli or mixed green salad and beer go well with this simple dish that's ideal for casual entertaining.

| | | |
|---|---|---|
| 3 lb | Italian sausage | 1.5 kg |
| 1 | onion, chopped | 1 |
| 4 cups | sliced mushrooms (about 1 lb/500 g) | 1 L |
| ¼ cup | all-purpose flour | 50 mL |
| 2 cups | light sour cream | 500 mL |
| 1¼ cups | beef stock | 300 mL |
| ½ cup | chopped fresh parsley | 125 mL |
| ½ lb | frozen puff pastry, thawed | 250 g |
| | *Glaze:* | |
| 1 | egg | 1 |
| 1 tbsp | cold water | 15 mL |

Remove sausage from casing. In very large skillet (or 2 smaller skillets), brown meat over medium heat, breaking up with spoon. Drain off fat.

Add onion and mushrooms; cook, stirring, for 3 minutes. Stir in flour; cook, stirring, for 2 to 3 minutes or until browned. Gradually add sour cream and beef stock; simmer over low heat for 30 minutes. Stir in parsley.

Transfer to 12-cup (3 L) casserole. Refrigerate long enough for any remaining fat to harden on surface; remove and discard fat.

Roll out pastry and place over casserole, sealing and crimping edges. Cut leftover scraps of pastry into decorations; cut hole in centre of crust to let steam escape and surround with pastry decorations. (Pie can be prepared to this point, covered lightly with foil and refrigerated for 24 hours.)

Glaze: Stir together egg and water; brush over pastry, both over and under decorations. Bake in 425°F (220°C) oven for 10 minutes. Reduce heat to 350°F (180°C); bake for 20 minutes longer or until pastry is brown and filling is bubbly. Makes 8 to 10 servings.

# Three-Bean Sausage Chili with Tomato-Avocado Salsa

I love sausage and beans; so I couldn't resist combining a bunch of different beans with Italian sausage in this great chili. If you like, instead of the salsa, top with a dollop of sour cream and chopped fresh coriander or green onions. Serve with a green salad and corn bread.

| | | |
|---|---|---|
| 1 tbsp | olive oil | 15 mL |
| 1 lb | hot or mild Italian sausage | 500 g |
| 1 | EACH onion and sweet red and green pepper, cut in ½-inch (1 cm) chunks | 1 |
| 2 | jalapeño peppers, chopped | 2 |
| 2 | cloves garlic, minced | 2 |
| 1 tbsp | EACH chili powder and paprika | 15 mL |
| 2 tsp | ground cumin | 10 mL |
| 1 tsp | dried oregano | 5 mL |
| 1 | can (28 oz/796 mL) crushed tomatoes in purée or diced tomatoes | 1 |
| 1 | EACH can (19 oz/540 mL) red kidney beans, chick-peas and black beans, drained and rinsed | 1 |
| 1 tbsp | red wine vinegar or fresh lime juice | 15 mL |
| | Salt and pepper | |
| | Tomato-Avocado Salsa (recipe follows) | |

In large heavy saucepan, heat oil over medium-high heat; brown sausage, turning occasionally, about 10 minutes. Remove and cut into ½-inch (1 cm) thick slices.

Pour off all but 2 tbsp (25 mL) drippings from pan; cook onion for 5 minutes. Add sweet and jalapeño peppers; cook for 1 minute. Stir in garlic, chili powder, paprika, cumin and oregano; cook for 30 seconds.

Stir in tomatoes, kidney beans, chick-peas and black beans; simmer, covered, for 15 to 20 minutes for flavors to blend. Add sausage; simmer for 10 minutes. Stir in vinegar. Add salt and pepper to taste. Makes 4 to 6 servings.

# Tomato-Avocado Salsa:

| | | |
|---|---|---|
| 1 | tomato, seeded and diced | 1 |
| 1 | avocado, peeled and diced | 1 |
| ¼ cup | diced red onion | 50 mL |
| 2 tbsp | chopped fresh coriander | 25 mL |
| 2 tbsp | fresh lime juice | 25 mL |
| | Salt and pepper | |

In small bowl, toss together tomato, avocado, onion, coriander, lime juice, and salt and pepper to taste. Makes about 1¼ cups (300 mL).

# Zesty Sausage Stew

Serve this hearty, quick-cooking stew with noodles or creamy mashed potatoes and a green salad.

| | | |
|---|---|---|
| 1 lb | country-style or farmer's sausage | 500 g |
| 2 | onions, coarsely chopped | 2 |
| 2 | cloves garlic, minced | 2 |
| 1 | sweet green pepper, coarsely chopped | 1 |
| 1 | can (28 oz/796 mL) tomatoes | 1 |
| ¼ cup | chopped fresh parsley (approx) | 50 mL |
| 1 tsp | dried basil | 5 mL |
| ¼ tsp | EACH dried oregano and pepper | 1 mL |

Cut sausage into bite-size pieces. In large saucepan, brown sausage over medium-high heat, about 10 minutes, stirring often. Remove with slotted spoon and set aside.

Pour off all but 2 tbsp (25 mL) drippings from pan; cook onions, garlic and green pepper over medium heat, stirring often, for 5 minutes. Stir in tomatoes, parsley, basil, oregano and pepper.

Return sausage to pan. Simmer, uncovered and stirring occasionally, for 30 minutes. Taste and adjust seasoning. Serve sprinkled with additional parsley. Makes 4 servings.

# Lentil and Sausage Stew

Grate cheese over this hearty, nutritious stew and serve with crusty bread and a green salad or coleslaw.

| | | |
|---|---|---|
| 1 cup | red lentils (8 oz/250 g) | 250 mL |
| 2 tbsp | vegetable oil | 25 mL |
| 1 lb | Italian sweet sausage or farmer's sausage, sliced | 500 g |
| 2 | carrots, sliced | 2 |
| 1 | onion, chopped | 1 |
| 3 cups | sliced mushrooms (about ½ lb/250 g) | 750 mL |
| 1 | clove garlic, minced | 1 |
| 2½ cups | beef or chicken stock | 625 mL |
| 2 tbsp | wine vinegar | 25 mL |
| 1 | small bay leaf | 1 |
| ¼ tsp | EACH dried thyme and oregano | 1 mL |
| 1 cup | drained canned tomatoes | 250 mL |
| 1 cup | sliced zucchini | 250 mL |
| | Pepper | |
| ¼ cup | chopped fresh parsley | 50 mL |
| 1½ cups | shredded Cheddar cheese | 375 mL |

Sort and rinse lentils; set aside.

In large heavy saucepan or Dutch oven, heat oil over medium-high heat; cook sausage for 15 to 20 minutes or until cooked through. Remove with slotted spoon and set aside.

Pour off all but 2 tbsp (25 mL) fat from pan. Add carrots, onion, mushrooms and garlic; cook over medium heat until softened, 3 to 5 minutes. Stir in stock, vinegar, bay leaf, thyme, oregano and lentils; bring to boil over high heat. Cover, reduce heat to low and simmer for 15 minutes.

Add tomatoes, zucchini, and pepper to taste; simmer for 10 to 15 minutes or until lentils and zucchini are tender but still hold their shape. Discard bay leaf. Stir in sausage and parsley. Sprinkle with cheese; cover and cook over low heat for 5 minutes or until cheese melts. Makes 4 to 6 servings.

# Lamb

# Lamb Shanks Braised with Figs and Root Vegetables

Serve this easy, full-flavored stew on couscous studded with lots of chopped fresh coriander.

| | | |
|---|---|---|
| 4 | lamb shanks | 4 |
| | Salt and pepper | |
| ⅓ cup | all-purpose flour | 75 mL |
| 2 tbsp | olive oil | 25 mL |
| 3 | cloves garlic, minced | 3 |
| 2 tsp | EACH dried basil and paprika | 10 mL |
| 1 tsp | EACH dried thyme, ground cumin and ground coriander | 5 mL |
| 1 cup | dry red wine | 250 mL |
| 2½ cups | chicken stock | 625 mL |
| ½ cup | chopped drained canned tomatoes | 125 mL |
| 1 | pkg (8 oz/250 g) dried figs | 1 |
| 2 tbsp | butter | 25 mL |
| 1 tbsp | packed brown sugar | 15 mL |
| 2 | EACH onions, carrots, parsnips and white summer turnips, peeled and cut in 1-inch (2.5 cm) cubes | 2 |

Lightly sprinkle lamb with salt and pepper to taste; coat all over with flour. In large Dutch oven, heat half of the oil; brown shanks, in batches and adding more oil when needed. Remove to plate.

Stir in any remaining flour, garlic, basil, paprika, thyme, cumin and coriander; cook over medium heat for 1 minute, stirring. Stir in wine; bring to boil, scraping up any brown bits from bottom of pan. Stir in 1½ cups (375 mL) of the stock and tomatoes. Return shanks and any juices. With scissors, cut stems from figs; quarter figs and add to stew. Bring to boil; cover and bake in 350°F (180°C) oven for about 2 hours or until lamb is very tender, stirring occasionally.

Meanwhile, in deep skillet or shallow stovetop casserole, melt butter and sugar over medium heat; stir in onions, carrots, parsnips and turnips until coated. Sprinkle with salt and pepper to taste. Add remaining stock and bring to boil. Bake, uncovered and stirring occasionally, in 350°F (180°C) oven for about 45 minutes or until vegetables are tender. Stir into cooked shanks. (Stew can be cooled, covered and refrigerated for up to 2 days; reheat slowly on stovetop, stirring often, or in 350°F/180°C oven, covered, for 30 minutes or until bubbly.) Makes 4 servings.

# Braised Lamb Shanks with Olives

Serve this bistro-style meal with steamed rice sparked by raisins and almonds or pine nuts.

| | | |
|---|---|---|
| 1 tbsp | olive oil | 15 mL |
| 4 | lamb shanks | 4 |
| | Salt and pepper | |
| 2 | onions, chopped | 2 |
| 2 | cloves garlic, minced | 2 |
| 1 cup | white wine or chicken stock | 250 mL |
| 2 tbsp | liquid honey | 25 mL |
| Pinch | EACH cayenne pepper, cinnamon, cloves and nutmeg | Pinch |
| 4 | carrots, halved and cut lengthwise in quarters | 4 |
| 1 | fennel bulb (or 4 celery stalks), coarsely chopped | 1 |
| 1½ cups | pitted olives | 375 mL |

In Dutch oven or deep ovenproof skillet, heat oil over medium-high heat; brown shanks on all sides, sprinkling lightly with salt and pepper to taste. Remove to plate.

Reduce heat to medium; cook onions and garlic for 5 minutes. Add wine and bring to boil; boil for about 5 minutes or until slightly reduced.

Meanwhile, mix together honey, cayenne, cinnamon, cloves and nutmeg; brush over shanks. Add carrots and fennel to pan; place shanks on top. Cover and bake in 350°F (180°C) oven for 1½ hours or until tender. (Shanks can be cooled, covered and refrigerated for up to 1 day or frozen for up to 2 months. Thaw in refrigerator; reheat slowly).

Scatter olives around shanks; cook for 10 more minutes. Makes 4 servings.

# Lamb Shanks with White Beans

Serve this easy version of a favorite combination with crusty bread and a creamy carrot-cabbage slaw. Since there are three people in our household right now, I find the New Zealand Spring Lamb packages of three shanks just right; however, the other ingredients will accommodate four nicely too.

| | | |
|---|---|---|
| 1 tbsp | olive oil | 15 mL |
| 3 | lamb shanks | 3 |
| | Salt and pepper | |
| 1 | can (14 oz/398 mL) tomatoes, chopped | 1 |
| ½ cup | chopped fresh parsley | 125 mL |
| ½ tsp | EACH dried savory and thyme | 2 mL |
| ¼ tsp | crumbled dried rosemary | 1 mL |
| 1 cup | chicken stock | 250 mL |
| 9 | cloves garlic, halved | 9 |
| 1 | can (19 oz/540 mL) white pea (navy) beans, drained and rinsed | 1 |
| Pinch | hot pepper flakes | Pinch |

In shallow stovetop casserole, heat oil over medium-high heat; brown lamb shanks well, sprinkling lightly with salt and pepper to taste. Remove and set aside.

Pour off any fat from pan. Add tomatoes, parsley, savory, thyme and rosemary; bring to boil, scraping up any brown bits from bottom of pan. Reduce heat and simmer, uncovered, for 12 minutes. Add stock and garlic; return to simmer.

Return lamb and any juices to pan; cover and bake in 325°F (160°C) oven for about 2¼ hours or until lamb is very tender, turning shanks occasionally.

Transfer shanks to warm platter; tent with foil to keep warm. Remove any fat from cooking liquid. Add beans, hot pepper flakes, and salt and pepper to taste; simmer, uncovered, for 10 minutes, stirring often. Spoon around lamb. Makes 3 servings.

# Classic Lamb Stew with Caramelized Root Vegetables

The sauce is rich and dark, and the lamb mild-tasting in this delicious stew. Crusty bread and a green salad are all you need to make it an easy meal for family or entertaining. If using frozen lamb, it's easier to cube if you don't thaw it completely.

| | | |
|---|---|---|
| 2½ lb | boneless lamb shoulder | 1.25 kg |
| 2 tsp | granulated sugar | 10 mL |
| ½ tsp | salt | 2 mL |
| ¼ tsp | pepper | 1 mL |
| ¼ cup | vegetable oil (approx) | 50 mL |
| 2 tbsp | all-purpose flour | 25 mL |
| 2½ cups | beef stock | 625 mL |
| 1 tbsp | tomato paste | 15 mL |
| 2 | cloves garlic, minced | 2 |
| ¼ tsp | dried thyme | 1 mL |
| 1 | bay leaf | 1 |
| 3 | EACH carrots and potatoes, peeled and cut in 1-inch (2.5 cm) pieces | 3 |
| 2 | white turnips (or half small rutabaga), cut in 1-inch (2.5 cm) pieces | 2 |
| 2 | small onions, cut in 8 wedges each | 2 |
| 1 cup | frozen green peas | 250 mL |
| ¼ cup | chopped fresh parsley | 50 mL |

Cut lamb into 1½-inch (4 cm) cubes. In small bowl, stir together sugar, salt and pepper.

In large Dutch oven or flameproof casserole, heat 1 tbsp (15 mL) of the oil over medium-high heat; brown lamb, in batches, sprinkling with half of the sugar mixture and adding more oil as needed. With slotted spoon, remove lamb to bowl.

Add flour to pan; cook, stirring, until browned. Gradually stir in stock, tomato paste, garlic, thyme and bay leaf; bring to boil, scraping up any brown bits from bottom. Return meat and any juices to pan. Cover tightly and bake in 325°F (160°C) oven for 45 minutes, stirring occasionally.

Meanwhile, in large skillet, heat 2 tbsp (25 mL) oil over medium heat; cook carrots, potatoes, turnips and onions, stirring and sprinkling with remaining sugar mixture, until lightly colored, about 7 minutes. Add to stew; cook 30 minutes longer or until lamb and vegetables are tender. Discard bay leaf. Stir in peas; cook for 5 minutes. Serve sprinkled with parsley. Makes 8 servings.

# Bistro-Style Lamb and Beans with Garlic Crust

This is the type of casserole I love serving to company with a salad and a fruit dessert. Its ingredient list is lengthy but not exotic, and all the steps to its making are quite easy.

| | | |
|---|---|---|
| 1 lb | dried white pea (navy) beans (2 cups/500 mL) | 500 g |
| 6 | carrots, sliced | 6 |
| 4 | onions, chopped | 4 |
| 1 | bouquet garni* | 1 |
| ¼ lb | salt pork or bacon, diced | 125 g |
| 2¾ lb | lean boneless lamb (preferably shoulder) | 1.375 kg |
| ⅓ cup | all-purpose flour | 75 mL |
| | Salt and pepper | |
| 2 tbsp | olive oil | 25 mL |
| 2½ cups | beef stock | 625 mL |
| ¼ cup | tomato paste | 50 mL |
| 1 tbsp | Dijon mustard | 15 mL |
| 1 | large head garlic, cloves peeled and halved | 1 |
| 1 tsp | EACH crumbled dried rosemary, thyme and marjoram | 5 mL |
| | *Garlic Crust:* | |
| ¼ cup | butter | 50 mL |
| 3 | large cloves garlic, minced | 3 |
| 12 | French baguette slices (½-inch/1 cm thick) | 12 |
| 1 tbsp | Dijon mustard | 15 mL |

Sort and rinse beans. In medium saucepan, cover beans with 6 cups (1.5 L) water; let soak overnight in refrigerator. (Or cover with water and bring to boil; boil for 2 minutes. Remove from heat; cover and let stand for 1 hour.)

Drain beans; cover again with cold water and bring to boil. Add half each of the carrots and onions; add bouquet garni. Reduce heat and simmer, covered, for about 40 minutes or until beans are tender but not mushy. Drain and discard bouquet garni.

Meanwhile, in large saucepan, cook salt pork over medium-high heat until browned and crisp. With slotted spoon, remove to drain on paper towels. Add remaining carrots and onions to pan; cook for 5 minutes over medium heat; remove to bowl.

Meanwhile, trim lamb and cut into 2-inch (5 cm) pieces. In sturdy bag, combine flour, ½ tsp (2 mL) salt and ¼ tsp (1 mL) pepper; add lamb and shake to coat well. Add 1 tbsp (15 mL) of the oil to pan; brown lamb in batches and adding more oil as needed. Add to vegetables in bowl.

Add stock, tomato paste, mustard, garlic, rosemary, thyme and marjoram to pan; bring to boil, scraping up any brown bits from bottom of pan. Return lamb, vegetables and pork to pan; bring to boil. Reduce heat, cover and simmer for about 1 hour or until meat is tender.

Stir in cooked beans and vegetable mixture; transfer to 12-cup (3 L) casserole. (Recipe can be prepared to this point and refrigerated for up to 2 days or frozen. Thaw in refrigerator and reheat gently before proceeding.)

Garlic Crust: In large skillet, melt butter over low heat; stir in garlic. Spread bread with mustard; arrange in garlic butter. Heat for 3 to 5 minutes, turning slices over, until butter is absorbed; arrange over lamb mixture. Bake, uncovered, in 350°F (180°C) oven for 30 to 40 minutes or until bubbly and crust is golden brown. Makes 10 servings.

---

\* **Bouquet garni: Tie 1 tbsp (15 mL) thyme sprigs or 1 tsp (5 mL) dried thyme, 3 parsley sprigs and 2 bay leaves inside ribs of 2 short stalks celery.**

# Greek-Style Lamb Shoulder Fricassée

Instead of cutting the lamb into the usual cubes for stew, I've left it whole and cooked it until it falls off the bone. Serve with orzo (rice-like pasta) and a yogurt cucumber salad.

| | | |
|---|---|---|
| 1 | bone-in lamb shoulder (about 3 lb/1.5 kg) | 1 |
| 1 tbsp | olive oil | 15 mL |
| 2 | onions, sliced | 2 |
| 4 | cloves garlic, minced | 4 |
| 1 tbsp | tomato paste | 15 mL |
| 2 tsp | grated lemon rind | 10 mL |
| 1 tsp | dried oregano | 5 mL |
| Pinch | EACH allspice and cinnamon | Pinch |
| 2 cups | chicken stock | 500 mL |
| 1 | can (398 mL) artichoke bottoms or hearts | 1 |
| | Salt and pepper | |
| 1 cup | crumbled or cubed rinsed feta cheese | 250 mL |
| 2 tbsp | chopped fresh parsley | 25 mL |

Trim lamb and place, meat side up, in shallow roasting pan; brown in 500°F (260°C) oven for 10 minutes, turning once.

Meanwhile, in large saucepan, heat oil over medium-high heat; cook onions, stirring often, for 3 minutes or until softened. Stir in garlic, tomato paste, lemon rind, oregano, allspice and cinnamon; cook for 30 seconds. Pour in stock and bring to boil; remove from heat.

Drain and rinse artichokes under cold running water; drain, quarter and add to stock mixture. Pour over lamb. Cover and bake in 325°F (160°C) oven for 3 to 3½ hours or until meat is very tender. (Recipe can be prepared to this point, cooled, covered and refrigerated for up to 24 hours. Remove any fat from surface. Reheat slowly on stovetop or in 325°F/160°C oven for about 30 minutes or until heated through.)

Remove meat to heated platter; tent with foil to keep warm. Skim off any fat from pan juices; pour through strainer into clean saucepan, reserving onions and artichokes. Boil juices for 10 minutes to thicken; add reserved vegetables. Season with salt and pepper to taste.

Slice meat and arrange on platter; sprinkle with cheese and parsley. Pour juices over top or serve in heated sauceboat alongside. Makes about 4 servings.

# Moroccan Braised Lamb

In Morocco, I was lucky enough to encounter *mechoui,* a basic element of Moroccan cooking. A whole sheep is spiced and roasted, then brought to the table in its entirety. More often, however, there were lamb *tagines*—melt-in-your-mouth stews flavored with the complex combination of spices at which Moroccans are so adept. Accompany this dish with couscous, and if you freeze it, add the almonds as you reheat the thawed stew.

| | | |
|---|---|---|
| 2½ lb | boneless lean lamb shoulder, cut in 1-inch (2.5 cm) cubes | 1.25 kg |
| | All-purpose flour | |
| | Salt and pepper | |
| ⅓ cup | olive oil (approx) | 75 mL |
| 2 | EACH carrots and onions, chopped | 2 |
| 1 | sweet green pepper, chopped | 1 |
| 4 | cloves garlic, minced | 4 |
| 1½ tsp | EACH ground cumin and cinnamon | 7 mL |
| 1 tsp | ground coriander | 5 mL |
| ½ tsp | dried thyme | 2 mL |
| ¼ tsp | saffron threads, crumbled | 1 mL |
| 2 cups | beef stock | 500 mL |
| 2 tbsp | tomato paste | 25 mL |
| 1 | can (19 oz/540 mL) chick-peas, drained and rinsed | 1 |
| ¼ cup | each seedless raisins and slivered almonds | 50 mL |
| | Grated rind of 1 lemon | |
| 2 tbsp | fresh lemon juice | 25 mL |

Coat lamb with flour, shaking off excess; sprinkle lightly with salt and pepper. In large Dutch oven, heat 2 tbsp (25 mL) of the oil over medium-high heat; brown lamb, in batches and adding more oil as needed. Transfer to bowl.

Add carrots, onions and green pepper to pan; cook over medium heat for 3 minutes. Add garlic; cook for 3 minutes. Stir in cumin, cinnamon, coriander, thyme and saffron; cover and cook for 1 to 2 minutes or until fragrant.

Stir in stock and tomato paste; bring to boil, stirring. Return lamb and any juices to pan. Add chick-peas, raisins, almonds, and lemon rind and juice; cover and bake in 350°F (180°C) oven for about 2½ hours or until lamb is very tender. Makes 6 to 8 servings.

# Mixed Grill Supper

Prepare and marinate lamb chops and an array of colorful vegetables overnight, then with a few minutes under the broiler, supper is ready in less time than it takes to stop for a pizza on the way home from work—great for a weeknight dinner guest.

| | | |
|---|---|---|
| 4 | loin lamb chops | 4 |
| 1 | clove garlic, halved | 1 |
| 1 tbsp | Dijon mustard | 15 mL |
| 2 | small zucchini | 2 |
| 2 | potatoes, peeled | 2 |
| 12 | mushroom caps | 12 |
| 3 tbsp | olive oil | 45 mL |
| ½ tsp | paprika | 2 mL |
| ¼ tsp | EACH dried thyme and rosemary | 1 mL |
| Pinch | EACH cayenne and black pepper | Pinch |
| 1 | tomato | 1 |
| | Salt | |

Trim excess fat from chops and slash edges; rub all over with cut sides of garlic. Spread mustard over chops. Place in shallow nonmetallic baking dish just large enough to hold meat and vegetables in single layer.

In saucepan of boiling salted water, cover and cook zucchini for 5 minutes; remove with tongs and set aside. Add potatoes to pot; cook for about 20 minutes or just until fork-tender. Cut zucchini and potatoes in half lengthwise; arrange, cut sides up, in dish with chops. Surround with mushrooms.

Stir together oil, paprika, thyme, rosemary, cayenne and black pepper; drizzle over chops and vegetables. (Recipe can be prepared to this point, covered and refrigerated for up to 24 hours. Let stand at room temperature for 30 minutes.)

Reserving any oil mixture, arrange meat and vegetables on lightly greased broiler pan; brush oil mixture over tomato and add to pan. Broil 4 inches (10 cm) from heat, turning chops once, for 8 to 10 minutes or until lamb feels soft but springy when pressed with finger. Season meat and vegetables with salt to taste. Makes 2 servings.

# Grilled Eggplant Moussaka

In many restaurants in Greece, diners are invited to go back into the kitchen to look over the day's fare set out in steam tables. More than once, although I love the wonderful textures and flavors in the dish, I was put off by the ubiquitous moussaka because it seemed greasy. Here, grilling the eggplant not only gives it a delicious smoky flavor but also greatly reduces the amount of oil needed. Served with a big green salad and crusty rolls, moussaka is great for entertaining because it's best baked right through and reheated—terrific for potluck, chalet or cottage feasting.

| | | |
|---|---|---|
| 2 lb | lean ground lamb, beef, veal or a combination | 1 kg |
| 2 | onions, chopped | 2 |
| 4 | cloves garlic, minced | 4 |
| 1 tbsp | cinnamon | 15 mL |
| 2 tsp | dried oregano | 10 mL |
| 1 tsp | granulated sugar | 5 mL |
| 1 | can (14 oz/398 mL) whole tomatoes | 1 |
| 1 cup | dry red wine | 250 mL |
| | Pepper | |
| 3 | eggplants | 3 |
| ¼ cup | olive oil (approx) | 50 mL |
| | *Bechamel:* | |
| 3 cups | milk | 750 mL |
| ¼ cup | butter | 50 mL |
| 3 | eggs | 3 |
| ¼ cup | all-purpose flour | 50 mL |
| ½ tsp | nutmeg | 2 mL |
| | Salt and pepper | |
| 2 cups | grated kasseri cheese or freshly grated Parmesan cheese | 500 mL |

In large skillet, cook lamb over medium-high heat, breaking up with spoon, for 3 to 4 minutes or until just beginning to brown. Add onions and garlic; cook, stirring occasionally, for 10 minutes. Drain off fat. Season with cinnamon, oregano and sugar; cook for 1 minute. Stir in tomatoes, wine and pepper to taste, breaking up tomatoes with spoon; simmer, uncovered and stirring often, for 25 to 30 minutes or until thickened.

Meanwhile, peel eggplants and cut crosswise in ½-inch (1 cm) thick slices. (It's not necessary to salt slices.) Brush both sides lightly with oil. Place on grill over medium-high heat; grill until tender, about 10 minutes, turning once.

Bechamel: In small saucepan, heat 2 cups (500 mL) of the milk with butter until bubbles appear around edge. Remove from heat.

In medium saucepan, beat together eggs, remaining milk, flour, nutmeg and pinch of salt until smooth. Place over medium heat and, stirring constantly, slowly add warm milk in thin stream. Cook, stirring, until boiling and thickened. Season with pepper to taste. Set aside.

Arrange half of the eggplant in 13- x 9-inch (3 L) glass baking dish, overlapping if necessary. Spread with lamb mixture. Sprinkle with half of the cheese. Top with remaining eggplant. Pour Bechamel over top; sprinkle with remaining cheese. Bake in 300°F (150°C) oven for 1 hour.

Cool, cover and refrigerate overnight. Let stand at room temperature for 30 minutes. Bake, uncovered, in 350°F (180°C) oven for 30 minutes or until browned and bubbly. Makes 8 servings.

---

**When using a cheese like Parmesan, be sure you buy the real thing and grate it just before adding. Pathetic ground versions found on shelves in the supermarket are soapy and salty. In a dish like this that calls for so much of the cheese, the results would be inedible.**

# Julia Aitken's Liverpool Lamb and Potato Hot Pot

My friend and my former food editor at *Homemaker's Magazine,* Julia Aitken, is responsible not only for this comfort dish but also for its interesting introduction. "This easy layered casserole, similar to Lancashire Hot Pot, comes from the port city of Liverpool in the south of that English county, where it's known as Scouse (pronounced to rhyme with mouse). The name derives from a Scandinavian dish called *labskaus,* a one-pot meal that was commonly cooked in ships' galleys. The name became shortened and anglicized, and since so many Liverpudlians were seafarers, the inhabitants of the city came to be known as 'scousers' and the dialect spoken there as 'scouse.' The dish was originally made with mutton or neck of lamb (scrag-end), but this version uses more tender and readily available lamb shoulder. Serve it with the traditional accompaniment, pickled red cabbage."

| | | |
|---|---|---|
| 1 | boneless lamb shoulder (2 to 3 lb/1 to 1.5 kg) | 1 |
| 1½ lb | baking potatoes (such as Yukon Gold), peeled and thinly sliced | 750 g |
| 1 tsp | EACH dried thyme and rosemary Salt and pepper | 5 mL |
| 2 | large onions, chopped | 2 |
| 1 cup | beef stock | 250 mL |
| 1 tbsp | butter, melted | 15 mL |

Trim lamb of visible fat; cut meat into 1-inch (2.5 cm) cubes. Set aside one-third of the best-looking potato slices for top of casserole.

Place one-third of the lamb in deep 12-cup (3 L) casserole; sprinkle with one-third each of the thyme and rosemary, and a little salt and pepper. Scatter one-third of the onions over lamb; top with one-third of the potatoes. Repeat layers twice. Arrange reserved potato slices over top.

Carefully pour stock into casserole; brush potatoes with butter. Cover tightly and bake in 325°F (160°C) oven for 2 hours or until lamb and potatoes are very tender. Uncover and cook for about 30 minutes or until golden brown. Serve in wide bowls. Makes 4 to 6 servings.

# Fish and Seafood

# Summer Party Paella

Chuck-full of summer vegetables and herbs, this make-ahead paella is just right for casual entertaining. Vary the seafood according to what you like and what is fresh at the market. If you wish, use fish pieces or clams instead of, or in addition to, the shrimp or mussels. Don't be put off by the lengthy ingredient list; paella is simple to prepare. Serve with crusty bread and a mixed leaf salad with corn and green onions.

| | | |
|---|---|---|
| 2 lb | chicken thighs or drumsticks, skinned | 1 kg |
| | Salt and pepper | |
| 2 tbsp | olive oil | 25 mL |
| 1 lb | chorizo or other spicy sausage, thinly sliced | 500 g |
| 1 | Spanish onion, quartered and thinly sliced | 1 |
| 1 | sweet red pepper, cut in strips | 1 |
| 1 | jalapeño pepper, minced | 1 |
| 3 | tomatoes, peeled, seeded and chopped | 3 |
| 1 | small zucchini, diced | 1 |
| 2 | cloves garlic, minced | 2 |
| 1 tbsp | fresh thyme leaves (or 1 tsp/5 mL dried) | 15 mL |
| 2 tbsp | minced fresh oregano | 25 mL |
| 1½ cups | Arborio rice | 375 mL |
| ¼ tsp | crumbled saffron threads | 1 mL |
| 3½ cups | boiling fish stock or chicken stock | 875 mL |
| 1 lb | mussels | 500 g |
| ½ lb | medium shrimp | 250 g |
| 2 cups | green peas | 500 mL |
| ¼ cup | chopped fresh parsley | 50 mL |
| 1 | lemon, cut in wedges | 1 |

Season chicken with salt and pepper. In large skillet, heat half of the oil; brown chicken all over, in batches and adding remaining oil as needed. Transfer to paella pan or large shallow casserole. Add sausage to skillet; brown for about 7 minutes. Add to paella pan.

Drain off all but 2 tbsp (25 mL) fat from skillet; cook onion, and red and jalapeño peppers over medium heat for 10 minutes. Add tomatoes, zucchini, garlic, thyme, half of the oregano, ¼ tsp (1 mL) salt and pinch of pepper; cook for 10 minutes, stirring often. Remove from heat. Stir in rice and saffron. Arrange around chicken and sausage. (Recipe can be prepared to this point, covered and refrigerated for up to 1 day. Let stand at room temperature for 30 minutes before proceeding.)

Stir stock into chicken mixture and bring to boil; reduce heat to low and simmer, covered, for 20 minutes or until rice is almost tender.

Meanwhile, scrub mussels, removing beards; discard any that do not close tightly. Shell and devein shrimp, leaving tails intact. (Seafood can be covered with damp tea towel and refrigerated for up to 4 hours.)

Add mussels to chicken mixture; cover and steam for 5 to 7 minutes or until mussels open. Discard any that do not open. Add shrimp and peas; cover and cook for 5 to 7 minutes or until shrimp are pink and juices run clear when chicken is pierced. Serve garnished with parsley, remaining oregano and lemon wedges. Makes 6 servings.

---

**Hint: Instead of cooking Paella, you can bake it. After adding rice and stock to pan, cover and bake in 375°F (190°C) oven for 25 minutes. Arrange mussels, shrimp and peas on top; bake, covered, for 15 minutes or until mussels open.**

# Mediterranean Pie

Images of the sun-soaked Mediterranean are sure to brighten any dull day when you serve this shrimp, olive and feta cheese pie. A spinach salad and crusty bread complete the light supper or lunch.

| | | |
|---|---|---|
| 2 tbsp | olive oil | 25 mL |
| 1 | small onion, finely chopped | 1 |
| 4 | tomatoes, peeled, seeded and chopped | 4 |
| ½ cup | dry white wine or chicken stock | 125 mL |
| ½ tsp | dried oregano | 2 mL |
| ¼ tsp | pepper | 1 mL |
| Pinch | hot pepper flakes | Pinch |
| 1 lb | shrimp, peeled, deveined and coarsely chopped | 500 g |
| ½ cup | coarsely chopped pitted black olives | 125 mL |
| 2 tbsp | chopped fresh parsley | 25 mL |
| ½ cup | unsalted butter, melted (approx) | 125 mL |
| 16 | sheets phyllo pastry (about ⅔ lb/350 g) | 16 |
| ½ lb | feta cheese, rinsed, drained and crumbled | 250 g |

In large skillet, heat oil over medium heat; cook onion until softened, about 3 minutes. Add tomatoes, wine, oregano, pepper and hot pepper flakes; cook, uncovered, for about 10 minutes or until thickened. Add shrimp; cook for 3 minutes or until pink. Remove from heat. Stir in olives and parsley. Cool.

Brush bottom and sides of 13- x 9-inch (3.5 L) baking dish with some of the butter. Keeping remaining phyllo covered with waxed paper and damp tea towel to prevent drying out, line dish with 1 sheet of the phyllo, pressing firmly into corners and up sides of dish. Brush with butter, being sure to coat corners and sides. Repeat with 7 more sheets, brushing each with butter.

Spoon shrimp mixture evenly over pastry; sprinkle with feta. Top with 1 sheet phyllo and brush with butter. Repeat with remaining sheets, brushing each with butter. Trim excess pastry.

Bake in 300°F (150°C) oven, brushing occasionally with remaining butter if pastry begins to dry out, for about 45 minutes or until puffy, crisp and golden. (Pie can be cooled, covered and refrigerated for up to 24 hours. Let stand at room temperature for 30 minutes. Brush with butter and reheat, uncovered, in 300°F/150°C oven for 20 to 30 minutes.) Cut into squares to serve. Makes 6 to 8 servings.

# Salmon and Wild Rice Pie

If pastry-making is not your forté, you can still make this colorful pie. Cheat and use two store-bought frozen deep-dish pie shells. Thaw them 20 minutes and invert the second over top of the filling. Serve with sour cream mixed with a little chopped fresh dill.

| | | |
|---|---|---|
| ¾ cup | wild rice | 175 mL |
| 2 tbsp | butter | 25 mL |
| 4 | green onions, sliced | 4 |
| ½ lb | mushrooms, sliced (2½ cups/625 mL) | 250 g |
| 2 | stalks celery, diced | 2 |
| 2 tbsp | snipped fresh dill (or 2 tsp/10 mL dried dillweed) | 25 mL |
| 2 tbsp | chopped fresh parsley | 25 mL |
| 1 tsp | salt | 5 mL |
| ¼ tsp | pepper | 1 mL |
| 4 | cans (each 7½ oz/213 g) sockeye salmon | 4 |
| 4 | eggs | 4 |
| 1¼ cups | light sour cream | 300 mL |
| | Pastry for deep 10-inch (25 cm) double-crust pie (see Never-Fail Big-Batch Pastry, page 142) | |
| 1 tsp | milk | 5 mL |

Rinse rice in sieve. In small saucepan, cover rice with 4 cups (1 L) cold water; bring to boil. Reduce heat, cover and simmer for 45 minutes or until just tender. (Do not overcook.) Drain and transfer to large bowl.

Meanwhile, in large skillet, melt butter over medium heat; cook onions, mushrooms and celery for about 10 minutes or until mushroom liquid is evaporated, stirring often. Cool and add to rice along with dill, parsley, salt and pepper.

Drain salmon well and break into large chunks. Gently stir into rice. Taste and adjust seasoning if necessary. (Filling can be prepared to this point, covered and refrigerated for up to 8 hours.) In small bowl, beat 3 of the eggs; blend in sour cream. Pour into rice mixture and gently combine.

On lightly floured surface, roll out half of the pastry and line deep 10-inch (25 cm) pie plate. Spoon in filling and pat down. Roll out remaining pastry. Moisten rim of shell and cover with top pastry. Trim and flute edge.

Beat remaining egg with milk; brush over pastry. Cut steam vents in top. Bake in 400°F (200°C) oven for 15 minutes. Reduce heat to 375°F (190°C); bake for about 35 minutes longer or until crust is golden brown. Let stand for 30 minutes before serving. Makes 6 to 8 servings.

# Salmon and Potato Strata

Potato slices replace the usual bread in this homey and economical main dish.
Serve with buttered green peas and chili sauce.

| | | |
|---|---|---|
| 1 | can (7½ oz/213 g) red sockeye salmon | 1 |
| 2 | stalks celery, sliced | 2 |
| 1 | onion, chopped | 1 |
| 4 | eggs | 4 |
| 1⅓ cups | milk | 325 mL |
| ¾ tsp | EACH paprika and salt | 4 mL |
| ½ tsp | EACH pepper and dried tarragon | 2 mL |
| 4 | potatoes, peeled and thinly sliced | 4 |
| ½ cup | dry bread crumbs | 125 mL |
| ¼ cup | chopped fresh parsley | 50 mL |
| 2 tbsp | butter, cut in bits | 25 mL |

In large bowl, mash salmon with juices and bones; stir in celery, onion, eggs,
milk, paprika, ½ tsp (2 mL) salt, pepper and tarragon until well mixed.

In greased 8-cup (2 L) casserole, arrange half of the potato slices; sprinkle
with remaining salt. Pour salmon mixture over top; layer with remaining potato
slices.

Stir together crumbs and parsley; sprinkle on potatoes. Dot with butter. Bake,
uncovered, in 350°F (180°C) oven for 1 hour and 15 minutes or until potatoes
are tender. Makes 4 servings.

# Salmon-Colcannon Pie

Colcannon is an Irish dish combining potatoes and cabbage in such a delightfully comforting way that I serve it often throughout the winter months as a side dish. Here it becomes part of a delicious pie, the ingredients for which you probably have on hand.

| | | |
|---|---|---|
| 4 | potatoes, peeled and halved | 4 |
| 4 cups | coarsely shredded cabbage | 1 L |
| 2 | onions, sliced | 2 |
| ¼ cup | butter | 50 mL |
| ½ tsp | salt | 2 mL |
| ¼ tsp | pepper | 1 mL |
| Pinch | mace | Pinch |
| | Pastry for 9-inch (23 cm) double-crust pie (see Never-Fail Big-Batch Pastry, page 142) | |
| 2 tbsp | chopped fresh parsley | 25 mL |
| 1 | can (7½ oz/220 g) sockeye salmon | 1 |
| 1 | egg yolk | 1 |
| 1 tbsp | cold water | 15 mL |

In large saucepan of boiling salted water, cook potatoes, covered, for 15 minutes. Add cabbage and onions; cook, uncovered, for 10 to 15 minutes or until vegetables are tender. Drain, keeping vegetables in pan.

Shake pan over medium heat until excess moisture has evaporated, 1 to 2 minutes. Mash vegetables with butter, salt, pepper and mace. Let cool.

On lightly floured surface, roll out half of the pastry and line 9-inch (23 cm) pie plate. Spread potato mixture evenly over pastry; sprinkle with parsley. In small bowl, mash salmon with juices and bones; spread over potato mixture. Roll out remaining pastry. Moisten rim of shell and cover with top pastry. Trim and flute edges; cut large slits in top.

Beat egg yolk with water; brush over pastry. Bake in 425°F (220°C) oven for 10 minutes. Reduce heat to 350°F (180°C); bake for 30 to 40 minutes longer or until golden brown. Makes about 6 servings.

# Bean and Salmon Supper

Here's a great dish for carrying to the cottage or out to the backyard for lazy summer eating. Accompany with crusty bread and serve fruit for dessert. The bean mixture will taste better if made a day ahead.

| | | |
|---|---|---|
| 1 | can (19 oz/540 mL) white pea (navy) beans, drained and rinsed | 1 |
| ½ cup | chopped fresh parsley | 125 mL |
| 4 | green onions, thinly sliced | 4 |
| 2 | stalks celery, sliced | 2 |
| ⅓ cup | diced sweet red pepper | 75 mL |
| 2 | cloves garlic, minced | 2 |
| ⅓ cup | EACH fresh lemon juice and olive oil | 75 mL |
| ½ tsp | dry mustard | 2 mL |
| | Salt and pepper | |
| 1 | can (7½ oz/220 g) sockeye salmon | 1 |
| | Leaf lettuce | |

In large bowl, gently toss together beans, parsley, green onions, celery and red pepper. Stir together garlic, lemon juice, oil, mustard, and salt and pepper to taste; pour over bean mixture and toss to combine. (Beans can be prepared to this point, covered and refrigerated for up to 24 hours. Bring to room temperature.)

Drain salmon well; break into chunks and mash any bones. Toss with bean mixture. Taste and adjust seasoning if necessary. Serve in lettuce-lined bowl or plates. Makes 4 servings.

# Tuna Burritos

A new take on burritos combines tuna, chick-peas and crunchy vegetables in a warm cheesy wrapper. Add a salad and some bottled salsa for an inexpensive and popular supper or lunch.

| | | |
|---|---|---|
| 1 tbsp | vegetable oil | 15 mL |
| 1 | onion, chopped | 1 |
| 2 | cloves garlic, minced | 2 |
| 2 | stalks celery, diced | 2 |
| 1 cup | diced sweet green pepper | 250 mL |
| 1 | can (19 oz/540 mL) chick-peas | 1 |
| 2 tsp | chili powder | 10 mL |
| ½ tsp | EACH dried oregano and ground cumin | 2 mL |
| ¼ tsp | hot pepper sauce | 1 mL |
| ¼ cup | fresh lime or lemon juice | 50 mL |
| 4 | large (10-inch/25 cm) flour tortillas | 4 |
| 1 | can (6 oz/170 g) tuna, drained and flaked | 1 |
| 1 cup | shredded Cheddar or Monterey Jack cheese | 250 mL |

In large skillet, heat oil over medium heat; cook onion for 3 minutes. Add garlic, celery and ¾ cup (175 mL) of the green pepper; cook, stirring often, for 5 minutes.

Drain chick-peas, reserving ¼ cup (50 mL) of the liquid. Rinse chick-peas and add to skillet along with chili powder, oregano, cumin and hot pepper sauce. Heat through, mashing chick-peas with potato masher. Stir in lime juice and reserved liquid; heat through.

Spread evenly over each tortilla, leaving 1-inch (2.5 cm) border. Sprinkle with tuna pieces and roll up. Place, seam side down, in greased 13- x 9-inch (3 L) baking dish; cover tightly with foil and bake in 400°F (200°C) oven for 15 minutes.

Sprinkle with cheese; bake, uncovered, for about 3 minutes or until cheese melts. Garnish with remaining green pepper. Makes 4 servings.

# Supper Tuna Burgers

Cooking for one or two can be a challenge. These whole-meal burgers, piled into pitas along with cucumber and sprouts, make a great supper when there's no time to fuss. For the coating, you can use whatever crackers you have on hand—soda, whole wheat, sesame; you'll need about ½ cup (125 mL).

| | | |
|---|---|---|
| 1 | can (7 oz/198 g) tuna, drained | 1 |
| 10 | soda crackers, finely crushed | 10 |
| ⅓ cup | light mayonnaise | 75 mL |
| ½ tsp | dried dillweed | 2 mL |
| ¼ tsp | dried oregano | 1 mL |
| | Salt and pepper | |
| ¼ cup | plain yogurt | 50 mL |
| ¼ tsp | paprika | 1 mL |
| 1 tbsp | vegetable oil | 15 mL |
| 2 | pita breads | 2 |
| | Cucumber slices and alfalfa sprouts | |

In bowl, flake tuna finely; stir in half of the crumbs, ¼ cup (50 mL) of the mayonnaise, half of the dillweed, the oregano, and salt and pepper to taste; shape into 2 patties.

Spread remaining crumbs on waxed paper or in shallow bowl. Press patties into crumbs to coat. (Patties can be covered and refrigerated for up to 6 hours.)

In small bowl, stir together remaining mayonnaise, yogurt, remaining dill, paprika, and salt and pepper to taste. (Refrigerate if making ahead.)

In large skillet, heat oil over medium-low heat; cook patties for about 3 minutes per side or until golden. Cut pita breads in half and warm in toaster; open to form pocket. Cut each hot tuna patty in half; place in pocket along with cucumber, some of the sauce and a few sprouts. Makes 2 servings.

# Cod and Potato Gratin

Dried salt cod looks quite strange as it lies in some corner of a Portuguese or Caribbean grocery store, but when soaked to desalt and plump it, the flavor is mild and somewhat sweet. Baked with onions and potatoes, it is a delightful Portuguese specialty. It's one I couldn't miss including in my book because of the Azorean heritage of my city, Cambridge, Ontario, and my enjoyment of the dish on trips to Portugal itself.

| | | |
|---|---|---|
| 1 lb | skinless dried salt cod | 500 g |
| 4 | potatoes (about 1½ lb/750 g) | 4 |
| 2 tbsp | olive oil | 25 mL |
| 1 | large Spanish onion, thinly sliced | 1 |
| 2 tbsp | butter | 25 mL |
| 2 tbsp | all-purpose flour | 25 mL |
| 1½ cups | milk | 375 mL |
| | Salt, black pepper and cayenne pepper | |
| ⅓ cup | chopped fresh coriander or parsley | 75 mL |
| 12 | black olives (preferably oil-cured) | 12 |
| 1 cup | shredded Gruyère cheese | 250 mL |

Rinse salt cod well under cold running water. Place in bowl; cover with cold water and plastic wrap. Refrigerate for at least 24 hours, changing water several times.

Drain, rinse well and drain again. Place in deep skillet and cover with cold water; bring to boil. Reduce heat, cover and simmer for 4 to 5 minutes or just until fish flakes when tested with fork. Drain and rinse well, then flake, removing any bones. (Good-quality salt cod fillets should contain none.)

Meanwhile, in saucepan of boiling salted water, cook potatoes until almost tender. Drain, cool and thinly slice, peeling if desired. Gently mix with cod.

In large skillet, heat oil over medium heat; cook onion, stirring often, for about 8 minutes or until limp and golden but not browned. Gently mix with cod.

In small saucepan, melt butter over medium heat; whisk in flour and cook, stirring constantly, for 2 minutes. Slowly whisk in milk; cook, stirring, until smooth and thickened, about 5 minutes. Season with salt, pepper and cayenne to taste. Gently combine with cod mixture.

Spread in 8-cup (2 L) shallow casserole. Sprinkle with pepper to taste and coriander. Dot with olives. Sprinkle with cheese. (Casserole can be prepared to this point, covered and refrigerated for up to 1 day. Let stand at room temperature for 30 minutes before heating.)

Bake, uncovered, in 350°F (180°C) oven for 35 to 40 minutes or until golden on top and bubbly. Makes about 6 servings.

# Cod Baked with Tomatoes and Feta

This easy fish casserole is alive with the flavors of the Mediterranean. Serve with a tossed salad and crusty bread to mop up all the delicious juices.

| | | |
|---|---|---|
| 1 lb | cod fillets | 500 g |
| 3 tbsp | all-purpose flour (approx) | 45 mL |
| 2 tbsp | olive oil | 25 mL |
| 1 cup | crumbled feta cheese (about ¼ lb/125 g) | 250 mL |
| 1 | onion, chopped | 1 |
| 3 | cloves garlic, minced | 3 |
| 1 | sweet green pepper, chopped | 1 |
| 1 | can (19 oz/540 mL) tomatoes | 1 |
| ½ cup | pitted black olives | 125 mL |
| ½ tsp | dried oregano | 2 mL |
| Pinch | EACH hot pepper flakes and granulated sugar | Pinch |
| 2 tbsp | minced fresh parsley | 25 mL |
| | Salt and pepper | |

Cut cod into serving-size portions; pat dry. Dredge lightly in flour.

In large skillet, heat half of the oil over medium-high heat; brown cod lightly on both sides. Arrange in 8-inch (2 L) square baking dish; sprinkle with feta. Set aside.

Pour remaining oil into skillet; cook onion, garlic and green pepper, stirring, until softened, about 4 minutes. Add tomatoes, crushing with fork; stir in olives, oregano, hot pepper flakes and sugar. Bring to boil; reduce heat to medium-low and simmer, stirring often, until thickened, about 10 minutes.

Add parsley; season with salt and pepper to taste. Spoon over fish. (Dish can be prepared to this point, cooled, covered and refrigerated for up to 8 hours. Add 5 minutes to baking time.) Bake, uncovered, in 375°F (190°C) oven for about 15 minutes or until bubbly. Makes 4 servings

# Greek-Style Shrimp with Rice

I've added hot cooked rice to a classic Greek shrimp and tomato dish called *Garides me Saltsa* for a more complete whole-meal stew that's tossed with enough feta cheese to create a pleasant briny flavor. Crusty bread and a leafy green salad simply dressed with oil and vinegar are the perfect accompaniments.

| | | |
|---|---|---|
| 2 tbsp | olive oil | 25 mL |
| 2 | cloves garlic, minced | 2 |
| 3 cups | diced peeled fresh tomatoes (or one 28 oz/796 mL can) | 750 mL |
| ¾ cup | dry white wine | 175 mL |
| 2 tbsp | chopped fresh parsley | 25 mL |
| ½ tsp | dried oregano | 2 mL |
| | Salt and pepper | |
| 1½ lb | large shrimp | 750 g |
| ¼ lb | feta cheese, cut in ¼-inch (5 mm) cubes | 125 g |
| ½ cup | parboiled rice | 125 mL |

In large deep skillet or shallow casserole, heat oil over medium heat; cook garlic for 2 minutes, stirring.

Stir in tomatoes, wine, half of the parsley, oregano, and ½ tsp (2 mL) each salt and pepper; bring to boil. Reduce heat and simmer, uncovered, until thickened, about 10 minutes. (Recipe can be prepared to this point, covered and refrigerated for up to 1 day. Bring to simmer before proceeding.)

Peel and devein shrimp, leaving last tail segment on. Sprinkle with salt and pepper to taste. Add to tomato mixture; cook over medium heat for about 5 minutes or until pink. Stir in cheese. Taste and adjust seasoning.

Meanwhile, in saucepan, cover and cook rice in 1 cup (250 mL) water for about 20 minutes or until tender and water is absorbed. Spoon into broad shallow bowls; top with shrimp mixture. Sprinkle with remaining parsley. Makes 4 servings.

# Seafood and Broccoli Lasagna

This elegant lasagna makes a delicious brunch or supper buffet, accompanied by crusty whole wheat rolls and a salad of Boston lettuce and cherry tomatoes.

| | | |
|---|---|---|
| 6 | lasagna noodles | 6 |
| 1 lb | sole fillets | 500 g |
| 3 cups | milk | 750 mL |
| 1 lb | broccoli | 500 g |
| ¼ cup | butter | 50 mL |
| ½ lb | mushrooms, sliced (2½ cups/625 mL) | 250 g |
| ⅓ cup | all-purpose flour | 75 mL |
| ½ tsp | salt | 2 mL |
| Pinch | EACH pepper and nutmeg | Pinch |
| ¼ cup | whipping cream | 50 mL |
| 2¼ cups | shredded Swiss cheese | 550 mL |
| ¾ lb | cooked shrimp | 375 g |
| ½ cup | freshly grated Parmesan cheese | 125 mL |

In large pot of boiling salted water, cook lasagna until al dente. Drain and refresh under cold water; drain and set aside on clean tea towels.

In shallow saucepan, bring sole and milk to simmer; cook, covered, for 5 minutes or just until fish starts to flake when tested with fork. Reserving hot milk, drain fish well. Set aside.

Meanwhile, peel and slice broccoli stems; divide florets into bite-size pieces. In large pot of boiling salted water, cook broccoli for 2 minutes; drain and refresh under cold water. Drain well and set aside on paper towels.

In saucepan, melt butter over medium heat; cook mushrooms for 3 to 5 minutes or until softened. Add flour; cook over low heat for 2 minutes, stirring, without browning. Gradually whisk in reserved hot milk, salt, pepper and nutmeg; cook over medium heat, stirring, until thickened. Reduce heat to low; slowly stir in cream. Remove from heat. Taste and adjust seasoning. Stir in 1 cup (250 mL) of the Swiss cheese. Lightly coat bottom of greased 13- x 9-inch (3 L) glass baking dish with some of the sauce. Flake sole; stir together with shrimp and remaining sauce.

Arrange 3 lasagna noodles in baking dish; spoon thin layer of fish mixture over top, spreading carefully to cover noodles. Arrange broccoli on top; dot with a few tablespoons of sauce. Stir ¼ cup (50 mL) of the Parmesan cheese into remaining Swiss cheese; sprinkle half over broccoli. Top with 3 more lasagna noodles; top with remaining fish mixture. Sprinkle with remaining Swiss cheese mixture. Top with remaining Parmesan. (Lasagna can be prepared to this point, covered and refrigerated for up to 8 hours. Let stand at room temperature for 30 minutes.)

Bake, covered, in 350°F (180°C) oven for 30 minutes. Uncover and bake for 10 to 15 minutes or until golden brown on top. Makes 6 to 8 servings.

# Vegetarian

# Vegetarian Black Bean Chili

Dice the vegetables coarsely for this colorful meatless meal. And for a change, why not serve it on roasted sweet potato cubes or split whole baked potatoes? It's also great on rice. Whatever you serve it on, top with a dollop of low-fat sour cream and a sprinkling of Cheddar.

| | | |
|---|---|---|
| 1 | medium eggplant | 1 |
| | Salt | |
| 2 tbsp | vegetable oil | 25 mL |
| ¼ lb | mushrooms, quartered (about 1½ cups/375 mL) | 125 g |
| 1 | onion, chopped | 1 |
| 1 | carrot, diced | 1 |
| 1 tbsp | chili powder | 15 mL |
| 2 | hot peppers, minced (or ½ tsp/2 mL cayenne) | 2 |
| 3 | cloves garlic, minced | 3 |
| 1 tsp | EACH dried oregano, basil and ground cumin | 5 mL |
| 1 | EACH sweet red and green pepper, cubed | 1 |
| 1 | can (28 oz/796 mL) tomatoes | 1 |
| 1 | can (19 oz/540 mL) black beans, drained and rinsed | 1 |
| 1 | can (12 oz/341 mL) whole kernel corn | 1 |
| 2 | stalks celery, sliced | 2 |
| 2 | small zucchini, cubed | 2 |

Cut unpeeled eggplant into ½-inch (1 cm) cubes; place in colander. Sprinkle lightly with salt; let stand for 30 minutes to drain off any bitter juices. Rinse and drain.

In large saucepan, heat oil over medium heat; cook eggplant, mushrooms, onion, carrot, chili powder and hot peppers for 7 minutes. Stir in garlic, oregano, basil, cumin and sweet peppers; cook for 3 minutes, stirring often.

Stir in tomatoes with juices, beans, corn and celery; bring to simmer, breaking up tomatoes. Reduce heat to low; cover and cook for 20 minutes. (Chili can be prepared to this point, covered and refrigerated for up to 1 day; reheat gently.)

Add zucchini; cook, uncovered, for about 6 minutes or until chili has thickened and zucchini is tender but still crisp. Taste and add salt if necessary. Makes 4 servings.

# Confetti Corn and Chili Pie

Serve this easy, meatless main dish with a salad of crisp greens, orange slices, avocado slices and black olives.

| | | |
|---|---|---|
| ⅓ cup | butter | 75 mL |
| 2 | cloves garlic, minced | 2 |
| 2 | eggs | 2 |
| 4 cups | kernel corn (frozen or canned, drained, about 1 lb/500 g) | 1 L |
| 4 cups | shredded Monterey Jack or mild Cheddar cheese (about 1 lb/500 g) | 1 L |
| 1 | can (114 mL) sliced jalapeño peppers, drained | 1 |
| Half | sweet red pepper, diced | Half |
| 1 tsp | ground cumin | 5 mL |
| ¼ tsp | EACH salt and pepper | 1 mL |
| Pinch | hot pepper flakes | Pinch |
| 10 | sheets phyllo pastry | 10 |
| | Light sour cream | |
| | Bottled salsa | |

In small saucepan, melt butter with garlic; simmer gently for 5 minutes.

Meanwhile, in large bowl, beat eggs; add corn, cheese, jalapeño peppers, red pepper, cumin, salt, pepper and hot pepper flakes.

Brush 13- x 9-inch (3 L) glass baking dish lightly with melted garlic butter. Keeping remaining phyllo covered with waxed paper and damp tea towel to prevent drying out, line dish with 1 sheet phyllo, pressing into corners and up sides of dish. Brush lightly with garlic butter. Repeat with 4 more sheets, brushing each lightly with butter.

Spoon corn mixture evenly over pastry; fold pastry over filling. Top with 5 more sheets of pastry, brushing each lightly with butter and tucking excess down into sides of pan with blunt knife or spatula. (Pie can be covered with waxed paper and refrigerated for up to 6 hours. Let stand at room temperature for 30 minutes before baking.)

With sharp knife, cut slit through top layers of pastry for steam vent. Bake in 350°F (180°C) oven for 45 minutes or until golden brown. Cut into squares to serve with sour cream and salsa. Makes 6 to 8 servings.

# Gratin of Creamed Spinach and Eggs

When you think there's absolutely nothing in the house for supper, look in the freezer for spinach and cook up a few eggs for this comforting casserole. It's better with fresh spinach, of course. Cook just until wilted and squeeze dry.

| | | |
|---|---|---|
| 3 tbsp | butter | 45 mL |
| 1 cup | fresh bread crumbs | 250 mL |
| 1 | onion, sliced | 1 |
| ¼ cup | all-purpose flour | 50 mL |
| 2 cups | milk | 500 mL |
| ½ tsp | EACH salt and nutmeg | 2 mL |
| ¼ tsp | pepper | 1 mL |
| 1 | pkg (10 oz/300 g) frozen chopped spinach, thawed and squeezed dry | 1 |
| ½ cup | freshly grated Parmesan cheese | 125 mL |
| 6 | hard-cooked eggs | 6 |
| 1 cup | slivered ham (optional) | 250 mL |

In large saucepan, melt butter; remove 1 tbsp (15 mL) and toss with bread crumbs. Set aside. Add onion to pan; cook over low heat, stirring often, for 5 minutes or until softened.

Add flour; cook, stirring, for 1 minute. Gradually whisk in milk, salt, nutmeg and pepper; cook, stirring, over medium heat for about 3 minutes or until thickened and bubbly. Add spinach and cheese; cook for 1 minute.

Quarter eggs lengthwise; place, cut side up, in greased 6-cup (1.5 L) shallow baking dish. Sprinkle with ham if using. Spoon spinach mixture over top. Sprinkle with bread crumbs; bake in 375°F (190°C) oven for about 20 minutes or until heated through and browned. Makes 4 servings.

# Vegetable Lasagna

I've had people tell me this moist and hearty vegetarian version has been their favorite lasagna recipe since it appeared in *Homemaker's Magazine* several years ago. Serve with garlic bread and a crisp green salad.

| | | |
|---|---|---|
| 2 tbsp | vegetable oil | 25 mL |
| 2 | onions, chopped | 2 |
| 2 | cloves garlic, minced | 2 |
| ½ lb | mushrooms, sliced | 250 g |
| 1 | sweet green pepper, chopped | 1 |
| 1 | can (28 oz/796 mL) plum tomatoes | 1 |
| 1 | can (14 oz/398 mL) tomato sauce | 1 |
| 2 | carrots, shredded | 2 |
| ¼ cup | chopped fresh parsley | 50 mL |
| 1 tsp | EACH dried basil, oregano, granulated sugar and salt | 5 mL |
| ¼ tsp | pepper | 1 mL |
| Pinch | hot pepper flakes | Pinch |
| 1 | pkg (10 oz/284 g) fresh spinach | 1 |
| 15 | lasagna noodles | 15 |
| 2 | eggs | 2 |
| 1 lb | low-fat ricotta cheese, drained if necessary | 500 g |
| Pinch | nutmeg | Pinch |
| 1 lb | part-skim mozzarella cheese, shredded | 500 g |
| 1 cup | freshly grated Parmesan cheese | 250 mL |

In medium saucepan, heat oil over medium heat; cook onions, garlic, mushrooms and green pepper, stirring often, for 5 minutes. Add tomatoes with juice, cutting up tomatoes as finely as possible, tomato sauce, carrots, parsley, basil, oregano, sugar, salt, pepper and hot pepper flakes. Bring to boil; cover, reduce heat and simmer for 30 minutes, stirring occasionally.

Meanwhile, in heavy saucepan, cook spinach, covered, with just the water clinging to leaves after washing, for 2 to 5 minutes or until just wilted. Drain well in sieve and let cool enough to handle; squeeze out any moisture with hands. Chop finely and set aside.

In large pot of boiling salted water, cook noodles according to package directions. Drain and rinse with cold water; drain again and spread out on clean tea towels.

In food processor, whirl eggs, ricotta cheese, nutmeg and cooked spinach until fairly smooth.

Spread one-quarter of the tomato sauce in greased 13- x 9-inch (3.5 L) baking dish. Arrange one-quarter of the noodles in single layer on top, cutting 1 noodle in half lengthwise to fit end. Spread with one-third of the ricotta mixture, then one-quarter of the tomato sauce, one-third of the mozzarella and one-quarter of the Parmesan. Repeat layers twice. Arrange remaining noodles on top; spread with remaining tomato sauce and sprinkle with remaining Parmesan cheese. (Lasagna can be prepared to this point, covered and refrigerated for up to 24 hours. Bake for 10 to 15 minutes longer.)

Bake, uncovered, in 350°F (180°C) oven for 30 minutes. Cover with foil and bake for 10 to 15 minutes or until hot and bubbly. Let stand for 10 minutes before cutting into squares to serve.

(Lasagna can be cooled, well wrapped and frozen for up to 2 months. Bake frozen in 350°F/180°C oven, covered, for 1½ hours.) Makes 10 to 12 servings.

# Roasted Summer Vegetable Lasagna

You can make this delicious lasagna any time of the year, of course, but it is extra good when fresh local vegetables are at their best.

| | | |
|---|---|---|
| 2 | EACH small eggplants and zucchini | 2 |
| 2 | sweet peppers (yellow or red or a combination) | 2 |
| 1 | onion | 1 |
| ½ lb | mushrooms, sliced (2½ cups/625 mL) | 250 g |
| ½ lb | cherry tomatoes (1½ cups/375 mL) | 250 g |
| 4 | cloves garlic, crushed | 4 |
| 2 tbsp | olive oil | 25 mL |
| 1 tsp | dried basil | 5 mL |
| ½ tsp | EACH dried oregano and rosemary Salt and pepper | 2 mL |
| ½ cup | chopped fresh parsley | 125 mL |
| 2 tbsp | EACH butter and all-purpose flour | 25 mL |
| 2½ cups | milk | 625 mL |
| Pinch | nutmeg | Pinch |
| 1 cup | freshly grated Parmesan cheese | 250 mL |
| ½ lb | lasagna noodles | 250 g |
| ¼ lb | mozzarella cheese, shredded (1 cup/250 mL) | 125 g |

Cut eggplants and zucchini into 1-inch (2.5 cm) cubes. Cut peppers and onion into 1-inch (2.5 cm) squares. Arrange in large shallow pan along with mushrooms and tomatoes. Dot with garlic; sprinkle with oil, basil, oregano, rosemary, and salt and pepper to taste. Toss to coat well and spread out in pan. Roast in 450°F (230°C) oven for about 30 minutes or until vegetables are tender, stirring twice. Stir in parsley.

Meanwhile, in small saucepan, melt butter over medium heat; stir in flour and cook, stirring, for 2 minutes. Gradually whisk in milk; cook, stirring, until thickened and smooth. Season with nutmeg, and salt and pepper to taste. Stir in half of the Parmesan cheese.

In large pot of boiling salted water, cook noodles according to package directions. Drain and rinse with cold water; drain again and spread out on clean tea towel.

Spread very thin layer of sauce in greased 13- x 9-inch (3.5 L) baking pan. Top with single layer of noodles, one-quarter of the sauce, one-third of the vegetable mixture and one-third of the mozzarella. Repeat layers twice starting with noodles and ending with sauce. Sprinkle with remaining Parmesan cheese. (Lasagna can be prepared to this point, covered and refrigerated for up to 24 hours. Let stand at room temperature for 30 minutes.)

Bake, covered, in 350°F (180°C) oven for 20 minutes; uncover and bake for 10 minutes or until golden and bubbly. Let stand for 10 minutes before cutting into squares to serve. Makes 6 to 8 servings.

# Curried Harvest Vegetables with Lentils

Lentils, which don't require the long soaking and cooking of dried beans, form the low-cost, high-fibre, low-fat base for a quick and colorful curry. Serve on hot rice (preferably basmati) and accompany with a favorite chutney. Follow with a hot apple crisp or baked apples and yogurt.

| | | |
|---|---|---|
| 1 cup | dried red lentils | 250 mL |
| 2 tbsp | vegetable oil | 25 mL |
| 2 | onions, chopped | 2 |
| 2 | cloves garlic, minced | 2 |
| 1 tbsp | EACH ground cumin and ground coriander | 15 mL |
| 2 tsp | turmeric | 10 mL |
| ½ tsp | pepper | 2 mL |
| ¼ tsp | hot pepper flakes | 1 mL |
| Pinch | EACH cinnamon and cloves | Pinch |
| 2½ cups | chicken or vegetable stock | 625 mL |
| 2 tbsp | fresh lemon juice | 25 mL |
| 2 | carrots | 2 |
| 1 | small winter squash | 1 |
| 1 | small cauliflower | 1 |
| 1 | sweet red pepper | 1 |
| ½ lb | green beans | 250 g |
| | Salt | |
| ½ cup | peanuts | 125 mL |

Sort and rinse lentils; set aside.

In large saucepan, heat oil over medium heat; cook onions and garlic for about 3 minutes or until softened. Stir in cumin, coriander, turmeric, pepper, hot pepper flakes, cinnamon and cloves; cook, stirring, for 30 seconds. Stir in lentils to coat well. Stir in stock and lemon juice; bring to boil. Reduce heat, cover and simmer for 5 minutes.

Meanwhile, cut carrots into 1-inch (2.5 cm) thick slices. Peel squash and cut into 1-inch (2.5 cm) cubes. Cut cauliflower into small florets. Cut red pepper into thin strips. Trim beans and cut in half.

Stir carrots, squash and cauliflower into lentil mixture; bring to boil. Reduce heat, cover and simmer for 5 minutes. Stir in red pepper and beans; simmer for 5 minutes. Stir in salt to taste and peanuts. Cook, uncovered, for 5 minutes or until vegetables are tender and lentils have formed thick sauce. Taste and adjust seasoning. (Curry can be made up to 1 day ahead if you undercook vegetables slightly. It will thicken if made ahead; thin with more stock or water if desired and reheat gently, stirring often.) Makes 4 to 6 servings.

**\*Hint: Choose a squash that's relatively easy to peel such as butternut. Pepper squash, with all its ridges, is more difficult.**

# Vegetable Couscous

This easy, flavorful dish combines couscous, a North African grain, with a spicy vegetable stew. Look for instant couscous in the rice section of most large supermarkets or in bulk-food stores.

| | | |
|---|---|---|
| 2 tbsp | vegetable oil | 25 mL |
| 1 | onion, cut in 2-inch (5 cm) chunks | 1 |
| 1 tbsp | minced fresh ginger | 15 mL |
| ½ tsp | EACH paprika, pepper, turmeric and ground cumin | 2 mL |
| Pinch | cayenne | Pinch |
| 1 | clove garlic, minced | 1 |
| 3 | carrots, cut in 2-inch (5 cm) chunks | 3 |
| 3 | parsnips, cut in 2-inch (5 cm) chunks | 3 |
| 2 | small turnips, peeled and cut in wedges | 2 |
| 2 | tomatoes, peeled and quartered | 2 |
| 1 | can (19 oz/540 mL) chick-peas, drained and rinsed | 1 |
| 2½ cups | chicken or vegetable stock | 625 mL |
| 2 cups | sliced green beans | 500 mL |
| ½ cup | seedless raisins | 125 mL |
| | Salt | |
| 1 cup | couscous | 250 mL |

In large wide heavy saucepan, heat oil over medium heat; cook onion for 2 minutes. Add ginger, paprika, pepper, turmeric, cumin and cayenne; cook for 3 minutes, stirring often.

Add garlic, carrots, parsnips, turnips, tomatoes, chick-peas and stock; bring to boil. Reduce heat to low; simmer, covered, for 15 minutes or until vegetables are almost tender.

Add beans and raisins; cook, uncovered, for 10 minutes or until beans are tender-crisp and liquid has thickened slightly. Season with salt to taste. (Stew can be prepared to this point, cooled, covered and refrigerated for up to 1 day. In this case, just cook 5 minutes after adding beans. Reheat gently.)

Meanwhile, in medium saucepan, boil 1½ cups (375 mL) water; add couscous and ½ tsp (2 mL) salt. Remove from heat. Let stand, covered, for 5 minutes or until couscous is tender and water is absorbed; fluff with fork. Spoon onto large heated platter; make well in centre. Spoon in vegetable mixture. Makes 4 servings.

# Garden Paella

This comforting rice dish is not only pretty, but nutritiously chock-full of vegetables and other good things.

| | | |
|---|---|---|
| 2 tbsp | olive oil | 25 mL |
| 1 | sweet red pepper, cut in strips | 1 |
| 1 | onion, finely chopped | 1 |
| 2 | cloves garlic, minced | 2 |
| 2 | tomatoes, peeled and chopped | 2 |
| 1½ cups | Arborio or other short-grain rice | 375 mL |
| 3 cups | chicken or vegetable stock | 750 mL |
| ¾ tsp | salt | 4 mL |
| ¼ tsp | saffron threads, crushed | 1 mL |
| 1 lb | asparagus | 500 g |
| ½ cup | sliced unblanched almonds | 125 mL |
| 2 | hard-cooked eggs, cut in wedges | 2 |
| | Pepper | |

In large deep skillet, heat oil over medium-high heat; cook red pepper, onion and garlic for 5 minutes, stirring occasionally. Add tomatoes; cook for about 3 minutes, stirring constantly, until thickened and most of the liquid has evaporated. Remove from heat.

Stir in rice to coat. Stir in stock, salt and saffron. Return skillet to heat; bring to boil. Reduce heat to low; simmer, covered, for 15 minutes or until rice is almost tender.

Cut each asparagus spear into thirds; arrange over rice. Cook, covered, for 5 to 8 minutes or until rice and asparagus are tender and liquid is absorbed. With fork, stir in almonds. Serve garnished with eggs and sprinkled with pepper to taste. Makes 4 to 6 servings.

# Mexican Tortilla Casserole

Layers of bean chili, tortillas, salsa and cheese will make this casserole a hit with younger family members. If corn tortillas are unavailable, substitute one 210-gram package corn tortilla chips. There's no need to fry them.

| | | |
|---|---|---|
| 2 tbsp | vegetable oil | 25 mL |
| 2 | onions, chopped | 2 |
| 1 | sweet green pepper, finely chopped | 1 |
| 3 | cloves garlic, minced | 3 |
| 1 | jalapeño pepper, minced | 1 |
| 1 | can (19 oz/540 mL) tomatoes | 1 |
| 1 tbsp | chili powder | 15 mL |
| 1 tsp | ground cumin | 5 mL |
| ½ tsp | EACH salt, pepper and dried oregano | 2 mL |
| ¼ tsp | hot pepper flakes | 1 mL |
| 2 | cans (19 oz/540 mL each) black beans, drained and rinsed | 2 |
| 12 | corn tortillas (6-inch/15 cm) Oil for frying | 12 |
| 1 | jar (455 mL) salsa | 1 |
| ½ lb | Monterey Jack cheese, shredded (2 cups/500 mL) Sour cream or plain yogurt | 250 g |

In large saucepan, heat 2 tbsp (25 mL) oil over medium heat; cook onions, green pepper, garlic and jalapeño pepper for 5 minutes.

Stir in tomatoes with juices, breaking up with spoon, chili powder, cumin, salt, pepper, oregano and hot pepper flakes; bring to boil. Reduce heat and simmer, uncovered, for 20 minutes, stirring occasionally. Stir in beans; simmer for about 10 minutes or until most of the liquid is evaporated. Set aside. (Chili can be cooled, covered, and refrigerated for up to 2 days.)

Cut tortillas into 1-inch (2.5 cm) wide strips. In large skillet, add oil to depth of ¼ inch (5 mm); heat over medium-high heat. Add single layer of tortilla strips; fry, turning once, for 1 to 2 minutes or until golden and crisp. Drain on paper towels. Repeat with remaining tortilla strips.

Spread one-quarter of the salsa in 13- x 9-inch (3 L) glass baking dish. Top with one-third of the tortilla strips, half of the black bean chili, then one-third of the cheese. Repeat layers once. Top with one-quarter of the salsa, then remaining tortillas, cheese and salsa. Bake, covered, in 400°F (200°C) oven for 20 to 40 minutes or until heated through. Serve with sour cream. Makes 6 servings.

# Tomato and Cheese Tart

On a recent visit to Southwestern France, we had a wonderful supper at a farmer's home near the house we were renting. Beatrice Scheuber made this easy but pretty tart into a main course by adding chopped smoked ham after the mustard. I think it makes a lovely main course for lunch either way. Garnish with a fresh sprig of one of the herbs if available.

|         | Pastry for 9-inch (23 cm) pie shell (See Never-Fail Big-Batch Pastry, page 142) |         |
|---------|------------------------------------------------|---------|
| 1 cup   | cherry tomatoes (about 20), halved             | 250 mL  |
| 1 tbsp  | Dijon mustard                                  | 15 mL   |
| ½ lb    | Gruyère cheese, shredded                       | 250 g   |
| 1 tsp   | dried basil                                    | 5 mL    |
| ¼ tsp   | dried thyme                                    | 1 mL    |
| Pinch   | pepper                                         | Pinch   |
| 1 tbsp  | olive oil                                      | 15 mL   |

On lightly floured surface, roll out pastry and ease into 9-inch (23 cm) tart tin, pushing down into corners. Trim edges. Prick all over bottom with fork; bake in 400°F (200°C) oven for 10 minutes. Prick again if necessary; bake at 375°F (190°C) for 15 minutes or until pale golden. Cool on rack.

Place tomatoes, cut side down, on paper towels; set aside to drain.

Spread crust with mustard; sprinkle with half of the cheese. Top with tomatoes, cut side up; sprinkle with basil, thyme, pepper and remaining cheese. Drizzle with oil. Bake in 375°F (190°C) oven for about 30 minutes or until cheese melts. Cool slightly on rack. Remove sides of pan; cut into wedges to serve. Makes 4 servings.

# Baked Italian Beans

Simple and easy, this low-cost meatless casserole is packed with the robust flavors you associate with good old-fashioned spaghetti. Serve with a crisp green salad and Italian bread.

| | | |
|---|---|---|
| 2 tbsp | vegetable oil | 25 mL |
| 2 | carrots, coarsely chopped | 2 |
| 2 | stalks celery, coarsely chopped | 2 |
| 2 | cloves garlic, minced | 2 |
| 1 | onion, coarsely chopped | 1 |
| 1 | sweet green pepper, diced | 1 |
| 1 | can (28 oz/796 mL) tomatoes | 1 |
| 1 | can (5½ oz/156 mL) tomato paste | 1 |
| 1 tsp | EACH dried oregano and basil | 5 mL |
| Pinch | EACH hot pepper flakes and granulated sugar | Pinch |
| ½ cup | freshly grated Parmesan cheese Salt (optional) | 125 mL |
| 1 | EACH can (19 oz/540 mL) white kidney beans and chick-peas, drained and rinsed | 1 |
| 1½ cups | shredded mozzarella cheese | 375 mL |
| 2 tbsp | butter | 25 mL |
| 1 cup | fresh bread crumbs | 250 mL |
| ¼ cup | chopped fresh parsley | 50 mL |

In large saucepan, heat oil over medium heat; cook carrots, celery, garlic, onion and green pepper until softened, about 7 minutes.

Stir in tomatoes with juices, tomato paste, 1 tomato paste can of water, oregano, basil, hot pepper flakes, sugar and 2 tbsp (25 mL) of the Parmesan cheese. Taste, adding salt if desired. Bring to boil; reduce heat and simmer, uncovered and stirring often, for 20 minutes or until slightly thickened.

Stir in beans and chick-peas; cook for 15 minutes to soften peas. Taste and adjust seasoning. Transfer to greased 13- x 9-inch (3 L) glass baking dish. Sprinkle mozzarella over top.

Melt butter; stir in remaining Parmesan cheese, bread crumbs and parsley. Sprinkle evenly over mozzarella. (Recipe can be prepared to this point, covered and refrigerated for up to 1 day. Let stand at room temperature for 30 minutes before heating.)

Bake in 375°F (190°C) oven for 20 to 30 minutes or until bubbly. Makes 4 to 6 servings.

# Vegetable Pot Pie

No one will miss the meat in this delightful pie, which is really a dinner of new vegetables under wraps. Serve with a salad of spinach and sweet red pepper strips.

| | | |
|---|---|---|
| ¼ cup | butter | 50 mL |
| 1 | pkg (10 oz/280 g) pearl onions, peeled | 1 |
| ½ lb | EACH tiny mushrooms, mini carrots and mini new red potatoes (unpeeled) | 250 g |
| 1½ cups | vegetable or chicken stock | 375 mL |
| ½ tsp | EACH crumbled dried sage, rosemary, salt and pepper | 2 mL |
| 1 cup | green peas (fresh or frozen) | 250 mL |
| 3 tbsp | all-purpose flour | 45 mL |
| 1½ cups | hot milk | 375 mL |
| Pinch | nutmeg | Pinch |
| 1 cup | coarsely shredded Swiss cheese | 250 mL |
| Half | pkg (411 g) frozen puff pastry, thawed | Half |
| 1 | egg | 1 |

In large shallow saucepan, melt half of the butter over medium heat; cook onions, mushrooms, carrots and potatoes for 5 minutes or until browned. Stir in stock, sage, rosemary, salt and pepper; bring to boil. Reduce heat and simmer, uncovered, for 15 to 20 minutes or until vegetables are just tender-crisp. Boil for 3 minutes to reduce stock to about ½ cup (125 mL). Stir in peas.

Meanwhile, in medium saucepan, melt remaining butter over medium heat; stir in flour and cook for 2 minutes, stirring. Gradually whisk in milk, nutmeg, and salt and pepper to taste; cook, stirring, until thickened and smooth. Stir in cheese. Stir into vegetable mixture. Transfer to deep 9-inch (23 cm) pie plate or shallow casserole just big enough to hold mixture. Let cool.

Roll out pastry and fit over pie, turning under excess. Beat egg with 1 tbsp (15 mL) water; brush over top. Make decorations if desired with bits of pastry, place on crust and brush with egg wash. With tip of sharp knife, make several small slashes in pastry. Bake in 400°F (200°C) oven for 20 to 25 minutes or until mixture is bubbly and top golden brown. Makes 6 servings.

# Spicy Bean Enchiladas

This fast vegetarian meal is so easy to put together that even first-time cooks will have no trouble. Pass a bowl of low-fat sour cream for everyone to spoon over his or her enchilada.

| | | |
|---|---|---|
| 1 tbsp | vegetable oil | 15 mL |
| 1 | EACH onion and sweet green pepper, chopped | 1 |
| 3 | cloves garlic, minced | 3 |
| 1 tbsp | EACH ground cumin and chili powder | 15 mL |
| 2 tsp | dried oregano | 10 mL |
| Pinch | hot pepper flakes | Pinch |
| 1 | can (19 oz/540 mL) kidney beans, drained and rinsed | 1 |
| 1 cup | bottled salsa | 250 mL |
| 4 | flour tortillas (10-inch/25 cm) | 4 |
| ½ cup | shredded Cheddar cheese | 125 mL |

In nonstick skillet, heat oil over medium-high heat; cook onion and green pepper for 5 minutes or until softened, stirring often. Add garlic, cumin, chili powder, oregano and hot pepper flakes; cook, stirring, for 2 minutes. Add beans and mash coarsely. (Recipe can be prepared to this point, covered and refrigerated for up to 1 day; reheat gently.) Stir in half of the salsa; cook for 5 minutes, stirring often.

Spoon mixture evenly down centre of each tortilla and roll up. Place, seam side down, in lightly greased 11- x 7-inch (2 L) baking dish. Spoon remaining salsa over top; sprinkle with cheese.

Cover with foil; bake in 450°F (230°C) oven for 10 minutes. (Or cover with waxed paper and microwave at High for 5 minutes.) Makes 4 servings.

# Baked Garden-Fresh Potato

Raid the salad crisper and you'll find most of the ingredients for this comforting supper—one I love to make myself when I come home late from a meeting. You can multiply the recipe for any number of people. If baking the potatoes in a microwave, remember to increase the time by a couple of minutes for each extra potato. I've suggested a toaster oven for a single serving, but it's certainly worth heating the regular oven if cooking for a few people.

| | | |
|---|---|---|
| 1 | baking potato (½ lb/250 g) | 1 |
| ¼ cup | EACH shredded Cheddar cheese and freshly grated Parmesan cheese | 50 mL |
| ¼ cup | EACH diced sweet green pepper and coarsely chopped mushrooms | 50 mL |
| Pinch | dried oregano or Italian seasoning | Pinch |
| Half | tomato, diced | Half |
| 2 tbsp | plain low-fat yogurt | 25 mL |
| Pinch | EACH salt and pepper | Pinch |

Scrub potato and prick in several places with fork. Place on paper towel; microwave at High for 6 to 7 minutes or until tender. (Or bake in 400°F/ 200°C toaster oven for 1 hour.)

Set aside 2 tbsp (25 mL) of the Cheddar. In bowl, stir together remaining Cheddar, Parmesan, green pepper, mushrooms, oregano and tomato. Push to 1 side of bowl.

Cut cooked potato in half and scoop out pulp to empty side of same bowl. Mash pulp with yogurt; stir into cheese mixture. Mound in potato shells and place on microwaveable serving plate. Microwave at High for 3 to 4 minutes. (Or place on ovenproof dish and bake in 400°F/200°C toaster oven for 15 to 20 minutes or until heated through.) Sprinkle with reserved Cheddar, salt and pepper. Makes 1 serving.

# Eggplant Gratinée

Even those who say they do not like eggplant will ask for seconds. Serve with toasted pita wedges and a cucumber salad with yogurt dressing.

| | | |
|---|---|---|
| 1 | large eggplant (about 1¼ lb/625 g) | 1 |
| | Salt and pepper | |
| 3 tbsp | olive oil (approx) | 45 mL |
| ½ lb | mushrooms, sliced (2½ cups/625 mL) | 250 g |
| 1 | onion, chopped | 1 |
| 1 | clove garlic, minced | 1 |
| 1 | can (19 oz/540 mL) tomatoes, chopped | 1 |
| 1 tsp | EACH dried basil and granulated sugar | 5 mL |
| Pinch | dried thyme | Pinch |
| ½ lb | provolone or mozzarella cheese, coarsely shredded (about 2 cups/500 mL) | 250 g |
| | Chopped fresh parsley | |

Peel eggplant and cut into ½-inch (1 cm) thick slices. Sprinkle both sides lightly with salt; spread in single layer on paper towels. Weigh down with heavy weight (cutting board, for instance) for 20 to 30 minutes.

Meanwhile, in large skillet, heat 1 tbsp (15 mL) of the oil over medium heat; cook mushrooms for 5 minutes. Remove with slotted spoon and set aside. Add 1 tbsp (15 mL) oil to skillet; cook onion and garlic for 3 minutes or until softened. Stir in tomatoes, basil, sugar and thyme; bring to boil. Reduce heat to medium-low; cook for about 15 minutes or until slightly thickened, stirring often.

Pat eggplant slices dry; brush both sides lightly with oil. Place on grill over medium-high heat or broil until tender, about 10 minutes, turning once. Add to sauce; cook gently, stirring often, for about 5 minutes or until eggplant is quite soft and limp. Stir in mushrooms, and salt and pepper to taste.

Pour half into greased deep 6-cup (1.5 L) baking dish; sprinkle with half of the cheese. Repeat layers. (Casserole can be prepared to this point, covered and refrigerated for up to 8 hours. Let stand at room temperature for 30 minutes.)

Bake, covered, in 400°F (200°C) oven for 20 minutes. Uncover and bake for 5 to 10 minutes or until bubbly. Serve sprinkled with parsley. Makes 4 servings.

---

*Hint: Sprinkling a large eggplant with salt will eliminate any bitterness and excessive moisture. I have done various experiments with salting eggplant. If you are using smaller eggplant or long thin Oriental ones, it makes no difference whether you salt or not.

# Eggs and Lighter Fare

# Quick Cassoulet

Having spent much time in Southwest France where this traditional country dish appears on every restaurant menu, I was keen on trying my hand at making it. I did so a few times for my New Year's Eve gatherings. Authentic cassoulet is, without doubt, absolutely delicious but has lots of fat and does take days to prepare. This quick fat-reduced version saves on time and has a wonderful flavor too.

| | | |
|---|---|---|
| 4 lb | duck | 2 kg |
| 1 lb | garlic farmer's sausage | 500 g |
| 1 tsp | vegetable oil | 5 mL |
| 4 | cloves garlic, minced | 4 |
| 2 | onions, coarsely chopped | 2 |
| ½ cup | dry white wine | 125 mL |
| 1 | can (28 oz/796 mL) crushed tomatoes | 1 |
| ½ tsp | EACH dried thyme and savory | 2 mL |
| 2 | bay leaves | 2 |
| Pinch | granulated sugar | Pinch |
| | Salt and pepper | |
| 4 | cans (19 oz/540 mL each) white pea (navy) beans | 4 |
| 2 cups | fresh bread crumbs | 500 mL |
| ⅓ cup | chopped fresh parsley | 75 mL |

Remove any loose fat from duck; cut duck into small serving-size pieces and set aside. Place backbone, wing tips, neck and giblets in medium saucepan. Cover with 3 times as much cold water; bring to boil. Reduce heat to medium-low; simmer, partially covered, for 1 hour. Set aside.

Meanwhile, cut sausage into ½-inch (1 cm) thick slices. In large flameproof casserole, heat oil over medium-high heat; brown sausage for 5 minutes. Remove with slotted spoon; drain on paper towels.

In same casserole, in 2 batches, brown duck pieces well on all sides to render as much fat as possible. Remove duck and set aside. Pour out and reserve all but 2 tbsp (25 mL) drippings.

Add garlic and onions to casserole; cook, stirring, over medium heat for 5 minutes. Stir in wine; bring to boil, scraping up brown bits from bottom of pan. Stir in tomatoes, thyme, savory, bay leaves, sugar, and salt and pepper to taste. Return sausage and duck pieces to pan; bring to boil. Cover and reduce heat to medium-low; simmer for 1½ hours or until meat is very tender, stirring often.

Drain and rinse beans. Add to casserole along with enough duck stock (about 1 cup/250 mL) from simmering bones to make very moist, but not soupy, mixture. Discard bay leaves. (Recipe can be prepared to this point, covered and refrigerated for up to 2 days or frozen for up to 3 months, storing drippings separately.)

In medium bowl, combine bread crumbs, parsley and ¼ cup (50 mL) reserved drippings; sprinkle evenly over casserole. (Recipe can be prepared to this point, covered and refrigerated for up to 1 day. Add 10 minutes to heating time.)

Bake, uncovered, in 350°F (180°C) oven for about 45 minutes or until bubbly and golden-brown crust has formed. Makes 10 to 12 servings.

# Sharon's Old-Fashioned Baked Beans with Apple Garnish

My assistant, Sharon Boyd, gets requests for these Quebec-style beans when she caters her husband's office parties. Sometimes she cuts whole apples into thick wedges instead of halves and places them in an overlapping ring around the outside edge of the beans. The beans are great with creamy cabbage salad. To make this vegetarian, omit salt pork; if you wish, sprinkle shredded cheese on for the last five minutes.

| | | |
|---|---|---|
| 4 cups | dried white pea (navy) beans | 1 L |
| 12 cups | cold water | 3 L |
| 2 | large onions, sliced | 2 |
| ½ lb | salt pork, diced | 250 g |
| ⅔ cup | chili sauce | 150 mL |
| ½ cup | molasses | 125 mL |
| 1 tbsp | cider vinegar | 15 mL |
| 2 tsp | dry mustard | 10 mL |
| 1½ tsp | salt | 7 mL |
| 1 tsp | pepper | 5 mL |
| 4 | apples (unpeeled), cored and halved crosswise | 4 |
| ½ cup | packed brown sugar | 125 mL |
| ⅓ cup | butter, softened | 75 mL |
| ⅓ cup | dark rum (optional) | 75 mL |

Sort and rinse beans. In large saucepan, cover beans with 12 cups (3 L) water; let stand overnight.

Drain beans, cover again with cold water and bring to boil; reduce heat and simmer, covered, for 30 minutes. Reserving cooking liquid, drain.

In 12-cup (4 L) casserole or bean pot, layer half of the onions, half of the beans and half of the pork. Repeat layers. Stir together chili sauce, molasses, vinegar, mustard, salt, pepper and enough reserved liquid to make mixture pourable. Pour over beans and add enough additional liquid just to be visible. Cover and bake in 275°F (140°C) oven for 6 hours, checking occasionally and adding a bit more liquid or water as needed to keep it just visible.

Cover beans with apples, cut side up. Cream together sugar and butter; spread over apples. Bake, uncovered, in 325°F (160°C) oven for 1 hour or until apples are tender. If using, pour rum over top just before serving. Makes about 12 servings.

# Eggs Creole

Inexpensive and quick to make, hard-cooked eggs become a main course when napped with a spicy tomato sauce. Serve over parsleyed rice and accompany with a crisp green salad.

| | | |
|---|---|---|
| 2 tsp | vegetable oil | 10 mL |
| 2 tbsp | chopped onion | 25 mL |
| ½ lb | mushrooms, sliced (2½ cups/625 mL) | 250 g |
| 1 | stalk celery, chopped | 1 |
| 1 | large carrot, grated | 1 |
| 1 | can (28 oz/796 mL) tomatoes, chopped | 1 |
| ½ tsp | EACH dried oregano and basil | 2 mL |
| ¼ tsp | dried thyme | 1 mL |
| Pinch | cayenne pepper | Pinch |
| | Salt | |
| ¾ cup | diced ham | 175 mL |
| 6 | hard-cooked eggs, halved | 6 |

In large skillet, heat oil over medium heat; cook onion, stirring occasionally, for 2 minutes or until softened. Add mushrooms; cook, stirring, for 2 minutes.

Stir in celery, carrot, tomatoes, oregano, basil, thyme, cayenne, and salt to taste; bring to boil. Reduce heat and simmer, stirring occasionally, for 30 to 35 minutes or until thickened. Stir in ham. (Recipe can be prepared to this point, covered and refrigerated for up to 1 day. Bring to room temperature.) Gently stir in eggs; heat through. Makes 6 servings.

# Eggs in Curry Sauce

Serve for brunch or lunch with basmati rice and your favorite chutney.

| | | |
|---|---|---|
| 2 tbsp | butter | 25 mL |
| 1 | leek (white part only), thinly sliced | 1 |
| 1 | clove garlic, minced | 1 |
| 2 tbsp | all-purpose flour | 25 mL |
| 2 tsp | good-quality curry powder | 10 mL |
| ½ tsp | ground cumin | 2 mL |
| ¼ tsp | ground coriander | 1 mL |
| 1 cup | chicken stock | 250 mL |
| ½ cup | dry white wine or additional stock | 125 mL |
| 1 | apple, peeled and chopped | 1 |
| 1 cup | peas (fresh or thawed) | 250 mL |
| ½ cup | light cream | 125 mL |
| 8 | hard-cooked eggs | 8 |
| 2 tbsp | chopped fresh parsley | 25 mL |
| | Salt and pepper | |

In saucepan, melt butter over medium-high heat; cook leek and garlic for 1½ minutes or until softened but not browned. Stir in flour, curry powder, cumin and coriander; cook, stirring, for 1 minute. Gradually stir in stock and wine.

Add apple; simmer over medium heat, stirring occasionally, for 10 minutes. Stir in peas and cream; cook for 1 minute. Add eggs and parsley; cook for 1 to 2 minutes or until heated through. Season with salt and pepper to taste. Makes 4 servings.

# Pizza Pot Pie

Like an upside-down pizza, this pie would be great as a family night supper at home or away because you can prepare most of it ahead of time and it's a bit more substantial than a pizza. If you're carrying it to the cottage or chalet, take the dough in one plastic bag and all the other ingredients in another. Pizza dough is available in many supermarkets; or approach your neighborhood pizza parlor. Or, make the super easy recipe that follows.

| | | |
|---|---|---|
| ½ lb | pepperoni, thinly sliced | 250 g |
| ½ lb | mushrooms, sliced (2½ cups/625 mL) | 250 g |
| 1 | sweet green pepper, coarsely diced | 1 |
| ½ cup | sliced green olives | 125 mL |
| ½ cup | freshly grated Parmesan cheese | 125 mL |
| 2 | green onions, sliced | 2 |
| 1 | small hot chili, sliced (or ¼ tsp/1 mL hot pepper flakes) | 1 |
| 1 tsp | anchovy paste, or 2 anchovy fillets, chopped (optional) | 5 mL |
| ½ tsp | dried Italian herb seasoning | 2 mL |
| 1 | can (14 oz/398 mL) pizza sauce | 1 |
| 1 lb | part-skim mozzarella cheese, shredded (4 cups/1 L) | 500 g |
| 1 lb | pizza dough | 500 g |

In wide shallow 8-cup (2 L) baking dish (preferably about 11 inches/28 cm in diameter), combine pepperoni, mushrooms, green pepper, olives, Parmesan cheese, green onions and chili.

Combine anchovy paste, herb seasoning and pizza sauce; gently stir into pepperoni mixture, spreading evenly in dish. Sprinkle with mozzarella cheese. (Recipe can be prepared to this point, covered and refrigerated for up to 1 day.)

On lightly floured surface, roll out dough 2 inches (5 cm) larger than dish; place on top and fold under at sides. Place on baking sheet; bake in 425°F (220°C) oven for 20 to 25 minutes or until top is golden brown and sounds hollow when tapped with knuckle. Cut top into wedges and spoon out filling to serve. Makes 4 to 6 servings.

# Easy Pizza Dough

Quick and easy to make when the pizza urge hits, the dough can be wrapped in plastic wrap, placed in a plastic bag and refrigerated for up to 8 hours or frozen for up to 2 months. Double the recipe if desired.

| | | |
|---|---|---|
| Pinch | granulated sugar | Pinch |
| ⅔ cup | warm water | 150 mL |
| 2 tsp | active dry yeast | 10 mL |
| 2 tbsp | vegetable oil | 25 mL |
| 1½ cups | all-purpose flour (approx) | 375 mL |
| ½ tsp | salt | 2 mL |

In small bowl, combine sugar and water; sprinkle with yeast and let stand in warm place until bubbly and doubled in volume, about 5 minutes. Stir in oil.

In large bowl, mix together flour and salt. Make well in centre of flour mixture; pour in yeast mixture. With fork, gradually blend together to form dough. With floured hands, gather into ball.

Turn out onto lightly floured surface; knead for about 5 minutes, adding just enough extra flour to make soft, slightly sticky dough. Place in greased bowl, turning once to grease all over. Cover bowl with greased waxed paper and tea towel. Let stand in warm draft-free place until tripled in size, 1½ to 3 hours.

Punch down dough and form into ball. Turn out onto lightly floured surface and cover with bowl; let stand for 10 minutes. Roll out dough into 12-inch (30 cm) circle. Makes about 1 lb (500 g), enough for one 12-inch (30 cm) pizza crust.

# Cheddar–Corn Impossible Pie

When you think there's nothing in the house for supper, or when relatives suddenly appear for Sunday lunch, here's the answer. The flour mixture in this vegetable-packed dish magically forms a very thin tender base for its zesty custard filling. Serve with chili sauce or bottled salsa and a cabbage-carrot slaw.

| | | |
|---|---|---|
| 2 tbsp | dry bread crumbs | 25 mL |
| 10 | slices bacon, cooked and crumbled | 10 |
| 1 cup | shredded mild Cheddar cheese | 250 mL |
| 1 | onion, finely chopped | 1 |
| Half | sweet green pepper, diced | Half |
| 1 cup | corn kernels | 250 mL |
| ¼ tsp | pepper | 1 mL |
| Pinch | EACH salt and cayenne pepper | Pinch |
| ½ cup | all-purpose flour | 125 mL |
| 1 tsp | baking powder | 5 mL |
| 2 tbsp | shortening | 25 mL |
| 4 | eggs | 4 |
| 2 cups | milk | 500 mL |

Grease 10-inch (25 cm) quiche pan or pie plate; sprinkle with bread crumbs. Combine bacon, Cheddar, onion, green pepper, corn, pepper, salt and cayenne; sprinkle over bread crumbs.

In bowl, stir together flour and baking powder; cut in shortening until in fine crumbs. Add eggs and milk; whisk just until smooth. Pour over bacon mixture.

Bake in 350°F (180°C) oven for 45 to 50 minutes or until knife inserted near centre comes out clean. Let stand for 5 minutes. Makes 4 servings.

# Risotto Primavera

Primavera means springtime, and this delicious risotto certainly celebrates the season with lots of fresh vegetables. Although I love risotto, I always hesitate serving it to company since I don't want to be in the kitchen stirring and missing any conversation. This pressure cooker method lets you make it in a fraction of the normal time. If you don't have a pressure cooker, you will have to add the stock about ½ cup (125 mL) at a time, stirring constantly, for about 15 minutes. Start the meal with a nice array of antipasti (olives, marinated roasted peppers, raw vegetables, assorted salami and the like) and accompany the risotto with Italian bread.

| | | |
|---|---|---|
| 1 tbsp | olive oil | 15 mL |
| 1 | large onion, chopped | 1 |
| 2 | cloves garlic, minced | 2 |
| 1½ cups | Arborio rice | 375 mL |
| 4 cups | hot chicken stock (approx) | 1 L |
| | Salt | |
| 1 lb | asparagus, cut in 1-inch (2.5 cm) pieces | 500 g |
| ¼ lb | sliced prosciutto, chopped | 125 g |
| 1 cup | frozen peas, thawed | 250 mL |
| 4 | green onions, sliced | 4 |
| ¼ cup | chopped fresh basil | 50 mL |
| 2 cups | freshly grated Parmesan cheese | 500 mL |
| | Pepper | |

In 16- to 24-cup (4 to 6 L) pressure cooker, heat oil over medium heat; cook onion and garlic for 2 minutes. Stir in rice to coat well. Stir in 3½ cups (875 mL) of the stock and pinch salt.

Lock lid in place; bring to high pressure over high heat. Lower heat just enough to maintain high pressure; cook for 5 minutes. Quickly reduce pressure according to manufacturer's instructions. Remove lid, tilting it away from you to allow any excess steam to escape. (Risotto will continue to absorb liquid at this point; add more stock to keep it soupy if necessary.)

Stir in asparagus and half of the prosciutto; cook over medium heat, stirring constantly and adding more stock if needed to keep it soupy, for 5 minutes or until rice is tender but slightly firm and mixture is creamy. Stir in peas and green onions; cook, stirring, for 2 minutes.

Stir in half of the basil, remaining prosciutto and 1½ cups (375 mL) of the cheese. Season with salt and pepper to taste. Serve garnished with remaining basil. Pass remaining cheese separately. Makes 4 servings.

# Brunch

# Wild Mushroom, Leek and Prosciutto Strata

I love having a main-course do-ahead casserole for brunches because all there is to do the day of the party is pop the dish in the oven, then delight in its aroma while it cooks. Although the ingredient list and method seem somewhat lengthy, the strata is quite quick to assemble. This type of layered egg-cheese-bread dish has been around since the turn of the century; the name "strata" probably appeared in the '70s because of the layering.

| | | |
|---|---|---|
| 12 | slices homemade-style dry bread (Italian loaf) | 12 |
| 4 cups | light cream (or 2 cups/500 mL EACH light cream and milk) | 1 L |
| ¼ cup | butter | 50 mL |
| 4 | leeks (white and 1 inch/2.5 cm) of pale green), thinly sliced | 4 |
| ½ lb | shiitake mushrooms,* stemmed and cut in ¼-inch (5 mm) wide strips | 250 g |
| ½ lb | thinly sliced prosciutto, cut in ¼-inch (5 mm) strips | 250 g |
| ¼ cup | EACH chopped fresh parsley and thyme or marjoram (or combination) | 50 mL |
| 2 cups | shredded Gruyère cheese (about 8 oz/250 g) | 500 mL |
| 6 | eggs | 6 |
| 2 tsp | dry mustard | 10 mL |
| | Pepper | |

Spread dry bread out in large shallow dish; pour cream over top. Set aside to let soak.

In large deep skillet, melt three-quarters of the butter over medium heat; cook leeks until softened, about 8 minutes. Add mushrooms; cook for 5 minutes. Add prosciutto; cook for 2 or 3 minutes. Reserving 1 tbsp (15 mL) of the parsley, stir fresh herbs into leek mixture; set aside.

Gently squeeze moisture from bread, reserving cream in bowl. (Don't worry if it breaks up.)

In greased shallow 12- x 8-inch (3 L) baking dish, arrange one-third of the bread, top with half of the leek mixture, then one-third of the cheese. Repeat layers once. Arrange remaining bread on top. (Don't worry if bread doesn't cover each layer.)

To cream in bowl, add eggs, mustard, and pepper to taste; whisk until combined. Pour over bread layer. Sprinkle with remaining cheese; dot with remaining butter. Sprinkle with reserved parsley. Cover well and refrigerate overnight.

Bake, uncovered, in 325°F (160°C) oven for 35 to 45 minutes or until top is golden brown and knife inserted in centre comes out clean. Makes 8 servings.

---

**\*Hint: If unavailable, substitute portobello mushrooms or 2 oz (50 g) dried shiitake mushrooms or morels. If using dried mushrooms, soak in hot water until softened, about 30 minutes. Drain and squeeze out excess moisture, discarding hard stems.**

# Harvest Strata

This colorful and easy casserole makes a great brunch for weekend houseguests.

| | | |
|---|---|---|
| 6 | slices homemade-style white bread | 6 |
| | Butter | |
| 2 cups | shredded old Cheddar cheese (8 oz/250 g) | 500 mL |
| 1 | sweet red pepper, diced | 1 |
| 3 | green onions, sliced | 3 |
| 1 | small zucchini, diced | 1 |
| 4 | eggs | 4 |
| 2½ cups | milk | 625 mL |
| 1 tsp | EACH dry mustard and Worcestershire sauce | 5 mL |
| ½ tsp | EACH salt and dried thyme | 2 mL |
| 2 tsp | dried basil | 10 mL |
| | Pepper | |

Butter bread on 1 side; cut into ½-inch (1 cm) cubes. Arrange in greased shallow 11- x 7-inch (2 L) baking dish. Sprinkle with cheese. Scatter red pepper, onions and zucchini on top.

In bowl, whisk together eggs, milk, mustard, Worcestershire sauce, salt and thyme; pour over vegetables. Sprinkle with basil, and pepper to taste. Cover and refrigerate overnight.

Bake, uncovered, in 350°F (180°C) oven for 1 hour or until golden. Makes 6 servings.

# Shrimp and Cheese Strata

This easy strata makes a special breakfast for holiday mornings.

| | | |
|---|---|---|
| 6 | slices homemade-style white bread | 6 |
| 3 tbsp | butter, melted | 45 mL |
| 1 cup | shredded Swiss cheese | 250 mL |
| 2 | green onions, chopped | 2 |
| 2 tbsp | snipped fresh dill | 25 mL |
| ½ lb | tiny cooked shrimp | 250 g |
| 3 | eggs | 3 |
| 1½ cups | milk | 375 mL |
| ½ cup | sour cream | 125 mL |
| ½ tsp | Dijon mustard | 2 mL |
| Pinch | salt | Pinch |

Cut each slice of bread in half diagonally; brush 1 side with butter. Arrange half of the bread, buttered side down, in ungreased 8-inch (2 L) square baking dish. Sprinkle with half each of the cheese, onions, dill and shrimp. Add remaining bread, buttered side up. Repeat layers.

In bowl, whisk together eggs, milk, sour cream, mustard and salt; pour over casserole. Cover and refrigerate overnight.

Bake, uncovered, in 350°F (180°C) oven for 45 to 60 minutes or until puffed and golden. Makes 6 to 8 servings.

# Breakfast Sausage and Cheese Bake

Serve with bottled salsa or chili sauce and warm flour tortillas for a breakfast perfect for friends.

| | | |
|---|---|---|
| 1 lb | Italian sausage | 500 g |
| 1 | onion, chopped | 1 |
| 4 | eggs | 4 |
| 1½ cups | milk | 375 mL |
| 1 tsp | EACH Dijon mustard and Worcestershire sauce | 5 mL |
| ¼ tsp | EACH salt, pepper and Tabasco sauce | 1 mL |
| 1½ cups | EACH shredded Swiss and Cheddar cheese | 375 mL |
| 8 | slices Italian or French bread | 8 |
| 1 tbsp | butter, cut in bits | 15 mL |

Remove sausage from casing. In large heavy skillet, cook sausage and onion over medium heat, breaking up sausage with fork, until sausage is cooked through, about 8 minutes. With slotted spoon, remove to drain on paper towels.

In large bowl, whisk together eggs, milk, mustard, Worcestershire sauce, salt, pepper and Tabasco. In medium bowl, combine Swiss and Cheddar cheeses.

Cut bread into ½-inch (1 cm) cubes. Arrange one-third of the bread in greased 8-cup (2 L) soufflé dish or deep casserole. Sprinkle with one-third of the cheese; top with all the sausage. Top with half of the remaining bread, then half of the remaining cheese. Top with remaining bread. Press layers slightly together; pour egg mixture over top. Sprinkle with remaining cheese; dot with butter. Cover and refrigerate overnight.

Bake, uncovered, in 350°F (180°C) oven for about 1 hour or until golden brown and set, and skewer comes out clean. Serve immediately. Makes 4 to 6 servings.

# Ham and Egg Pie

Our good friend Priscilla Hofmeister is one of those great houseguests who bring the makings for a meal during their stay. She often does breakfast for us, and it includes a bacon and egg pie. I've adapted the recipe to serve more people and substituted ham for the usual back bacon Priscilla includes. It's great served with chili sauce.

| | | |
|---|---|---|
| 1 | pkg (397 g) frozen puff pastry, thawed | 1 |
| 1 tbsp | Dijon mustard | 15 mL |
| ¾ lb | ham, thinly sliced | 375 g |
| 13 | eggs | 13 |
| 2 tbsp | EACH chopped green onions and fresh parsley | 25 mL |
| ¼ tsp | EACH salt and pepper | 1 mL |
| 1 tbsp | water | 15 mL |

Roll out half of the pastry about 1 inch (2.5 cm) bigger than bottom of 13- x 9-inch (3 L) glass baking dish; line bottom and part of the sides. Spread evenly with mustard; top with half of the ham. Break 12 of the eggs onto ham. With fork, prick yolks but do not stir yolks and whites together. Sprinkle with onions, parsley, salt and pepper; top with remaining ham.

Roll out remaining pastry; place on top, sealing edges onto bottom pastry. Beat remaining egg with water; brush over top. With tip of sharp knife, make small slashes in several places in top pastry. Bake in 400°F (200°C) oven for 25 to 30 minutes or until pastry is golden brown. Cut in squares to serve. Makes 10 to 12 servings.

# Goat Cheese and Sun-Dried Tomato Cheesecake

Serve thin wedges of this easy-to-make savory cheesecake warm or at room temperature over a bed of dressed greens for a delicious brunch dish. Or, merely garnish with halved cherry tomatoes and black olives and serve with fresh or dried fruit.

| | | |
|---|---|---|
| ¾ cup | all-purpose flour | 175 mL |
| ¼ cup | butter, softened | 50 mL |
| ¼ cup | toasted chopped walnuts | 50 mL |
| 1 | egg yolk | 1 |
| ¼ tsp | salt | 1 mL |
| ½ lb | mild goat cheese | 250 g |
| ¼ lb | cream cheese | 125 g |
| 3 | eggs | 3 |
| 1 tbsp | chopped fresh basil (or 1 tsp/5 mL dried) | 15 mL |
| ¼ tsp | hot pepper sauce | 1 mL |
| | Salt and white pepper | |
| ¼ cup | finely chopped oil-packed sun-dried tomatoes | 50 mL |

In 8-inch (2 L) springform pan, gently combine flour, butter, walnuts, egg yolk and salt with hands; pat evenly over bottom of pan. Bake in 350°F (180°C) oven for 10 minutes.

In food processor or bowl, beat together goat cheese, cream cheese, eggs, basil, hot pepper sauce, and salt and pepper to taste only until smooth and blended. Stir in tomatoes. Pour into crust; bake for 20 to 25 minutes or until almost set and starting to crack around outside yet still wobbly in centre.

Remove from oven. Immediately run sharp knife around inside of pan to prevent cheesecake from cracking upon cooling. Cool slightly to serve. (Cheesecake can be cooled completely, covered and refrigerated for up to 2 days. Let stand at room temperature for about 1 hour before serving.) Makes about 8 servings.

# Roasted Cherry Tomato Clafoutis

Traditional clafoutis (a kind of cakelike custard) is made with black cherries or other fruit to be served as a dessert. I've added cheese and chosen cherry tomatoes to make a savory version that would be just right for a company breakfast, perhaps with some back bacon and interesting bread.

| | | |
|---|---|---|
| 2 cups | cherry tomatoes (1 lb/500 g) | 500 mL |
| 2 tbsp | olive oil | 25 mL |
| 1 tbsp | chopped fresh thyme (or 1 tsp/5 mL dried) | 15 mL |
| 2 | cloves garlic, crushed | 2 |
| 2 tsp | granulated sugar | 10 mL |
| | Salt and pepper | |
| 1 cup | light cream | 250 mL |
| 3 | eggs | 3 |
| 2 tbsp | all-purpose flour | 25 mL |
| ½ lb | mozzarella cheese, shredded (about 2 cups/500 mL) | 250 g |

Remove stems from tomatoes. Arrange in single layer in shallow 6-cup (1.5 L) baking dish. Drizzle with oil; sprinkle with thyme, garlic, sugar, ½ tsp (2 mL) salt and ¼ tsp (1 mL) pepper. Roast in 400°F (200°C) oven for 10 to 15 minutes or until skin shrivels slightly.

In blender, blend cream, eggs and flour until smooth; pour over tomatoes. Sprinkle with cheese. Reduce temperature to 350°F (180°C); bake for about 25 minutes or until puffed and golden. Makes 4 servings.

# Watercress Frittata

Enjoy with chili sauce, toast triangles and a glass of white wine for a quick lunch, brunch or light after-theatre supper. You can have the egg mixture ready and everything chopped, grated or sliced ahead of time.

| | | |
|---|---|---|
| 4 | eggs | 4 |
| 2 | egg whites | 2 |
| ⅓ cup | freshly grated Parmesan cheese | 75 mL |
| ½ tsp | salt | 2 mL |
| Pinch | pepper | Pinch |
| 1 | bunch watercress | 1 |
| 1 tbsp | olive oil | 15 mL |
| 1 cup | sliced mushrooms | 250 mL |
| 2 | cloves garlic, minced | 2 |
| 2 | green onions, sliced | 2 |
| ½ tsp | dried basil | 2 mL |
| ¼ lb | mozzarella cheese, cut in thin strips | 125 g |

In bowl, whisk together eggs, egg whites, ¼ cup (50 mL) of the Parmesan, salt and pepper; set aside.

Remove enough watercress leaves to measure 1 cup (250 mL) packed; discard stems and set remaining sprigs aside for garnish.

In large ovenproof skillet, heat oil over medium-high heat; cook mushrooms, garlic, onions and basil until mushrooms are lightly browned, about 3 minutes. Add watercress; cook, stirring often, until leaves are wilted, about 2 minutes.

Remove skillet from heat and stir in remaining Parmesan. Spread evenly over bottom of skillet; pour egg mixture over top. Cook over medium heat for 1 minute; sprinkle with mozzarella. Place skillet under broiler; broil until cheese begins to brown, 2 to 3 minutes. Slide onto warm serving plate and cut into wedges to serve garnished with watercress sprigs. Makes 4 servings.

# Index